Mission Insite

Worship
Ways

Praise for *Worship Ways for the People Within Your Reach*

"Tom Bandy and Lucinda Holmes have written a very important book for anyone planning or leading worship. The book asks important questions, identifies a variety of approaches to worship, and invites readers to think missionally and purposefully as they plan and lead worship that helps worshipers to 'meet Jesus.' Our worship teams will be reading this book."
—Adam Hamilton, senior pastor, The United Methodist Church of the Resurrection

"This book will transform the way we think, plan, and come to worship. It is a timely, prophetic work boldly reclaiming that 'worship is God's purest form of mission.' Thank you Tom!"
—Jeff Hutcheson, presbytery pastor for mission and vision, Presbytery of San Francisco

"A provocative and helpful analysis for worship teams exploring why we worship and how best to connect people to God in a post-Christendom era. Recommended."
—Robert Schnase, author of *Five Practices of Fruitful Congregations* and *Seven Levers: Missional Strategies for Conferences*

"With clarity and razor sharp insight, *Worship Ways* explores what it takes to offer worship that is transformational, life enhancing, and dynamic. Bandy and Holmes identify seven types of mission-targeted worship, linking life-needs to faith and an experience of Christ. This guide will reform serious worship leaders, resulting in worshipers who fully encounter the sacred and connect with life-sustaining community. This could well be the most important book on how and why we worship in our time."
—Ian Price, Mediacom Education CEO

"*Worship Ways* is a valuable resource for those who plan worship and for those wanting to connect with the people God has given them in their communities. It is an essential guide for those who care about both."
—Lovett H. Weems Jr., Distinguished Professor of Church Leadership and Director, Lewis Center for Church Leadership, Wesley Theological Seminary, Washington, DC

"Move beyond the *worship wars* of the 1980s and 1990s to the *worship ways* of the contemporary generation . . . This book is an excellent balance of biblical theology, cultural analysis, statistical research, and practical tips to show how churches can missionally connect to their communities through worship."
—Page Brooks, professor, New Orleans Baptist Seminary

"*Worship Ways* recasts the concept of worship and offers a useful exploration of the specific kinds of worship that resonate with different demographic groups. It is essential reading for anyone who seeks to unravel the challenging new realities of worship."
—Tom Barlow, UnStuckChurch.net

Worship Ways

For The People Within Your Reach

THOMAS G. BANDY

WITH LUCINDA S. HOLMES

Abingdon Press™

Nashville

WORSHIP WAYS FOR THE PEOPLE WITHIN YOUR REACH

Library of Congress Cataloging-in-Publication Data

Bandy, Thomas G., 1950-
  Worship ways for the people within your reach / Thomas G. Bandy, with Lucinda Holmes.
    pages cm
  Includes bibliographical references.
  ISBN 978-1-4267-8807-9 (binding: soft back, trade pbk. : alk. paper) 1. Public worship.
2. Missions—Theory. I. Title.
  BV15.B365 2014
  264—dc23

                                                                          2014016988

14 15 16 17 18 19 20 21 22 23—10 9 8 7 6 5 4 3 2 1

MANUFACTURED IN THE UNITED STATES OF AMERICA

Contents

Acknowledgments

From Tom:

A lifetime of dialogue between church and culture has been shaped by so many people! I would like to particularly acknowledge the great influence of Paul Tillich on my thinking and writing and especially many colleagues in the North American, German, and French Tillich Societies that bring together professionals from all sectors.

I also thank the many Protestant, Catholic, Orthodox, and Pentecostal theologians, denominational leaders, and local pastors in all parts of the United States, Canada, Australia, New Zealand, and many regions in Europe that have influenced the synthesis of this book.

Special appreciation is due to the innovators and developers of www.MissionInsite.com and the demographic search engine that they have developed for churches and nonprofit organizations.

Finally, I am grateful for thousands of conversations with anonymous, ordinary people from every lifestyle imaginable, who have shared their spiritual yearnings and cultural insights in so many odd places, though such a diversity of media, simply because they are looking for God.

From Lucinda:

I dedicate this work to my husband, Cliff Meek, and my father, Lee Holmes, the two most important laymen of my life and calling. Cliff, my life partner in ministry with a calling as strong (and at times, even stronger!) and clear as mine. And to my dad, who passed along the power of telling a story and his greatest legacy to me, being a great man of the church.

Acknowledgments

I am grateful for every musician and worship team chairperson that I have served beside in my thirty-four years of ministry. Each of you has made me a better pastor and worship leader. I would like to thank and acknowledge the worship teams of the Crossroads and Bristol Hill United Methodist Churches, who have called forth a renaissance in my worship leadership and have told me the truth every day.

And lastly, I would like to acknowledge today's innovators of mission-targeted worship in the Kansas City area whom I have also drawn upon in my writing. The pastors and worship teams of the *Keystone/Revolution* United Methodist Church, *The Redemption Table* of Lee Summit, *Live Forward* Thursday evening experience at Church of the Resurrections, and the *Crosswords UMC* in Lansing are blessing people who yearn for God and who are underrepresented in today's mainline churches.

Authors' Note

Demographics trends are very fluid, and lifestyles are constantly changing. The names, descriptions, and search engine codes used by demographers to identify lifestyle groups and segments are frequently updated. We refer to the lifestyle groups and segments identified in Mosaic 2010 by Experian (www.Experian.com). This is available to churches through MissionInsite (www.MissionInsite.com), and this website also includes "Mission Impact," Tom's extensive commentary on ministry expectations for lifestyle segments.

Readers who refer to this book should regularly check for updates and changes to the names, descriptions, and codes of lifestyle groups and lifestyle segments. Many denominations subscribe to www.MissionInsite.com and provide access to their constituent congregations and agencies. Data is updated frequently.

Introduction

Why Worship?

Why worship? I mean, really, *why worship?* This is the deeper question that is really asked by the rapidly growing population of spiritually yearning, institutionally alienated people in Western culture today. This group includes people with no religious preference and "nones"; but it also includes a multitude of formerly active church members who are stepping further and further from regular worship attendance. What is the point? Why bother? Does it really matter? If Sunday morning worship suddenly ceased in our neighborhoods, towns, and cities, would anybody really miss it other than a handful of professionals who live off the income it generates?

We believe that worship design will never be able to get on the right track unless it answers this fundamental question. It is really a pre-Christian question for postmodern times. All the classic theological and cultural answers to this question are no longer valid in the current environment of religious skepticism and irrelevant churches. Why worship?

- Do we worship in order to reunite with friends, build community, and enjoy fellowship? No, because we can find intimacy in any number of ways and social medias, at more convenient times, and without artificial jargon

1

and oddball rituals getting in the way of authentic communication.

- Do we worship in order to empower social service through our prayers, contributions, and teamwork? No, because we can change the world around us more efficiently through social services, coordinate outreach more quickly through social media, and give more generously through micro-charities.

- Do we worship in order to learn about God, sharpen our moral views, and discern truth? No, because we can read a book (print, electronic, or audio), and we can take a seminar (or webinar), and we can connect with anyone in the world face-to-face, in an instant, and simply *ask our questions*.

- Do we worship in order to praise and adore God? No, because we are so broken, lost, lonely, worried, scared, alienated, and abused that it is unclear what we have to be grateful about; and if we have experienced a quantum of solace, our gratitude is probably given to a therapist, society for the arts, social service, hospice, government agency, or judicial proceeding.

From the point of view of the growing legion of disenchanted former religious people, there really isn't a point to worship. And from the point of view of public sectors that once partnered with the church (e.g., persuasive skeptics in public education, pure and applied sciences, broadcasting and media, nonprofit social service and health care, and law), the value of worship is lessening all the time.

Whenever we help churches explore the lifestyle segments that comprise their immediate and primary mission fields, we see a common pattern. The percentage of people who consider themselves spiritual is remarkably high, the percentage of people who think that faith is important is remarkably low, and the percentage of people who value worship attendance is somewhere in the middle.[1] How is it that faith commitment matters *less* than worship attendance? The answer is that for many today, worship has nothing to do with faith, and everything to do with fellowship, heritage, volunteering, and appreciation of unpopular music. These are all things that can be achieved more easily, with less overhead cost and more impact and enjoyment elsewhere.

If worship were simply cancelled and Sunday morning ceased to become the centerpiece of church experience, what would happen? This is not a radical, hypothetical question. It is, in fact, what is already happening both intentionally and unintentionally as the church struggles for "market share" in Western culture. Instead of spending resources in money and volunteer energy to run worship services for fewer and fewer people, denominations and religious institutions are converting themselves into faith-based nonprofits . . . and the emphasis is increasingly on being a nonprofit rather than being faith-based.

Yet the idea of worship lingers. It persists. It won't go away. Stripped of all the wordiness and liturgy, dogma and tradition, facilities and symbols, sacred egos and sacred cows, there remains a profound *desire for God*. If worship is simply understood as an experience of the *mysterium tremendum*, or "the touch of the Holy," or as Christians might say, the *real presence of God*, then the desire for that experience just won't go away. It is precisely because we are broken, lost, lonely, worried, scared, alienated, and abused that we long for a *more permanent* solution to the human condition.

After all, there is the *other* statistic emerging from demographic research. How is it that despite lack of faith commitment, worship just won't go away? The answer is that the vast majority of people consider themselves spiritual. They may not prefer any particular religion, but they do prefer to have a meaning and purpose for life. They are convinced that there must be more to living than the current emptiness, pointlessness, entrapment, and injustice that are part of what we now know as *normal experience*. Worship just won't go away.

As the anonymous Christian monastic author of *The Cloud of Unknowing* says, there is a thirst, hunger, or desire for the divine that ever escapes our comprehension and control and yet constantly impinges on our awareness. It keeps nudging us, or we keep bumping up against it, but however it flickers at the edge of our vision or teases our imaginations, it reinforces our sense of alienation and awakens our sense of longing.[2]

Church leaders have been so preoccupied with *how* to worship that they have failed to really explore *why anyone worships* in the first place. The conversation about worship in the era of Christendom assumed that we are all *religious insiders* trying to build consensus about the *best way to worship*. Church people gradually awakened to the reality that the religious insiders were very diverse, so the discussion about worship design focused on different worship styles. Churches tried to *reform, contemporize, blend,* and *multitrack* worship every which way. They tried different times, places, technologies, musical genres, images, and languages. Nevertheless, church leaders still clung to the assumption that there were religious *insiders* and *outsiders* . . . and however worship might be designed *stylistically*, it was still supposed to assimilate *outsiders* (visitors, newcomers, inquirers, and seekers) and make them *insiders*.

The game has changed. Today there are no insiders. All people—including church members—are *outsiders*. No one has an inside track to God's grace, so worship is really about thanksgiving for grace received. Everyone is a stranger to grace, so worship is really targeting a blessing that will address each individual's longing, and perhaps give them something to be thankful about on the way home or during the rest of the week. Nobody is an insider. Everybody is an outsider. Therefore, worship is an act of mission.

Worship as Mission

It's an intersection where God's grace and human anxiety meet. The experience may be a rendezvous with destiny or a collision with unstoppable love. The result may be an improved journey or a sharp turn. Worship is the purest form of God's mission, and God expects our collaboration to make it happen.

The last time the game changed like this was with the mission to the Gentiles (sometimes known as the apostolic age). Then, as now, institutional religion was losing credibility. Then, as now, worship attendance was criticized as boring or irrelevant. Then, as now, established religious leaders argued with one another about worship styles, theological purity, and political correctness. Then, as now, the growing population of spiritually yearning, institutionally alienated people didn't care about those debates. They simply longed for the immediacy of the Holy, and looked for a simple, clear, unambiguous experience of the real presence of God that would directly address the dilemmas of their current human condition.

Paul's mission to the Gentiles finally asked the *real* question: Why worship at all? What is the point? His frustration with the *insider/outsider* debates of the established religion of his day boiled over in Corinth (Acts 18:5-17). Paul makes his famous declaration: "From now on I will go to the Gentiles!" He leaves the traditional religious institution (which in our day is the established church), and literally goes next door to the private home of a Greek (Titus Justus) to establish an alternative worship experience.

Despite the fact (or perhaps *because* of the fact) that Paul brings several establishment leaders with him, persecution increases. He is attacked for persuading people to worship in ways that are contrary to polity, but litigation is dismissed by the secular authorities. Instead, Paul has a dream in which God encourages him not to be afraid but to speak boldly, "for there are many in this city who are my people."

Who are these people? These are the people who long for the immediacy of God's grace. A caveat to Paul's doctrine of justification by faith, rather than works, is the radical inclusiveness of God's love. There is no difference between institutional members and seekers, for "the same Lord is Lord of all and is generous to all who call on him" (Rom 10:12). Christ is neither up nor down, but *right here*.

Everyone is an outsider. All people (including church members) are strangers to grace. Worship is no longer about thanking God for entitlements. It is about blessing people who are yearning for mercy.

Worship and Lifestyle

The era of church shopping is over. The church growth movement thrived in the 70s, 80s, and 90s because Christian consumers were still motivated to "shop around" for the worship style they enjoyed. As we move deeper into the spiritual chaos of postmodernity, however, churches are no longer competitive in the religious marketplace. Yes, a handful of angry or disillusioned church veterans will still leave one church and go to another that they like better, but more and more will simply drift.

The *desire for God*, however, is stronger than ever. People still long for the touch of the Holy. They are still fascinated by the supernatural. They may doubt the existence of absolutes, but they still miss them. People are more aware than ever before of the sidetracks, roadblocks, and deadweights that dominate their lifestyles and make them cynical or desperate. They want to meet God face-to-face or heart-to-heart or person-to-person. They want to express their anger, plead for help, or just cling to something.

Worship to the pre- and postmodern seeker is any experience, in any time and place, when the power of God's grace intersects with the urgency of human need. This means that *worship* and *lifestyle* are mixing and merging today in unexpected ways.

The modern perception of life and faith (mid-fifteenth century extending through mid-twentieth century) was a time of rationalism. The sacred time, places, and experiences were separated from normal everyday living. More importantly, sacred ideas, emotions, and worldviews were separated from logical ideas, scientific analysis, and business. Eventually the latter belittled the former to such a degree that by the 1960s religion seemed about to be swallowed by an expanding secular city.[3]

Exactly what happened in the emergence of postmodern sensibilities may be complicated, but what is clear is that spirituality has made a comeback. The sacred is no longer separated from daily living, and worship is no longer a time out from the weekly routine. Now spirituality is a constant undercurrent to lifestyle, and anything and everything has a sacred side. Moreover, as society fragments and flows into more and more diverse microcultures, each group explores spirituality driven by distinct needs and questions.

At the time of this writing, the United States can be studied in nineteen distinct lifestyle groups and seventy-one different lifestyle segments.[4] This alone is about a 40 percent increase in diversity in just the past ten years. Each lifestyle segment represents distinct behavior patterns, relationships, social values, attitudes, and worldviews that can be tracked by habits of shopping, recreation, charitable giving, intimacy and family life, shifting career paths, wealth and debt, public policy debates . . . and yes, spirituality.[5]

The degree of alienation from religion, church, and traditional worship varies considerably from segment to segment. Very few segments can be said to be wholeheartedly supportive of institutional religion and traditional worship on Sunday mornings. Most are somewhere on the path of losing respect, stepping away, and finding good reasons not to go to church.

On the other hand, in varying degrees of intensity or enthusiasm, all lifestyle segments are exploring or incorporating spirituality in their daily lives. Segments differ in their life situations, needs, and yearnings, and differ in their ideas of faith community, preferences for ministry, and expectations of relevant worship. This requires churches to be radically adaptive, which is a behavior pattern quite contradictory to the modern denominational obsession with continuity, predictability, and franchise thinking. In the past, churches designed worship with an eye to uniformity, so that wherever a church member worshiped they would feel "right at home." Today churches are forced to design worship with an eye to diversity, so that wherever a seeker worships they will feel the real presence of Christ that addresses their personal and profound anxieties head-on.

The fragmentation of Western culture (and specifically the United States) into more and more lifestyle segments again parallels the experience of the ancient world in the apostolic age. Each city and region of the empire had its own distinct behavior patterns, relationships, social values, attitudes, and worldviews that probably could be tracked by habits of trade, leisure, generosity, intimacy and family life, guilds, freedom and slavery, public policy debates, and religion. Just as the Internet and immigration diversifies society today, so Roman roads and mass migrations diversified society even more in those days. The Philippians had different ideas of faith community, preferences for ministry, and expectations of relevant worship than the Corinthians, Ephesians, and so on. Paul's mission team couldn't just follow the strategic plan of conformity from the head office in Jerusalem to be effective. They had to learn to be radically adaptive. The worship changes alone were stressful.

The Touch of the Holy

The touch of the Holy can happen in the Eucharist, a personal testimony, a timely prayer, an unrehearsed word, a spontaneous kindness, the passing of the peace, or an outstretched fingertip.

Suddenly you feel the breath of the Spirit on your shoulder and the presence of Jesus at your side.

Just look at the riots in Ephesus and the uproar in Corinth![6]

In a world of such diversity, where worship and lifestyle merge, the only good worship is *worship that works*. Paul says that good worship is whatever motivates a seeker to confess with their lips that Jesus is Lord, and believe in their hearts that God raised him from the dead. That's it. Skip the requirements of circumcision and membership classes, and just get them close to Christ! Don't obsess over burnt offerings, politically correct liturgies, and three take-home insights from the sermon. So long as seekers are equipped to love kindness, do justice, and walk humbly with Jesus, worship is a success![7]

Worship as Compulsion

Why is spirituality alive and well among seventy-one distinct lifestyle segments . . . and more? If worship is no longer a duty, but a *compulsion*, what is it that *compels* otherwise busy and distracted people to worship?

Remember! We do not mean that in any *modern* sense that lifestyle segments feel compelled to *Sunday morning church attendance*. We mean, in the *postmodern* sense, that lifestyle segments feel compelled to *seek the immediacy of God*, or as Christians might say, *the real presence of Christ*. When, where, and how that occurs is up for grabs. It may happen with some predictability on Sunday morning, at a church building, with professionals presiding; but it may also happen unpredictably, at any time, even in the most mundane surroundings, surrounded by eager but incompetent seekers.

There are seven primary "life situations" that never go away.[8] These are like primary colors of the spiritual spectrum. There are innumerable hues or tints that may be possible, but these are blends of the primary colors that are fundamental properties of light. Similarly, there are many combinations of life situations that peculiar publics (lifestyle segments) might experience at any given time, place, or context. Yet these seven basic life situations are fundamental properties of existence, even though they may be blended in unique ways for each lifestyle segment in particular contexts.

These life situations represent the *compelling* sense of *urgency* that besets a lifestyle segment. This urgency is what *drives* people into spirituality. It is what *compels* people to seek God. And it is what *motivates* otherwise busy people to occasionally show up on Sunday morning at church.

The *lost* . . . looking for direction

The *lonely* . . . looking for rapport

The *trapped* . . . looking for deliverance

The *dying* . . . looking for renewable life

The *broken* . . . looking for healing

The *abused* . . . looking for vindication

The *discarded* . . . looking for compassion

If and when people of any given lifestyle segment visit a church on Sunday morning, they are *compelled* to be there as a result of a profound yearning. They are there for a reason, and it is not church shopping. They will base their decision *to return* to that church on whether or not what happens on Sunday morning (e.g., hospitality, worship, and significant conversations) addresses that urgency or not.

Moreover, they will probably make up their minds whether or not to return to church in the first thirty seconds after entering the door (when talking with the greeters); or in the last thirty minutes before exiting the door (when talking with refreshment servers and members). Even if the worship service itself leaves them ambivalent, the real proof of authenticity will emerge from the unrehearsed words and spontaneous actions that emerge from relationships. The relationships will determine whether or not people in any given lifestyle segment will "hang in" for worship long-term. The relationships will give them confidence that they will indeed experience the immediate and real presence of God that will address their desire for direction, rapport, deliverance, renewable life, healing, vindication, or compassion.

These life situations are linked to the classic descriptions of existential anxieties defined by psychologists and theologians.[9] Individuals in any lifestyle segment may or may not be aware of these hidden existential anxieties. Self-awareness can lead to acceptance and health, just as lack of self-awareness can lead to alienation and pathology.

Existential Anxieties	Resulting Life Situations	Catalyst for Acceptance
Emptiness	Lost, looking for direction	**Life Purpose and Destiny**
Meaninglessness	Lonely, looking for rapport	**Authentic and Truthful Relationships**
Fate	Trapped, looking for deliverance	**Liberation and Fresh Start**
Death	Dying looking for renewed life	**Confidence for Enduring Life**
Guilt	Broken, looking for healing	**Wholeness and Serenity**
Shame	Abused looking for vindication	**Advocacy and Justice**
Displacement	Discarded, looking for compassion	**Belonging and Comfort**

Note that there is a seventh anxiety added to the classic list. The anxiety of *displacement* is significant in the postmodern world of immigration, instant communication, and cross-cultural interaction that increasingly challenges the global village.

Individuals are beset by these anxieties. Each may dominate more or less, in different phases of life or circumstances, but these fundamental anxieties are inevitable as conditions or boundaries of existence. Ancient Christians might have called this set of existential anxieties "original sin." Postmodern Christians might call these anxieties "original dysfunction." This can be generalized for lifestyle segments.

- For example, some segments of "boomers" (especially those who are affluent, ambivalent about career, or surviving broken relationships) may be most *compelled* by emptiness to search for life purpose and destiny. Or, some segments of "echoes," many of whom are the grandchildren of the boomers, (especially those who are bullied or marginalized), may be most *compelled* by meaninglessness to search for authentic and truthful relationships.

- Similarly, some segments that are particularly vulnerable to alcohol or drug abuse or experience grinding poverty or excessive indulgence may be most *compelled* by feelings of fate or entrapment to seek liberation and a fresh start. Or some segments likely to be victims of prejudice or advocates of peace might be most *compelled* by abuse or shame to seek justice.

Certainly, these generalizations need to be tested in any given community or neighborhood. After all, people in any given lifestyle segment tend to gather in the same place. It is possible to use prayer walks, focus groups, and other forms of listening and observation to discern which anxieties dominate the life situation of a community at any given time.

FAQ

Lucinda: What do you mean by an *existential* anxiety?

Tom: The term refers to what is fundamental to our very existence as human beings. Whether we are aware of it or not, it is a condition with which we inevitably struggle in daily life.

Lucinda: What do you mean by an existential *anxiety*?

Tom: An anxiety is a profound ambiguity or uncertainty that dogs our daily living. It is the source of our conscious worries about life, such as emptiness, meaninglessness, fate, death, guilt, condemnation, and displacement.

Should our sensitivity to the existential anxieties and life situations of the public around us shape the design of worship? Of course! Each lifestyle segment in the postmodern world yearns to experience the immediacy of God in ways that are relevant to their life situations and wants to experience worship as a catalyst to acceptance. God may be experienced anytime, anywhere, but worship opportunities can be designed to be pregnant with the possibilities of acceptance.

In Christian perspective, every worship service is an incarnational event. The immediate grace of God meets the urgency of human need. The mystery of Christ, fully human and fully divine, is the very essence of worship. Worship is an encounter with Christ, and any encounter of Christ is worship. Yet Christ can be experienced by different people in different ways. We see countless examples of this in the Gospels. For some, Christ is experienced as teacher, for others as a moral example, and for others as a healer. For still others Christ is a mentor or righteous judge, while for others he brings forgiveness or compassion or belonging. All experiences are different; yet all experiences are authentically experiences of Christ.

The experience of Eucharist in Eastern Orthodoxy is perhaps the most ancient and continuous experience of an incarnational event. The very fact that the eucharistic liturgy is essentially unchanged from week to week, or century to century, makes it a remarkably pure lens through which to see the existential anxieties that compelled premodern people and drive the postmodern search for meaning. Worshipers enter the sanctuary from all walks of life, with their hearts on their sleeves, each one seeking (and hopefully receiving) the unique blessing they need from the cosmic Christ. That is why the worship experience is beyond words and profoundly mystical.

God's Power Changes Life!

A suffering woman stretches her hand to touch the hem of Jesus's garment as he passes. Immediately Jesus senses that power has flowed out and fixes upon the woman with his compassionate eyes. In an instant she falls to her knees and the whole truth of her life is revealed. And Jesus says, "Daughter, your faith has made you well. Go in peace!" (Mark 5:25-33).

Incarnation is any moment when God's power flows into your lifestyle and changes everything.

Incarnation means that the *fullness* of God is paradoxically revealed in the *limitations* of human experience. God is revealed not just in part, but *fully*. Ordinary human experience is still *ordinary*, and nothing more. The mystery defies explanation and control. In the ancient formula, Jesus the Christ is *fully* human and *fully* divine. Authentic worship is *utterly* holy and yet (paradoxically) shapeable or designable by church leaders who are faithful in their very fallibility.

We can now explore the postmodern merger of lifestyle and worship for explicitly Christian experience. This will give us clues to the future targeting of worship services and worship design.

Existential Anxieties:	Resulting Life Situations:	Catalyst for Acceptance:	Christ Experience:
Emptiness	Lost, Looking for direction	Life Purpose and Destiny	**Spiritual Guide**
Meaninglessness	Lonely, looking for rapport	Authentic and Truthful Relationships	**Perfect Human**
Fate	Trapped, looking for deliverance	Liberation and Fresh Start	**New Being**
Death	Drying, looking for renewed life	Confidence for Enduring Life	**Promise Keeper**
Guilt	Broken, looking for healing	Wholeness and Serenity	**Healer**
Shame	Abused, looking for vindication	Advocacy and Justice	**Vindicator**
Displacement	Discarded, looking for compassion	Belonging and Comfort	**Shepherd**

The mystery of Christ means, of course, that there are innumerable ways incarnation may be experienced. These seven experiences, however, correspond to the basic anxieties that are fundamental conditions of human existence.[10]

- Christ as "spiritual guide" is the catalyst for discerning purpose and destiny, as God mentors the lost to find direction.

- Christ as "perfect human" is the catalyst for shaping authentic and truthful relationships, as God models companionship for the lonely looking for rapport.

- Christ as "new being" is the catalyst for liberation and new starts, as God breaks people free from addiction or entrapment.

- Christ as "promise keeper" is the catalyst for confidence for enduring life, as God breaks the threat of death with the hope of eternity.

- Christ as "healer" is the catalyst for wholeness and serenity, as God forgives and repairs physical, relational, psychological, or spiritual brokenness.

- Christ as "vindicator" is the catalyst for righteousness, as God removes shame with self-esteem and social justice.

- Christ as "shepherd" is the catalyst for belonging, as God gathers displaced people into community and welcomes strays with compassion.

Christ is the catalyst for acceptance. Christian worship is authentic (insofar as it reveals the fullness of God) and successful (insofar as it blesses human participants with grace sufficient to their needs) when acceptance occurs. It is important to understand that acceptance has both a horizontal and vertical significance. The horizontal significance of acceptance means that love between and among the worshipers overflows as reconciliation, respect, and unity. The vertical significance of acceptance means that love between God and each worshiper overflows as forgiveness, compassion, and reunion. One might say that the "mix" of horizontal and vertical acceptance varies in each worship experience.

The difficulty, of course, is that one Sunday morning experience cannot be all things to all lifestyle segments. One strategy of hospitality cannot serve all life situations at once. One leadership deployment plan to create significant conversations between believers and seekers cannot be effective for everyone at the same time. And certainly one worship design can never reveal the full power and depth of God's blessing. The diversification of society into seventy-one (and more) lifestyle segments means that one size will not fit all.

Even Eastern Orthodoxy and other strongly eucharistic traditions face this challenge. The different existential anxieties that drive lifestyle diversity push even these churches to adjust, nuance, and

15

focus worship in ways unrelated to the Christian Year and specifically sensitive to the compulsions that drive people to seek God. It is not just what happens *in* worship, but also what happens *before* worship and *after* worship that counts. Indeed, it is the entire Sunday morning experience (before, during, and after "worship") that is in fact *WORSHIP*!

Up until the 1990s, "blended worship" was still possible in many US contexts (particularly in the South and the Midwest). "Blended worship" was a mix of styles and media based on generational assumptions or stereotypes. In the new millennium, however, the only way churches can effectively bless the diversity of publics is by diversifying hospitality before worship, nuancing or multitracking worship options, and intentionally shaping significant conversations after worship. This does not mean offering the same worship service in different styles. It means offering distinct mission-targeted worship choices to bless each different lifestyle segment. Churches must first focus the mission purpose of worship, and then pragmatically match worship style to the preferences of the expectant public.

The same adaptive approach is necessary for designing hospitality and opportunities for significant conversation. The greeting and refreshments strategy that works well with one lifestyle segment will not work with another. The strategy to create significant interaction between mature Christians and open-minded seekers will also be different for each lifestyle segment.

Insofar as experience of the real presence of Christ occurs on Sunday morning, this means that the "Sunday morning experience" must be more carefully planned than ever before. However, our intention is not just to change the way you *plan worship*. We want to change the way you *come* to worship and *think about* worship. Set aside whatever you thought you knew about "good worship," and open yourself to worship in the postmodern world that is radically different that anything we have expected or experienced in six hundred years of modernity and denominationalism.

Game Changers

Top 12 Reasons Worship Design Is Different in the
Post-Christendom World

1. Most people think worship is a waste of time. Yet stripped
   of all the wordiness and liturgy, dogma and tradition,
   facilities and symbols, sacred egos and sacred cows, there
   remains a profound desire for God.

2. Existential anxiety is what drives people to spirituality
   and compels people to seek God. And it is what motivates
   otherwise busy people to occasionally show up on Sunday
   morning at church.

3. Worship as an act of mission. It is the intersection of specific human yearning with relevant experiences of grace.
   For Christians, it is about experiencing the real presence
   of Christ.

4. Membership privilege is dead. There are no insiders and
   outsiders. Everyone is a stranger to grace. The only good
   worship is worship that works: targeting a public, blessing
   a person, and giving them hope.

5. The era of church shopping is over. Worship is not about
   assimilating members but blessing people. Worship is an
   encounter with Christ, and any encounter with Christ is
   worship.

6. People experience the mystery of Christ in different ways
   . . . all legitimate, just different. Jesus can be revealed as
   spiritual guide, perfect human, promise keeper, new being, healer, vindicator, or shepherd.

17

7. Worship is a total Sunday morning experience, from humble hospitality, through life-shaping communion, to significant mentoring. The real presence of Christ must be in each step.

8. Sunday morning worship is a microcosm of lifelong discipleship: meeting Christ, experiencing Christ, growing in Christ, walking with Christ, and living like Christ.

9. Worship design will never get on track unless it answers the fundamental question, "Why Worship?" It is not beginning with "How?" as in strategies and creative tactics, or "What?" as in a particular style of music or liturgy, but with the question "Why worship at all?"

10. Worship and lifestyle are mixing and merging today in unexpected ways. The challenge for worship design is not in music style or liturgical format but in offering distinct mission-targeted choices to bless different lifestyle segments in your community.

11. In a world of diversity, the only "good worship" is worship that works. Paul says that good worship is whatever motivates a seeker to confess with their lips that Jesus is Lord, and believe in their hearts that God raised him from the dead. So long as seekers are equipped to love kindness, do justice, and walk humbly with Jesus, worship is a success!

12. God's power is revealed to specific people, at the right time, in a relevant way, with lasting results. You can help or hinder the process. God will hold you accountable for the one or the other!

Self-Awareness Exercise

Complete this exercise *before* reading the rest of this book.
Discuss it. Save it.
Repeat this exercise *after* you finish reading this book.
Compare and discuss.
You can measure what you have learned and plan
the next steps in worship design.

The Big Question:	How was worship relevant to my life yesterday . . . and how is worship relevant to my life today . . . and how will it be relevant tomorrow?
What is my own life situation? Choose the two that best describe your current sense of urgency.	_____ Lost . . . and looking for direction _____ Lonely . . . and primarily looking for rapport _____ Trapped . . . and primarily looking for deliverance _____ Dying . . . and primarily looking for renewed life _____ Broken . . . and primarily looking for healing _____ Abused . . . and primarily looking for vindication _____ Discarded . . . and primarily looking for compassion
What is my compelling existential anxiety? Choose the two that best describe your current sense of urgency.	_____ Emptiness: Nothing is important and I'm not going anywhere! _____ Meaninglessness: Nobody loves me and everything is relative! _____ Fate: I'm trapped, doomed, and cannot escape! _____ Death: I'm aging, weakening, and afraid the end is near! _____ Guilt: I'm broken and can't be fixed; fallen and can't get up!

	____ Shame: I'm a victim and overwhelmed by low self-esteem! ____ Displacement: I'm rootless, homeless, and don't fit in anywhere!
What is my most recent, most powerful experience of Jesus Christ? Choose the two that best describe your current sense of joy.	____ Spiritual Guide: God is my mentor, enlightening my path. ____ Perfect Human: God is a perfect companion, a model to live by. ____ New Being: God is a higher power who has made me free. ____ Promise Keeper: God is everlasting, in whom I trust. ____ Healer: God is a miracle worker who has made me whole. ____ Vindicator: God is a righteous judge who has given me justice. ____ Shepherd: God is my keeper and protector, who gives me shelter.
How relevant is the worship service I usually attend?	____ Awesomely relevant, every time. ____ Mainly relevant, most of the time. ____ Occasionally relevant, some of the time. ____ Only relevant on special occasions. ____ Rarely relevant.
Bonus Question!	
What is my Lifestyle Segment?	Refer to Mission Impact (found at www.Mission Insite.com). Review the lifestyle segments and select the one with which you most empathize.
	If your church has access to the MissionInsite demographic search engine, enter your residential address and study the lifestyle segment(s) where you live.

20

Mission-Targeted Worship

God's intention is to rescue the alienated world, and restore the unity of creator and creation. This means that the church and all activities of the church are about mission. Even worship is about mission. This is one of the most radical and controversial implications of the transition to the postmodern world of demographic diversity.

The church has always tried to diversify worship choices. In the days when Christianity could claim authority over the passage of time, worship was diversified to focus on Christian seasons, Christian holy days, and theological themes that gave meaning to relatively stable, agrarian lives. In just the last hundred years, industrial and technological revolutions have eroded that authority, forcing the church to search for new ways to become relevant to ever more diverse and unstable societies.

First, the church diversified worship by time. Our great-grandparents and grandparents referred to the "early" or the "later" worship service. The former was usually simpler (perhaps without as much musical accompaniment), and the latter was usually more elaborate (perhaps including more music, drama, volunteers, and so on). However, each worship service had the same theme, liturgy, and sermon.

Next, the church diversified worship by generation. Silent and boomer generations began to refer to "traditional" and "youth" worship services. The former was weekly, standardized, and predictable, with sermons that exposited scripture and explained theology. The latter was occasional (or another than Sunday morning), topical, and creative, with sermons that commented on current affairs.

Church membership in North America peaked in the late 60s and early 70s. In the spiral downward, and responding to criticisms about boring and irrelevant worship, the church diversified worship *by style*. Boomers and busters began to refer to worship as "traditional" or "contemporary." Each option included young and old. Traditional worship usually honored veteran church members and held the prime-time Sunday morning slot between ten thirty and twelve o'clock. It blended denominational and local church customs but continued to be standardized, predictable, and more formal. Contemporary worship styles varied according to what leaders considered contemporary, which often seemed five to fifteen years out of date to the echo generation. Churches began seriously to consider other days, times, and locations; used new technologies and instrumentations; and explored interactive methods to deliver a message.

The postmodern attitude that emerged in the 90s and new millennium affected young and old. Seekers and members looked for substance beyond style and began asking the fundamental questions about the real point and purpose of worship. The real breakthrough, however, has been the discovery that existential anxiety, urgent life situations, and yearnings for incarnation were not just individual issues. These could be generalized as expectations—or yearnings—that defined life-style segments.

This is a matter of identifying *trends* rather than *certainties*, but it is possible to connect demographic and psychographic research to identify clues to the spiritual hopes and religious preferences of distinct microcultures.[1]

FAQ

Lucinda: Is any given theology more or less helpful in designing worship?

Tom: No, because worship does not emerge from theology. It emerges from the human condition of struggle and yearning that longs to be touched by the Holy.

Seeker sensitivity can now be taken to a new and more objective level. This no longer depends on the personal biases of a few observers, the popular assumptions of the media, or the best guesses of a church board. Spiritual hopes and religious preferences can be more objectively tracked by sophisticated demographic research. They still must be reality tested by listening strategies and interviews with local nonprofit organizations, but church leaders can now design worship options with more confidence that these will be *really relevant* to the publics they hope to bless.

There is a direct correlation between the changing circumstances of life and the kind of worship a particular public seeks. And there is a direct correlation between a lifestyle segment, the anxieties that motivate it, and the kind of worship in which it might participate. Worship design is a simple formula:

Seeker Sensitivity

+

Incarnational Experience

=

God's Blessing through Relevant Worship

It is important to understand the radical shift from modern religious sensibilities to postmodern spiritualities. In the modern world, the whole point of seeker sensitivity was to *attract* people *into* the institutional church. Worship leaders measured success by worship attendance and eventual program involvement. In the postmodern world, seeker sensitivity has a very different goal. The point is not to *attract* people, but to *bless* people. Church leaders evaluate success by counting changed lives and social impact that often has nothing to do with attendance and membership. Yes, seeker sensitivity that aims to *bless*

23

people first may also result in institutional growth but more as a side effect or an added benefit. Those who aim to bless the publics around them are in turn blessed.

The formula may be simple, but the design process for each option of worship is much more complex.

First of all, there are currently seventy-one or more lifestyle segments in the United States and Canada alone. In the most homogeneous rural areas and small towns, there will still be three to six distinctly different lifestyles segment that represent the greatest proportion of the population. In the most heterogeneous urban and urbanized areas, there may be ten to fifteen distinctly different lifestyle segments within a radius of just a few miles. Each lifestyle segment is driven by a different spiritual urgency, with reference to a different life situation. Their religious preferences for hospitality, worship, Christian education, small groups, and outreach and their preferences for facilities, technologies, symbol systems, and communication media may even be *contradictory*.

This means that the era of blended worship that worked effectively at the close of the modern age in the 80s and 90s won't work today. Blending works best if the goal is to *attract* people into the institution, so that a single hospitality strategy and worship service can include everybody. Today it is no longer possible to satisfactorily blend a "one-size-fits-all" experience. The public is too diverse, and the tolerance within each lifestyle segment to put up with the preferences of another lifestyle segment is too low.

FAQ

Lucinda: Are you saying that traditional worship is bad?

Tom: No, just limited. Whether you admit it or not, all worship is mission targeted. What we call traditional tends to be whatever option of worship the people *currently in the room* find meaningful. Mission is not about forcing people *outside* to adapt to the preferences of people *inside*.

The good news is that worship options don't all need to be expensive, technologically sophisticated, or labor intensive.

- Tom has discovered that even in remote parts of Canada, for example, among outports in Newfoundland and Labrador, and the isolated regions of America (e.g., Appalachia or Idaho), it is possible for even the smallest church to design two distinct worship options. One might be an educational, caregiving worship service on Sunday morning, addressing the anxieties of aging church veterans over death and brokenness and focusing on compassion and wholeness through formal liturgies, nineteenth-century hymnology, intercessory prayers, and traditional preaching. The other might be a rompin', stompin', Celtic or cowboy inspirational and coaching service in the evening, addressing the anxieties of being lost and entrapped through song and dance, spontaneous prayers, and lay witness.

- Lucinda has discovered that in small towns overtaken by urban sprawl in the United States, it is also possible for churches with few resources to develop multiple sites and multiple choices. One option might be a caregiving, healing worship service early Sunday morning, addressing the anxieties of loneliness and abuse and focusing on friendship and acceptance through informal traditions, passing the peace, and pastoral prayers. The other might be a coaching and transformational service later Sunday morning, addressing the anxieties of lostness and entrapment and focusing on lifestyle coaching and addiction recovery through video, drama, dialogue, and the laying on of hands.

Some options require salaried professionals, lots of volunteers, print and audio technologies, and wooden pews. Other options require unpaid volunteer expertise, a handful of friendly folks, computerized images, and a drama team. The one clear fact is that these services are designed separately, not blended. The formula for postmodern worship may be simple, but demographic and lifestyle diversity makes implementation complex.

The second reason a simple formula still requires complex implementation is that a church cannot give a blessing that it has not already experienced.

In other words, you can't give what you don't have. If the worship leaders have not personally experienced Christ as spiritual guide, perfect human, new being, promise keeper, healer, vindicator, or shepherd; then no matter how clever their techniques and tactics, they will never succeed in blessing seekers with direction, rapport, deliverance, new life, healing, vindication, or belonging. Worship design in the modern world was all about *program*. After all, the goal was to connect the visitor with an appropriate program so that he or she would join the church.

However, worship design in the postmodern world is all about *relationship*. The goal is to connect the seeker with an experience of Christ that changes his or her personal, family, and community lives.

Once again, this shift to postmodern seeker sensitivity is radical and stressful for veteran church leaders. In the old, modern world, worship needed to be designed by *professionals* in a *quest for quality*. Highly trained, paid experts needed to create high quality performances in order to attract people into the church. In the emerging, postmodern world, worship needs to be designed by *credible spiritual leaders* to encourage *authentic mentoring relationships*. Highly accountable, spiritually deep, and often unpaid leaders who can speak personally of both life struggle and spiritual victory shape intense (and sometimes unpolished) experiences to bless people as they leave the church.

The Altered Call

Tom: *When we experience the real presence of Jesus Christ, God simultaneously employs and shatters all cultural forms. The power and presence of God uses—and then surpasses—whatever worship tactic has facilitated the revelation.*

Lucinda: It all begins with you—pastor, priest, or planner. In stripping away my personal tastes in worship and stepping beyond my institutional boundaries and childhood comfort zones, I had to let go control. I had to admit my need to be seen as authoritative, competent, and "right all the time." When serving as an executive in a successful megachurch, my husband called me out: "You like the image of being at this church more than the ministry of this church. You like being the center of attention more than Christ being the center of attention." I denied it of course . . . the last red flag of addiction. I now call that "altar ego."

All worship leaders have an altar ego, even if we hide under the lowliness of poor self-esteem, public claims of unworthiness, or genuine doubt. Deep inside, we're in it for the ego, not the outreach. We can learn new skills, work harder, promise to be more humble, and even give up on excellence altogether, but the addiction is still there. We cannot make ourselves whole. We cannot help seekers experience Christ as the new being, healer, spiritual guide, perfect human, promise keeper, shepherd, or vindicator unless we have experienced it ourselves.

Stop before reading further! What needs to change about your altar ego in order for you to focus your altered calling to make Christ known?

Seven Options for Mission-Targeted Worship

There is an amazing ferment in creative worship design happening in the global Christian movement today. Most church leaders are unaware of this diversity because their peer influences tend to be limited denominational affiliation, local and regional connections, and cultural boundaries. Indeed, churches have often been the last *homogenous* communities based on shared demographics of age, race, economic status, and educational achievement left standing in the midst of communities that are now radically *heterogeneous*. Therefore, church leaders are often unaware of the creativity in worship occurring in local congregations across the city or across the street.

Protestant, Catholic, Pentecostal, and independent church leaders often assume uniformity, predictability, and continuity of worship within their traditions that really isn't true. Yes, this may alarm church officialdom that seeks to defend dogmatic purity and political correctness.

However, the urgency to create relevant worship that blesses the public with authentic, life changing, society-reforming experiences of Christ outweighs the risks in the hearts and minds of many mission-driven pastors. Their creativity may not be widely known within their institutions out of self-protection. Few books explore their innovations, because by the time a book is written, edited, released, and distributed it is out of date. Even the Internet captures only a fraction of this ferment, because video streaming is still not a high priority among many lifestyle segments.

FAQ

Lucinda: Should every worship service be inflexibly loyal to a historical pattern or common structure?

Tom: No, because that is unfaithful to the gospel. The experience of the real presence of Christ meeting the point of human yearning is all that is sacred. The pattern or structure is just a strategy and tactic that all too often becomes a sacred cow.

Tom has had a "macro" experience traveling and consulting across the United States, Canada, and Australia in nearly every state, province, and major center and coaching internationally among other cultures and contexts. Lucinda has had a "micro" experience innovating, leading, and training worship teams in urban, urbanizing, and transitional community contexts.

What we have discovered is that externally focused, mission-driven churches are giving up the fruitless task of diversifying worship *by style*. In part, this is because it simply doesn't work! Churches may succeed in attracting visitors to worship, but they fail miserably in transforming individual lives and positively changing social contexts. No matter how high the quality of worship, and how appealing the style of worship, the world *still* isn't any different because the church exists. This means that however *attractive* a church becomes, it cannot *sustain* participation. The public is not stupid! Indeed, its thirst for God is more urgent (and specific) than ever, and its perceptions of authenticity or hypocrisy are more acute than ever!

Moreover, church leaders have discovered that stress management over changes in worship style is simply not worth the effort. Church members are not stupid either! Their thirst for God is just as urgent (and specific), and their need for profound spiritual and missional rationale for change is ever more acute! Attraction is not enough. There must be a deeper reason to change worship than merely increasing attendance and potential financial support.

The Altered Call

Tom: Worship is mission. It is God's mission to rescue the estranged world one existential anxiety at a time.

Lucinda: Worship as mission is always with a particular people whom God has given us to bless with a relevant expression of Christ's grace. We cannot give to others what we have not experienced.

The tradition of Veronica on the Via Dolorosa wiping the face of Christ, his image now imprinted on her towel, came to me as a living prayer one night as I cleansed my face. With my cloth pressing his image into my very being, I no longer needed a false one. What are your deepest anxieties? What are your most powerful experiences of Christ? How have they continued to shape your calling?

The only justification for worship is that it addresses the critical life situations of people and resolves their existential anxieties. The only credible worship is an experience of Christ that is a catalyst for acceptance. This is why the terminology of "traditional" and "contemporary" worship is dropping out of use. Each worship option is now being described by its *anticipated impact to bless seekers*. Faithful church members are willing to go outside their comfort zones and do whatever it takes to change worship, *provided it really helps people experience the transforming power of Christ and changes society.*

Building on the table presented in the first chapter, we observe that there are seven basic kinds of mission-targeted worship services (at least in Western Christianity) today.

Worship Options	Life Situations Addressed	Catalyst for Acceptance	Christ Experience	Existential Anxiety Resolved
Coaching Worship	Lost Looking for Direction	Life Purpose and Destiny	Spiritual Guide	Emptiness
Educational Worship	Lonely Looking for Rapport	Authentic and Truthful Relationships	Perfect Human	Meaningless-ness
Transforma-tional Worship	Trapped Looking for Deliverance	Liberation and Fresh Start	New Being	Fate
Inspirational Worshp	Dying Looking for Renewal	Confidence for Enduring Life	Promise Keeper	Death
Healing Worship	Broken Looking for Healing	Wholeness and Serenity	Healer	Guilt
Mission-Connectional Worship	Abused Looking for Vindication	Advocacy and Justice	Vindicator	Shame
Caregiving Worship	Discarded Looking for Compassion	Belonging and Comfort	Shepherd	Displacement

The tactics for each worship option will be explored in detail in the coming chapters. We encourage readers not to make any assumptions (either with excitement or alarm) about the personnel, music, liturgy or drama, technology support, or financial resources that might be demanded by each option of worship. Tactics are very contextual. Exactly The tactics for each worship option will be explored in detail in the coming chapters. We encourage readers not to make any assumptions (either with excitement or alarm) about the personnel, music, liturgy or drama, technology support, or financial resources that might be demanded by each option of worship. Tactics are very contextual. Exactly how each worship option is implemented requires thorough research into the lifestyle segment that is likely to seek out any particular worship option.

The first step in targeting worship is to understand which lifestyle segments you are blessing now, and what kind of worship option you are currently doing. As we shall see later, it is usually only possible to blend two at most. Some pairs of worship choices are easier to blend than others, and some pairs of worship are nearly impossible to blend. You simply have to surrender any expectation to bless everybody with the same worship service.

The second step in targeting worship is to identify the next lifestyle segment God calls you to bless. Remember, the issue isn't whether you like it or even *want to do it*. The issue is that *they* yearn for it, and God *expects* you to set aside your personal likes and dislikes to bless others. Which is more important? Me first or God's mission?

Church planters often understand this more clearly than established church leaders. Planters have already targeted the lifestyle segment for whom their hearts burst and proceed from there. Their challenge is that once they have successfully focused and developed a worship service for the target lifestyle segment, they need to resist complacency, fall down on their knees, follow Jesus to a new lifestyle segment, and do it all over again.

Established church leaders often need to realize that the lifestyle segment(s) they are blessing now, and who are well represented in worship today, actually do not represent the largest lifestyle segments in the mission field around the church. Their challenge is to refocus mission on the largest lifestyle segments *in the community*, rather than spend all their resources on a relative minority in the community.

You can clearly see what has happened over the life cycle of many churches. They started out in a relatively homogeneous community, blessing the single largest lifestyle segment. Over time, this segment migrated or morphed, and the community itself radically diversified. However, the church continued repeating the same programs year after year as if nothing had changed. So entrenched do church people become in this habit that membership preferences become sacred cows. They talk about *faithfulness* and practice *unfaithfulness*.

Every turnaround church I know has overcome the stress of this change. They have added worship options to bless the lifestyle segments that are currently unrepresented or underrepresented in the church. They try to make the diversity of church participants *mirror* the proportionate lifestyle segment diversity of the mission field. They not only *talk* about faithfulness. They stake the parsonage and the pension plan on *faithfulness*.

My Church Exercise	
What kind of worship did I most value 10 years ago? Choose the two that best describe your past sense of urgency.	_____ Coaching Worship . . . helping me find purpose and destiny _____ Educational Worship . . . helping me find authentic & truthful relationships _____ Transformational Worship . . . helping me find freedom and a fresh start _____ Inspirational Worship . . . helping me be confident for enduring life _____ Healing Worship . . . helping me find wholeness and serenity _____ Mission-Connectional Worship . . . helping me find justice and self-esteem _____ Caregiving Worship . . . helping me find comfort and belonging

What kind of worship do I yearn for today? Choose the two that best describe your current sense of urgency.	_____ Coaching Worship . . . helping me find purpose and destiny _____ Educational Worship . . . helping me find authentic & truthful relationships _____ Transformational Worship. . . helping me find freedom and a fresh start _____ Inspirational Worship . . . helping me be confident for enduring life _____ Healing Worship . . . helping me find wholeness and serenity _____ Mission-Connectional Worship . . . helping me find justice and self-esteem _____ Caregiving Worship . . . helping me find comfort and belonging
What kind of worship best describes what our church does now? Choose the two that best describe the worship service currently offered.	_____ Coaching Worship . . . helping me find purpose and destiny _____ Educational Worship . . . helping me find authentic & truthful relationships _____ Transformational Worship . . . helping me find freedom and a fresh start _____ Inspirational Worship . . . helping me be confident for enduring life _____ Healing Worship . . . helping me find wholeness and serenity _____ Mission-Connectional Worship. . . helping me find justice and self-esteem _____ Caregiving Worship . . . helping me find comfort and belonging
Bonus Question!	
What do other members in my family think?	Share this same exercise with members of your immediate family (spouse and children, grandparents and grandchildren). Share this same exercise with members of your church family (groups for youth, women, men, and seniors; choirs or bands; regular, occasional, and holiday attendees).

Worship Option

Coaching Worship

Coaching worship is a topical service that gives practical advice for effective and fulfilling living. It glorifies God by helping God's people shape their personal and family lives (including careers, relationships, and even recreational activities) around Christian values.

The seekers that tend to gravitate to this kind of worship service often live in dramatically changing communities. These may be urban neighborhoods experiencing significant immigration, small towns overtaken by urban sprawl, or rural and remote communities experiencing sudden industrialization or resource development (like oil and gas exploration). Other seekers that gravitate to this kind of worship service often experience high stress from lives in transition or high mobility. These may include people who relocate frequently every few years due to career changes or people who routinely have long commutes from the suburbs to work.

Here are some of the lifestyle segments that are likely to value coaching worship and are also likely to travel some distance to find it. The identification code in **bold** is the index used by Experian for easy reference.[1] Church leaders can discover whether or not lifestyle segments such as these are a significant proportion of their mission field by using the search engine at www.MissionInsite.com.[2] The very names of the lifestyle segments can hint at their lifestyle preferences.

A03: Kids and Cabernet

Prosperous, middle-aged married couples with children, living
    child-focused lives in affluent suburbs

B07: Generational Soup

Affluent couples and multigenerational families living a wide
    range of lifestyles in suburbia

E20: No Place Like Home

Upper-middle-class, multigenerational households in exurban
    areas

F22: Fast Track Couples

Active, young, upper-middle-class couples and families living
    upwardly mobile lifestyles

M45: Diapers and Debit Cards

Young, working-class families and single-parent households
    living in small, established city residences

O55: Family Troopers

Families and single-parent households living near military bases

P56: Rolling the Dice

Middle-aged, midscale income singles and divorced individu-
    als in secondary cities

R67: Hope for Tomorrow

Young, lower-income African-American single parents in
    second-city apartments

S68: Small Town, Shallow Pockets

Older, downscale singles and empty nesters living in modest
    exurban small towns

It is important to stress that preference for coaching worship is *likely* but not *certain*. Individuals may gravitate to other mission-targeted worship services as unique and urgent situations emerge. For example, these mobile lifestyle segments living in transitioning communities are especially vulnerable to health crises that impact mobility (and therefore income, family stability, and so on). Therefore, they may shift their worship participation to healing worship. Similarly, these busy, multitasking people may experience periodic crises in relationships and questions about truth and shift their worship participation to educational worship. However, this is usually temporary, and they gravitate back to coaching worship, as described below.

Life Situation and Compulsion to Worship

The publics that gravitate to coaching worship commonly express feelings of "being lost" and are looking for a sense of direction. They are compelled to seek God due to anxieties over emptiness. Life seems more like a "rat race" than purposeful journey. The changes going on around them—or buffeting their stability like waves against the seashore—seem random and pointless. They yearn to see a bigger picture, gain clarity about God's plan, and find their own place in it.

The life situation and compulsion for coaching worship is revealed in the famous Andy Warhol painting from 1986, *Last Supper*.[3] He deliberately caricatures the famous Leonardo da Vinci painting of the same subject, but introduces contemporary and seemingly secular elements. It is said that Warhol painted this work in the context of a spiritual discipline that included boxing or martial arts. Motorcycles dominate the painting. A price tag for "$6.99" suggests skepticism of the institutional church, combined with longing for authentic religious experience. The bold phrase "The Big C" is a short form for "The Big C: Can the Mind Act as a Cancer Cure?" In general, the painting reveals the practical and pragmatic expectations these lifestyle segments have of spirituality. The difference between coaching worship and educational worship may be subtle, but it is very significant. As we shall see in the next chapter, educational worship addresses the anxiety of *meaninglessness*, and the tangible expression of that is *loneliness*. However, the

37

publics that gravitate to coaching worship are not necessarily lonely. They often come with friends and family and sit together in friendship circles, but making new friends and deepening relationships is not their primary goal. They appreciate the expertise of the presenter, but building a personal relationship with that person is not their primary goal. Their goal is more pragmatic. They are anxious because life seems *empty*, and the tangible expression of that is *feeling lost*. They often have many friends and are active in social media. Their problem is that they are lost in the crowd, unclear about where they are going, uncertain about what to do, and perhaps afraid of taking a first step.

These publics often have "attitude!" They appear more confident than they really are. They have little interest in why the world is like it is or who is right or wrong. They are interested in how to get things done and the related questions about what to do and when or where to do it.

Coaching worship is not theoretical, but practical. What helps these people find purpose and direction in daily living is the concrete advice on how to live. These people are less concerned about what happens at the end of time than what happens tomorrow at work or tonight when they quarrel with their children. Practical Christian values give them clear boundaries and benchmarks around which they can orient their lives. They are part of a *system* of Christian living that resolves many of the daily ambiguities in their decision making.

The Altered Call

Tom: *Successful coaching worship is not measured by attendance, but by the number of significant conversations.*

Lucinda: *The experience of Christ as spiritual guide compels us to link worship with individual mentoring and small groups. This alters the calling of many clergy who are used to expository preaching and classroom teaching. Worship leaders need to be mentors who have "been there, done that." Mentors don't pretend to know everything but are further down the road and willing to turn back and* *help those coming up behind. Their expertise gives reliable advice, but their life experience helps us discover potential and release gifts we never knew we had. Is that you?*

Coaching worship really began to emerge as a significant option in the late 70s and 80s, and parallels the rise of the "global village." Internet, immigration, and economics have been more challenging and unpredictable than ever before, redirecting careers, redefining intimacy, and reshaping environments. National borders and cultural assumptions are blurred by the emergence of multinational corporations and megalopoli. Coaching worship meets people in the "nitty-gritty" of daily living. It is not important to *understand* all this. It is important to *make it personal*. What does this mean *for me*? How do I have to change and adapt? How can I find my way to success and happiness when all the landmarks and benchmarks seem to have disappeared?

The advice provided in coaching worship is not always easy. It may persuade participants to dramatically change their career paths, intimate relationships, personal habits, and daily pursuits. Yet they are willing to risk upward mobility, marriage and family life, and even neighborhood reputation and financial success in order to live in a values system that lowers stress and encourages personal fulfillment. Despite the appearance of informality typical of a coaching worship service, these participants are just stepping aside from high-stress lives.

A closer look at the lifestyle segments that gravitate to this form of worship reveals that many participants are starting (or restarting) careers and families; blue collar or white-collar middle management; trained in applied sciences, trades, and occupational specializations; and still looking for a permanent home. The same lifestyle segments that gravitate to coaching worship may also watch a myriad of house-hunting, home-renovation, or property-flipping television programs. It is noteworthy that all such "homemaking" television programming provides a knowledgeable expert (who has "been there, done that") as a guide and host. In the same way, the worship leader of a coaching service is often an expert who gives practical advice about Christian living.

These people are not trying to find the courage to stake their lives on Christ; but rather, they are trying to find a method to shape their lifestyles around Christ. They yearn to experience Christ as a spiritual guide who can help them find their ways through the ambiguities of daily living. They seek Christ as a mentor who can be available 24-7, coach them through difficult and stressful circumstances, and help them make difficult decisions. Overall, Christ helps them see and accept their personal destiny.

What It Looks Like

Coaching worship is all about practical help for daily living. The topics address issues and concerns that occur and recur in the context of home, workplace, playground, and points in-between. Clearly, the specific topics are very contextual, and worship designers discover these "hot topics" through listening strategies in the neighborhood or community, conversations with social service and public education partners, and sensitivity to economic and social changes. The focus is very local, not global. It addresses the stresses and ambiguities that are experienced on a daily and weekly basis by a large number of people in the primary mission field.

This kind of worship is often advertised on an illuminated marquis outside the meeting space, in local newspapers in almost any section *except* the religion pages, and through local social service, public health, public education, and continuing education networks. The topic is usually changed weekly, but there may be a theme that lasts several weeks. The title usually begins, "How to . . ." For example, topics we have seen recently include:

- How to fight with your spouse and stay Christian
- How to merge two families in a remarriage
- How to help little children cope with a death in the family
- How to grow a small business with Christian values
- How to play competitive sports with Christian values

The worship experience is usually very informal. It encourages dialogue and conversation. It provides a variety of take-home resources and follow-up opportunities. Life context defines the questions, and a combination of practical expertise and biblical awareness provides the answers.

Clearly, this is not the kind of worship that many denominations encouraged in previous decades. It does not follow a common lectionary. It does not follow a Christian Year. If anything, it follows a pop-culture calendar that emphasizes holidays like Valentine's Day, March break, Mother's Day, Thanksgiving, and Halloween and addresses the personal and family stresses that often accompany such occasions. This service does not begin with scripture and apply it to daily life. It begins with daily life and searches scripture for an appropriate response. It is not developed by a pastor in search of a topic. It starts with a topic in search of an expert opinion.

FAQ

Lucinda: How do I get the topics?

Tom: Listen! Tactics include community focus groups and regular interviews with leaders in other sectors, like social service, health, business, career counseling, and so on. You can also use search engines like www.MissionInsite.com that provide specific psychographic insights into lifestyles and needs.

The people who attend coaching worship are motivated because the theme of the day *is their issue.* They are attracted by the topic, and they are blessed by clarity and insight into the right decisions and behaviors. Even if significant behavioral changes are required, participants find them both *meaningful* (clearly anchored in Christian values) and *reasonable* (clearly supported by experience and expertise). They may revisit a coaching worship the next time there is a topic that addresses their life issues, but they often remain in communication and provide ongoing support to a church that has a reputation for guiding people through the practical dilemmas of daily living.

Hospitality

The topic addresses the needs of very diverse publics. The gathering may include different ages, income brackets, races, and even languages. Participants represent diverse marriage and family statuses, education levels, occupational backgrounds, and even religious backgrounds. It is not uncommon to discover that frequent participants in a coaching service are *also* members of another church and occasionally worship there. Many people attend coaching worship with reluctance or misgivings. They may be inexperienced with, or alienated from, church as an institution. They may approach warily and sit in the back. They are often accompanied by a friend, family member, work associate, or a member of the church with whom they are acquainted socially.

This means that hospitality must be quite intentional and offer multiple options. Hospitality begins at least thirty minutes ahead of worship, even if the event is scheduled early in the morning. Greeters are trained to be radically accepting and nonjudgmental. They are trained to be sensitive to unique cultural dispositions in the treatment of children, women, elders, and so on. They are extraordinarily respectful of personal space but extremely cheerful and helpful. Individual greeters may even speak the rudiments of a second language. They are optimistic peacemakers and a nonthreatening presence.

Refreshments necessarily provide multiple choices. The refreshment area resembles a food court with multiple serving stations and plenty of room to stand or sit. There is usually ambient music in a genre popular in the local community, but the lyrics are compatible with Christian values. Refreshments tend toward comfort foods but whether they are fresh or packaged depends on the individual context. Servers are available (especially for children and seniors), but otherwise people help themselves.

Refreshments are available from thirty minutes prior to worship, throughout worship, and up to an hour following worship. People are free to carry food into the worship center and are encouraged to replenish their refreshments even during the worship program. Volunteers are always present in the "food court" to restock, manage waste, and converse with participants. There is usually a resource table or store where books, videos, and other resources relevant to the topic of the day can be purchased to take home.

Worship Format

Three basic principles guide the design of coaching worship. Keep it contextual. Keep it informal. Keep it simple. The constant temptation of traditionally trained clergy is to make worship too historical, formal, and complicated. Among the lifestyle segments most interested in coaching worship, those mistakes all suggest a lack of authenticity and hidden manipulation.

Keep it contextual. This means that the theme of the worship experience and the content of the message address urgent issues that recur frequently in the daily lives of participants. The music is in a genre, and uses the instrumentations, that are commonly appreciated by the participants and enjoyed in whatever media or manner that they normally enjoy them at home, bars, coffee shops, or any other venue. The message is practical and communicates tips and tactics that will make life better the minute they leave. Books, magazines, video, and other resources are either free or cheap, absolutely on target with the theme, and available to take home or access instantly.

Keep it informal. Conversation and interaction are constant and crucial. Audience participation is important. Drama, video, and music are integrated with the theme. Depending on the lifestyle segments involved, coaching worship can use stand-up comedy, games, and other forms of amusement that rely on irony to make a point. It is OK to laugh and cry, to leave the room for more coffee or a smoke, and to interrupt the speaker with a question. However, core values (positive behavioral expectations) are clearly displayed and communicated. Participants who behave badly or rudely will be held accountable by their peers as well as worship leaders.

Keep it simple. Since *simple* is a relative term, it might be more accurate to say *intuitive.* Every lifestyle segment finds different activities "intuitive" that another lifestyle segment might find foreign. For

43

example, computer-generated imaging and web surfing in the midst of worship is simple (i.e., intuitive) for some segments, and something seemingly simple like referring to an index in a book or brewing fresh coffee might be mind-boggling and counterintuitive to others. Make it easy for people. Never expect them to learn something in order to learn something else.

The formula of coaching worship is *music, message,* and *next steps.* All of that is surrounded by, and filtered through, relationships. Worship participants tend to sit in small groups and position their bodies to see, touch, and talk with others.

The first twenty minutes may be just music as if participants were at a small or informal concert. They usually don't sing, unless it is to join the band in a refrain, or participants are invited to volunteer for karaoke-style music. They will clap, move, dance, cheer, and applaud . . . and sometimes be utterly silent, lost in the lyric or the rhythm. Music may come and go during the experience and may be used to set the mood or anticipate the message.

Lucinda's Notes: You Can Do This!

Wirelessly streaming music to one or more powered speakers keeps the flow seamless from informal gathering to worship. Worship designers tend to use multipurpose space. Hardware does not need to be expensive, and it is usually portable. In my experience, a great Sunday morning DJ with ballroom dancing as a hobby has amazing playlists to fit every season.

For the fellowship gathering prior to worship, use instrumentals so that folks aren't shouting over it, and save the music with the most poignant lyrics that speak to the head and heart to just prior to the emcee's introduction and welcome.

Prerecorded music is also an effect closer to a coaching message; fade it for the closing words by the emcee and bring it up again as people leave.

The message may take as much as thirty minutes or more (especially if punctuated by dialogue, drama, or video clip). The Bible is a constant reference point, but exactly how it is used and how much weight of authority it is given varies according to the faith convictions of the church. A single passage or story sets the stage for the message, but the message itself relies on resources or expertise related to the subject at hand. As much as possible, the Bible is regarded as a manual for good living, rather than a theological treatise or historical account.

The "next step" is more important than any benediction or commissioning. The speaker points participants toward additional resources or opportunities that will equip them further to deal with whatever challenge is urgent. Worship often spotlights small group leaders or small group opportunities or identifies mentors in the audience who can be approached during refreshments following the service.

The bedrock beliefs of the church are communicated through words and symbols visible in the room, rather than embedded in any particular creed or rite. Prayers are generally brief or spontaneous. Eucharist may be celebrated (depending on the faith of the church and expectations of lifestyle segments participating) but tends to be brief, informal, and usually very open. Sometimes the elements are offered in different alternatives (wine and juice; wafers, bread cubes, loaves; sitting, standing, kneeling, and whatever is easy, simple, welcoming, and "intuitive").

FAQ

Lucinda: How do I close a coaching service?

Tom: Hand off! Finish worship by referring to next steps like short-term small groups to follow up on the topic, print and video resources for home, and guides and mentors in the refreshment center.

The topic dictates the program or presentation, and therefore the format will change from week to week. Aside from music, message, and next steps, worship is remarkably unpredictable. This may be unsettling for some church veterans who are used to consistency, but it is energizing for most seekers who look for creativity and relevance.

Worship Leadership

The two primary worship leaders can best be described as an "emcee" and a "coach." The pastor or priest is usually in the room, but may only make a brief appearance on stage to welcome people, pray briefly, or articulate the basic mission of the church. (The clergy may reappear if Eucharist is celebrated).

The emcee is usually a member of the church who readily and visibly identifies with the lifestyle segments in the room. In other words, the "emcee" resembles the demographic by age, gender, marital status, income, occupation, and lifestyle. He or she dresses, behaves, and speaks in whatever way is seen as normal by the rest of the people in the room. The worship service is so simple that not much needs to be introduced. The emcee may introduce the coach, lead the applause for a musician, formally announce an intermission for refreshments, and even offer some comic relief. The emcee may also itemize the next steps, introduce mentors and midweek small group leaders, or highlight a resource before everyone leaves.

The coach is the credible expert who provides the teaching or training. This may be the pastor, but often this is a nonordained church member or guest. Credibility depends on his or her reputation or competency around the particular topic of the day. These experts are often found in the community itself among business leaders, social service and health care workers, emergency response teams, legal advisers and financial managers, and so on. It is also possible to use video clips or record interviews with specialists or well-known leaders in any sector, on any topic.

However, expertise is not the only reason the coach is credible. The coach must also be compatible with, and intentionally honor, the values and beliefs of the church because the coach is not only an expert but also a role model.

Aside from expertise, the best coach is usually one who is readily perceived to be utterly reasonable, culturally sensitive, and spiritually alive. The coach offers both presentation and dialogue. There is always Q&A following his or her coaching. Sometimes the emcee will return to the stage to help manage the dialogue, and sometimes the coach will do it.

Lucinda's Notes: You Can Do This!

I'll never forget what happened one worship design meeting, after I had been struggling for weeks micromanaging each Sunday's announcements. This time the team went silent. I asked them, "What's wrong?" And then the words of both conviction and grace followed: "Well Lucinda, you just suck at that. Do what you do best and we'll take care of the rest."

What sweet freedom in the truth. I could now really enter into worship and not worry about the details and what comes next. I concentrated on the message and guiding the worshipers toward the next steps of a life in Christ. The team called me "the closer." Sometimes, it was to bring only the sacraments or a guided time of prayer or to introduce the testimony.

Since the topic dictates the program, and different program strategies require different personnel, the leadership of coaching worship often varies. Teams may become involved for drama, dance, cooking, crafts, and so on. The consistency is maintained by pastor/priest, emcee, and perhaps a musician. Sometimes a music or band leader also functions as an emcee. Sometimes a technician (e.g., a computer-imaging operator) is the emcee. This depends on the lifestyle segments involved and what kind of leader attracts their interest and respect.

Facilities and Technologies

Coaching worship requires a flexible space that encourages relationships, facilitates dialogue, and allows effortless movement of people. Therefore, a traditional sanctuary with fixed furniture, or an auditorium with row seating, is not useful. The facility can be as large as a church hall or as intimate as a coffee shop or pub. The size must be able to easily accommodate small groups of people sitting together (usually around a table), with plenty of space for people to move back and forth to refreshments.

The worship center needs to be immediately proximate to a refreshment center. There should be no hallways, stairs, or any obstacles in the way. In a large venue, the refreshment area might be a food court with multiple serving stations, but in a small venue it may just be a table with food and drink. However, there should be plenty of space for people to mingle and talk.

The quality of seating, table decorations, and room ambience depends largely on the lifestyle segments who are expected to participate. Since relationships and conversations are so important, it is obviously preferable that the room have color and comfort suitable to a warm environment where people are encouraged to relax and linger. However, even a gymnasium will do. Tables should include paper and pens for taking notes, and some lifestyle segments will expect sufficient electrical outlets to plug in laptops. Make sure that extension cords are secure and safe in the midst of traffic. Most lifestyle segments value Internet access, so the room should have Wi-Fi, with any access code plainly in view.

Coaching worship often relies on computer imaging to project images, videos, and key points of the coach's message. This can be either relatively simple or elaborate, and today both can be done with little expense. If music video replaces live music, a good sound system is vital. Dialogue with the speaker demands multiple microphones available around the room, although sometimes a simple, cordless, microphone can be shared by a runner who can bring the microphone to the questioner. It is vital that everyone can hear *all* the dialogue.

Lucinda's Notes: You Can Do This!

Great content can come from video-based Bible studies, selections from other presenters' messages available online, and non-church-based information and insight from the news, lifestyle, and entertainment industry.

Many megasized churches have reasonably priced teaching segments that are well edited for their satellite campuses. Always note the copyright restrictions, and give credit for your resources.

A stage (or raised platform or even just a high stool for the coach) is usually present. This is particularly important if live drama, musical performances, or other activities relevant to the topic of the day are used. This means that lighting and spotlighting can also be very helpful. Some venues make the stage portable because some coaching topics are enhanced by focusing attention to the center of the room.

Many of the lifestyle segments interested in coaching worship include families with young children. The facility needs to be family friendly, allowing easy access for strollers and special seating for expectant mothers. High-quality child care needs to be immediately proximate to the worship area, but sometimes children simply stay in the same room with the adults. This means that the worship space includes safe, comfortable, clean spaces for children to play in the same room, crayons and toys for older children at the tables with parents, and even infant diaper changing stations along one wall. If children are sharing the space, the environment might include sound baffles (banners, tapestries, or textiles to reduce echo effects).

There is no printed order of service. There may be handouts that provide outlines for the message, additional resources to take home, or occasionally exercises or conversation starters for each table group (if that is the technique chosen by the coach). Usually information about the message, further resources, and midweek small group opportunities are projected on screens before and after worship and during intermissions.

If Eucharist is included in worship, any necessary liturgy is brief, in common language, and projected on screens. Communionware is usually very simple and emphasizes symbolically how God can use very ordinary things for extraordinary purposes. The practical content, informality, and diverse participation of coaching worship usually implies extreme generosity that accepts both participation and nonparticipation without question.

Timing and Timeliness

Coaching worship follows the rhythm of daily and seasonal life for the specific lifestyle segments to be reached. It does not follow the traditional Christian Year of important church observances but the lived year as actually experienced by people in the mission field. This is because every holiday and season forces different kinds of stress on the lives of people. The point is always practical advice on how to live effectively as a Christian.

For example, coaching worship is usually sensitive to holidays like New Year's Day, Valentine's Day, Mother's Day, Thanksgiving, Halloween, and Christmas Eve. Coaching worship topics may focus on unique stresses regarding health, relationships, family dynamics, good parenting, budgeting, or other real issues that surface on such occasions.

Similarly, coaching worship is sensitive to annual shifts in lifestyle like summer holidays, fall public school changes, winter blahs, and spring madness. Worship designers are aware of the unique stresses associated with March break, vacation schedules, work regimens, student exams, the most common relocation months, and so on. (In the southern hemisphere many of these issues may be seasonally reversed.)

FAQ

Lucinda: How do I interface with the lectionary?

Tom: You can't. This is about *timely topics*, not timeless truths. Imposition of a theological agenda will be seen as inauthentic and even disrespectful.

Coaching worship is also very responsive to local emergencies or community transformations. Natural or home disasters, tragic deaths, and economic collapses are examples of negative events that provoke stress. The opening of a new hospital ward, launch of a new social program, celebration of a special day for the environment, or support for a sport or arts venue are examples of positive events that provoke a different kind of stress.

The day and time of coaching worship is clearly flexible and depends on the normative work, education, and recreation schedules of the lifestyle segments. Note this! The church adjusts the day and time of worship around the lifestyle segments' schedules and *never* expects them to adjust their schedules around the day and time of the worship.

In many contexts of the United States, Sunday continues to be a prime opportunity for worship. In that case, coaching worship is usually late Sunday morning at eleven and often includes lunch or takeout. This is because many of the younger lifestyle segments blessed by coaching worship stay up late on Saturday night or cope with small children on Sunday morning. Alternatively, coaching worship may be early Sunday evening and include wine or beer (if the core values of the church permit it) and dessert. This is because worship may rely on local semiprofessional musicians and artists for whom Sunday evening may be free.

Yet in more and more contexts, it is not safe to assume that Sunday is the best day or time. This is especially true if churches make coaching worship a monthly (rather than a weekly) opportunity. These churches will be even more radical in allowing the *topic* of the day to dictate the *time* and *place* of worship. One month it might be here and this time; another month it might be there at another time.

Measuring Success

The notion of measuring the success of a worship service may initially seem foreign to traditionally trained pastors and worship leaders. However, church leaders and members actually do measure success without realizing it. When the pastor, worship leader, or participant goes home (for example), their spouse, neighbor, or friend almost always asks, "How did it go?" "Was it a good worship service?" The answers may vary: "It was a good sermon." "I remember three points." "We clapped for the anthem." "There was a good crowd." "The offering was up." All these are measurements of success, but they may not be the *right things to measure*!

Like all programs of any organization, there is a way to measure the success of coaching worship. Leaders will usually evaluate every coaching worship experience within two to three days of the event. The reason they must be this intentional is that coaching worship lives or dies by its *immediate sensitivity* to the shifting trends of the mission field. Seeker sensitivity is everything.

Five key measures of success are the following:[4]

1. **The proportionate participation of targeted lifestyle segments:** One obvious measure of success is to calculate the percentage of participants that actually represent the lifestyle segments that are the intended target. For example, if worship is designed to bless young, working-class families and single parent households or young, lower-income African American single parents living in nearby apartments, then leaders can use focus groups, random exit interviews, or plain observation to determine if those people are indeed connecting with the worship service.

2. **The number of visitors in worship:** Coaching worship participation grows by word of mouth and through the invitation of members or current participants. It is an

outreach to nonmembers and often a first step into greater involvement with Christian lifestyle. A high proportion of participants should be first- or second-time visitors. Leaders can often discover this simply by asking new people to raise their hands, or identify themselves over coffee, in order to receive a free gift that is relevant to the topic of the day. This builds the database for future advertising of topical worship services.

3. **The number of significant conversations between leaders and participants:** Coaching worship provides lots of opportunities for relationship building and informal dialogue within worship—but also before worship, through intermission during worship, and after worship over refreshments. If successful, coaching worship should create a "buzz" of conversation that can be observed and overheard. This is enhanced when leaders (especially the emcee, musicians, dramatists, and tech teams) deliberately mingle with people and intentionally stimulate dialogue on topic. These significant conversations can be counted, reported back to the church, and used to customize the next worship experience to be even more effective.

4. **The number of midweek small groups:** Coaching worship is a motivational introduction to advice about daily living. It usually spotlights small group leaders and small group opportunities. Therefore, a high proportion of participants in any given coaching worship should show up in the following week(s) in a relevant small group at homes, restaurants, or even the church building. A rule of thumb is about 60 percent. If a low percentage of participants show up for small groups, this means that the coaching worship service has failed to really answer their questions or motivate their search. Participation in small groups is directly tied to the number of significant conversations after worship.

5. **The reputation growing in the community:** Coaching worship is intended to be practical and useful so that there are immediate and visible benefits in the daily living of participants at home, work, and play. Therefore, leaders can measure the buzz that it stimulates in the community. For example, there should be an awareness and appreciation of the coaching worship themes among social service, health care, law enforcement, municipal government, and other agencies. There may be positive recognition in the media and even positive feedback from businesses or industries.

These five key measures indicate *the right way to measure success* for coaching worship. They help worship designers make weekly or monthly adjustments to be more effective in blessing the lifestyle segments targeted in the community.

Compatible Worship Options
A church can only blend two of the seven options
of worship successfully.
What are the easiest and hardest blends for coaching worship?

Easiest Blend: Inspirational Worship
Difficult Blend: Educational Worship or Mission-Connectional Worship
Hardest Blend: Caregiving, Healing, or Transformational Worship

Worship Option

Educational Worship

Educational worship is a teaching service that informs, explains, and advocates doctrines, principles, ethical positions, and church policies to members of the church. It glorifies God by equipping church members to witness by word and deed to the gospel and its implications for belief and morality.

The seekers that tend to gravitate to this kind of worship service can come from many different lifestyle segments, but they tend to be of three clusters. Note that these three distinct lifestyle groups (and the segments they include) do not necessarily gravitate to the same hospitality, education, small group, and outreach programs. Although they may prefer a purposefully educational worship experience, they may not participate in the same *style* of educational worship or readily participate in the same church. Churches that are most successful in reaching all three groups of seekers tend to be in urban centers proximate to a university or college.

The first cluster of seekers tends to be older, wealthier (or at least with a financial status that insures stability and some luxuries), and educated with university or professional training. These people also tend to have longer residency in any given location, and participate in a phase of life that includes older children or empty nests. These lifestyle groups and segments include the following.[1]

Group A: Power Elite

The wealthiest households in the United States, living in exclusive neighborhoods, enjoying all that life has to offer

A01: American Royalty

Wealthy, influential, and successful couples and families living in prestigious suburbs

A02: Platinum Prosperity

Wealthy and established empty-nesting couples residing in suburban and in-town homes

A03: Kids and Cabernet

Prosperous, middle-aged married couples with children, living child-focused lives in affluent suburbs

A04: Picture-Perfect Families

Established families of child-rearing households living in wealthy suburbs

Group C: Booming with Confidence

Prosperous, established couples in their peak earning years living in suburban homes

C11: Aging of Aquarius

Upscale boomer-aged couples living in cities and close-in suburbs

C12: Golf Carts and Gourmets

Upscale retirees and empty nesters in comfortable communities

C13: Silver Sophisticates

Mature, upscale couples and singles in suburban homes

Group H: Middle-Class Melting Pot

Midscale, middle-aged, and established couples living in suburban and fringe homes

H26: Progressive Potpourri

Mature, multiethnic couples with comfortable and active lives in middle-class suburbs

H27: Birkenstocks and Beemers

Upper-middle-class, established couples living leisure lifestyles in small towns and cities

H28: Everyday Moderates

Midscale, multicultural couples and families living in midtier metro suburban settings

H29: Destination Recreation

Middle-aged, midscale couples in rural towns and fringe suburbs working to enjoy their active lifestyles

Group J: Autumn Years

Established, ethnically diverse, and mature couples living gratified lifestyles in older homes

J34: Aging in Place

Middle-class seniors living solid, suburban lifestyles

J35: Rural Escape

Older, middle-class couples and singles living comfortable lives in rural towns

J36: Settled and Sensible

Older, middle-class, and empty-nesting couples and singles in city neighborhoods

Group Q: Golden Year Guardians

Retirees living in settled residences and communities

Q62: Reaping Rewards

Relaxed, retired couples and widowed individuals in suburban homes living quiet lives

Q63: Footloose and Family Free

Elderly couples and widowed individuals living active and comfortable lifestyles

Q64: Town Elders

Stable, minimalist seniors living in older residences and leading sedentary lifestyles

Q65: Senior Discounts

Downscale, settled retirees in metro apartment communities

Worship designers should pay special attention to the demographic trends for these groups. Two of the most significant groups that gravitate to educational worship are gradually disappearing (Group J: Autumn Years and Group Q: Golden Year Guardians), and only three out of four segments, in only one of the many boomer lifestyle groups, seem to be primarily interested in educational worship (Group C: Booming with Confidence). Although there is interest among affluent and middle class lifestyle groups and segments (Group A: Power Elite and Group H: Middle Class Melting Pot), there is plenty of evidence that their attention for educational worship is increasingly competing with other lifestyle interests (e.g. travel, sports, nature, and so on).

The second cluster of seekers may be younger and less stable than the first cluster. They tend to have sufficient income to sustain a fulfilling life but not much extra. They also tend to be starting out, experimenting with ideas and behavioral norms, and relatively mobile and unattached. These lifestyle groups and segments include the following.[2]

Group K: Significant Singles

Middle-aged singles and some couples earning midscale incomes supporting active city styles of living

K37: Wired for Success

Young, midscale singles and couples living socially active city lives

K38: Gotham Blend

Mix of middle-aged and middle-class singles and couples living urban New York City–area lifestyles

K39: Metro Fusion

Ethnically diverse, middle-aged singles living urban, active lifestyles

Group O: Singles and Starters

Young singles starting out, and some starter families, in diverse urban communities

O51: Digital Dependents

Mix of generation Y and X singles that live digital-driven, urban lifestyles

O52: Urban Ambition

Mainly generation Y African American singles and single families established in midmarket cities

O53: Colleges and Cafes

Young singles and recent college graduates living in college communities

The lifestyle segments in each group value educational worship because it will help them test their thinking and behavior against Christian orthodoxy and Christian ethics. Unlike the previous cluster, they are less likely to simply *agree* with the teaching or conform to the behavioral norms. Instead, they will engage these insights critically and selectively. Their worship attendance may well be more sporadic, and they may not see a big difference between a *seminar* on theology and ethics and an *educational worship experience*. There are some segments belonging to the groups above that are not listed because they do not gravitate to educational worship as a first choice. Indeed, they may carry stereotypes that educational worship is *the only option* for worship and one that they categorically reject.

The third cluster that values educational worship is at the opposite extreme of affluence. They tend to be poor and struggling to survive. They also tend to be less educated (without high school diplomas) and work in blue-collar trades, subsistence farming or mining, or in industry and transportation.

Group S: Struggling Societies

Economically challenged mix of single, divorced, and widowed individuals in smaller cities and urban areas looking to make ends meet

S68: Small Town, Shallow Pockets

Older, downscale singles and empty nesters living in modest exurban small towns

S69: Soul Survivors

Older, downscale African American singles and single parents established in modest urban neighborhoods

S70: Enduring Hardships

Middle-aged, downscale singles and divorced individuals in transitional small town and exurban apartments

S71: Hard Times

Older, downscale and ethnically diverse singles typically concentrated in inner-city apartments

Educational worship is a form of continuing education and a path to self-improvement. It provides basic doctrinal principles that give the "Struggling Societies" lifestyle segments strength and unequivocal values that target behavior. In their case, education has a more rigorous, literal, or rote quality that is more disturbing than helpful to the second cluster of young, better educated, upwardly mobile people above and more radical than the first cluster wants.

Life Situation and Compulsion to Worship

The lifestyle segments that commonly gravitate to educational worship commonly express feelings of loneliness that overshadow even the sense of being lost that is so profound a motivator for coaching worship. Clearly there are similarities between people who feel lost and people who feel lonely, but in this case the dominant search is to find some *rapport* with the living truth about life. They are compelled to seek God due to anxieties about the potential *meaninglessness* of life. Whether they are surrounded by material wealth or aspiring to material wealth or missing material wealth altogether, they all have a sense that materialism itself is a dead end. They long to discover, and cling to, abiding theological principles and consistent ethical norms that make life worthwhile *despite* the presence or absence of material success.

As I noted in the previous chapter, the difference between educational worship and coaching worship is subtle but extraordinarily significant. Coaching worship addresses the anxiety of *emptiness*, and the tangible expression of that is *feeling lost*. Educational worship addresses the anxiety of *meaninglessness*, and the tangible expression of that is *feeling lonely*. Educational worship became particularly significant with the collapse of the old political and rationalistic worldview following the two world wars and the shattered illusions of the emerging nuclear age. The modern art of this period (e.g., Picasso's *Guernica*) combines surreal images with a desperate sense of alienation. Suddenly "being human" became an open question and life quest.

The traumas of the First and Second World Wars, and indeed subsequent experiences of mass murders, ethnic cleansings, purposeless violence, and random crime, combined with natural disasters and medical crises to elevate the problem of evil as the greatest dilemma for faith. *Guernica* captures this profound sense of meaninglessness that raises doubts about the existence or power of God and the inevitability of salvation history. I once visited an historic mainstream church near Boston Common that had a huge sign on the front door of the church: "Got Questions? So Do We!" This epitomizes the tension between certainty and skepticism, and the quest for absolutes, that is the focus for educational worship. Not surprisingly, the visual art displayed in the building is an extreme contrast between cubism like Picasso's *Guernica* and stained glass depicting classic biblical scenes.

The publics that gravitate to educational worship often bring with them a marked cynicism and skepticism about life, religion, and the future. They are less pragmatic and more speculative. They are very interested in *why* the world is like it is and *who* is right or wrong; but they are less interested in *how* to get things done or *when* and *where* to act. They are relatively confident in their skills. They just don't understand the *reasons*.

Educational worship, therefore, is more theoretical than practical (the reverse of coaching worship). It tends to be more conceptual, doctrinal, or even dogmatic; and it tends to be more rigid, demanding, or even fundamentalist about morals. These doctrines and morals may be very liberal or very conservative. The theologies explained and advocated in some educational worship may have radically different views about the authority of scripture, ordination, and sacraments, but worship is still about education. The public policies explained and advocated in educational worship may have radically different views about hot topics like war and peace, gun control, abortion, euthanasia, sexuality, and medical ethics, but worship is still about education.

FAQ

Lucinda: Is educational worship what many people mean by "traditional worship"?

Tom: There are two kinds of worship that are often considered "traditional," and this is certainly one of them. It often juxtaposes music that predates the twentieth century of doubt and expository sermons that engage the emerging age of skepticism.

The goal of educational worship is to *change your mind,* while the goal of coaching worship was to *alter your behavior.* Educational worship helps people make sense of the world. It explains, interprets, compares and critiques, and engages the mind. It creates intelligent, reflective Christians. Worship tends to be a function of continuing education. It tends to encourage rational reserve rather than emotional engagement. Faith is a matter of understanding and agreement.

It is important to understand, however, that anxiety about the potential meaninglessness of life does not just drive people to *creeds* but to *authentic relationships*. Assent to doctrines and ethical norms is important, but it is even more important that principles of faith and moral expectations are embodied in the pastor or priest, leaders and elders, and ultimately in the quality of relationships in the church. Note, for example, that educational worship routinely values *not only* the sermon and the liturgy *but also* a formalized process to "pass the peace" or "greet one another." This process is deliberately formulaic. It brings together the longing for abstract truth and the longing for personal authenticity. The most common reason that attendance in educational worship declines is not that the doctrines and ethical principles are not explained, but that the leaders and members are not perceived to live up to them. People remain committed to an agreement about truth but withdraw from the church when there is a credibility gap between "talking the walk and walking the talk."

The goal of educational worship, therefore, is to describe universal models of integrity that can be imitated by anyone, in any century, in any cultural context, and in any particular situation. This universality that is typical of educational worship contrasts sharply with the contextuality that is typical of coaching worship. This also helps us understand why the aesthetics of worship are so important. Worship brings people closer to classical paradigms of truth, goodness, and beauty. The relationship with God is both intimate and exalted. Beyond the complexity of worship is a simple truth: *God is love.*

This is why the incarnational experience we associate with educational worship is that of Christ the perfect human. The perfection of Christ is that he is the truth *and* the life. People yearn for the immediacy of God as truth personified. In coaching worship, Christ is the mentor who guides us through the ambiguities of daily living. But in educational worship, Christ is the model who demonstrates in his own self the eternal truths and consistent behavioral norms that are Christian. The publics who gravitate to coaching worship want to *walk with Jesus*, sensitive to the variations of time, place, people, and process. The publics who gravitate to educational worship want to *be like Jesus*, rising above any given context to a higher, purer, and enduring standard of faith.

FAQ

Lucinda: Why are friendships formalized in the passing of the peace so important?

Tom: People in these segments are not just looking for truth but for *embodied* truth. They look for perfection both in ideas and relationships. The nativity doctrine of the "Word made flesh" may be more important than the historical baby Jesus. Passing the peace is often formal because the person sitting next to them may be Christ incognito.

It is interesting to note that secular governments often have ambivalent attitudes toward educational worship. On the one hand, they see educational worship as an important means to assimilate immigrants into a new culture with shared language, ideals, and rituals. On the other hand, they fear educational worship because it also challenges political assumptions and cultural mores by comparing them to the standards of the Old and New Testaments. The goal of cultural homogeneity is often in tension with the possibility of prophetic critique.

What It Looks Like

Educational worship is all about assent and obedience to a particular set of theological principles and ethical norms. It is necessarily more abstract and general, because the teaching must be universally applicable. The liturgy includes generic prayers of confession and classical assurances of forgiveness. Sermons include abstractions and generalizations that must be particularized in illustrations and examples, but only to sharpen the point and match deductive reasoning with inductive evidence. Examples and illustrations tend to be historical or global (rather than personal or local) for this very reason. These illustrations demonstrate the universality of doctrines and norms over time and space.

Educational worship emphasizes sermon and liturgy. Even the prayers tend to be long and didactic—mini-sermons in their own right. Liturgy is important, and while language may be updated to contemporary speech, the liturgy still follows a consistent, orderly pattern. Worship follows a specific and theologically interpreted passage of time (the Christian Year), or orients around especially holy occasions. Sermons often follow a lectionary that has been determined by an ecclesiastical or professional hierarchy, supported by commentaries that interpret scriptures, explain doctrinal and ethical points, and suggest poignant illustrations. This insight is provided from the wider church and the tradition of faith, and this emphasizes the fact that truth is above and beyond the particular wisdom or communication ability of any given pastor or priest. Worship is, and should be, predictable from week to week and place to place.

FAQ

Lucinda: Do I have to rigorously follow a lectionary?

Tom: No, but you must have structure and predictability. You can customize your own lectionary. In my previous book, *Uncommon Lectionary*, I described a "Seeker Cycle" for beginners in the faith and a "Disciple Cycle" for more advanced faith formation. The former was shaped around the calendar year, while the latter was shaped around the Christian Year.

Educational worship tends to be more formal. It does not need to be old fashioned, but it does need to be structured. The participants are well managed. They are trained or told to stand, sit, kneel, speak, listen, or act. Therefore it has a presentational style. People tend to sit in rows, facing forward, with limited mobility, in order to focus on speakers or events taking place in front of them. Distractions are discouraged. Projection screens (if they are used at all) primarily provide words to songs, liturgical helps, or points from the sermon, but few still images and no videos. It is important to concentrate the mind on what is being said and follow a scripted dialogue between leader and participants. Membership training, in large part, is a matter of learning what to believe and how to participate in worship.

Modernity has encouraged the development and spread of educational worship, because it is seen as an extension of public education and a vehicle for social assimilation. Both denominations and governments favor educational worship because it is reasonable and controllable. Denominations can ensure that constituents around the globe are united around specific affirmations and viewpoints. Governments can rely on churches to peacefully welcome immigrants and help them adjust to new environments and to perpetuate acceptable behavior among an increasingly mobile population. Churches tend to be like a franchise and are interchangeable within the franchise. Wherever you go, you will feel right at home.

Lucinda's Notes from the Mission Field

A preacher and worship team developed a sermon series within the traditional lectionary entitled "Under the Son: Today's Cynicism and the Answer from Ecclesiastes," in order to address the anxiety over meaninglessness among the lifestyles in their university town. Each worship service posed a question. Music and liturgy were integrated with a study guide. Singing was spirited, but the words of the hymns were as important as the quality of the organ music and choir. The next sermon series explored different religions and answered the question "Is Jesus the Only Way?"

The people who attend educational worship are motivated as much by a desire to bond with like-minded people as a desire to deepen their understanding. They want to be with people who believe as they do and see the world as they do. Such people often express a core value for belonging and speak of the church as a family, even though the worship itself often feels rather formal and intellectual, prayers are often general and impersonal, and people do not tend to linger long. This is because belonging means identifying with a particular tradition, and family means agreement with certain principles. They experience Christ not only as a great teacher but also as role model and paradigm of truth.

In contrast to coaching worship, the people who participate in educational worship are trying to find the courage to stake their lives on Christ (and Christian principles in general); but they are less interested in shaping their lifestyles in particular. There is a critical distance between theory and praxis. Those who are affluent continue to be affluent; those aspiring to affluence continue to strive for success; and those who are poor continue to be opportunistic. Whether they are regular or irregular in attendance, they support the church because it preserves and teaches ideals, principles, and viewpoints that give meaning to life.

Hospitality

Educational worship tends to encourage lifestyle homogeneity. This is why the three clusters of lifestyle groups identified earlier may all prefer worship with an educational purpose, but may not be able to worship *together* in the *same worship service*. Churches are able to make some specific assumptions about visitors and participants that limit and focus hospitality strategies.

Greeters tend to be more formal. They welcome people, but do not try to emotionally engage with people. A friendly smile and a handshake are sufficient, because the motivation for worship is to *learn* something important rather than *change* one's pattern of living. Greeters do not want to intrude on the private space of members or appear pushy to visitors. Similarly, ushers are more concerned with distributing liturgical resources, facilitating attention, and reducing disturbances than with crisis intervention or caregiving. The biggest challenge is that the homogeneity encouraged by educational worship might encourage greeters and ushers to neglect visitors in favor of long-time acquaintances.

Refreshments associated with educational worship tend to provide either *healthy choices* or the *basics*. It is less important to provide multiple choices of sweets and drinks, because servers can make assumptions about community preferences. Older or more affluent lifestyle segments eat less, and select sugarless, fat-free, or nutritious snacks and drinks. Younger or less affluent lifestyle segments eat more, but readily accept day-old donuts or box store frozen foods and basic coffee, tea, and juice. A banquet table is not necessary, because people attracted to educational worship tend not to linger. It is sufficient that their belief and values systems have been reinforced or that they can take away important points or insightful illustrations for private reflection at home. If they linger, it is more likely to chat with friends than discuss the sermon.

Hospitality environments, however, can be very important. All of the clusters who gravitate to educational worship expect sufficient space for a variety of friendship circles to talk without bumping into each other or blocking access to serving stations. There also need to be opportunities to sit and place food on a table or opportunities to carry food to breakout rooms for Bible study or other adult education opportunities. A small urn and tray of food in the narthex is not sufficient. In addition, educational worship is enhanced by a resource table, bookstore, or library immediately proximate to the refreshment area. People are prone to browse books, purchase audio and videotapes, and search for devotional guides that are synchronized with the preaching schedule.

Worship Format

Here are the three basic principles the guide the design of educational worship: Keep it orthodox. Keep it orderly. Keep it thoughtful. In many ways, this is the classic seminary training for worship design and leadership that has been typical in the postwar period from the 1950s through the 90s. It parallels the development of preaching guided by a common lectionary that emerges especially in the 60s and 70s. This is why educational worship is one of two kinds of worship that are most often considered traditional by both members and pastors.

Keep it orthodox. The term has both a narrow and broad definition, and educational worship can be both. Narrowly defined, educational worship rigorously articulates and constantly repeats historic creeds, liturgies, and rites that are intentionally defended against misinterpretation or misapplication. More broadly, educational worship embeds a system of beliefs and values, celebrates a consistent form of worship, and relies on a distinct polity for decision making and design of worship. There is some room for local customs and idiosyncratic viewpoints, but on the whole educational worship is intended to articulate one message with one voice.

Keep it orderly. Every worship service follows a prescribed pattern. The specific prayers and readings may change (by season or lectionary), but the process is predictable: call to worship, confession and assurance, scriptures (often Old Testament, Epistle, and Gospel), sermon, Eucharist or prayers of intercession, benediction and commissioning. The offering is often ceremonial, representing rededication of one's life. The design of worship includes standard formulas of faith, historic wording for confession and assurance, routine prayers of intercession for the church and the world, traditional prayers (like the Lord's Prayer) using specific wording, prescribed scriptures relevant to the season or holy days of the year, and blessings that encapsulate a theological position.

Keep it thoughtful. The sermon or homily is usually very important, and it may be equally important that preachers or lay speakers be specifically authorized to address the congregation. Sermons may last twenty to thirty minutes or more. Unlike coaching worship (which starts with mission and selects a scripture address it), educational worship starts with scripture and seeks to interpret it and apply it. Doctrines are explained, ethical positions are defined, theological questions are explored, religions are compared, and the sacred is clearly contrasted with the secular. The Bible is less a manual for daily living, and more a summary of truth and ultimate principles.

The formula of educational worship is *continuity, predictability,* and *profundity.* All of that is filtered through the living model of credible pastors, liturgists, choirs and music directors, and other visible "actors" in the presentation. Their interaction and leadership demonstrates the significance of the teaching. Participants formally demonstrate Christian core values for civility and respect; the key relationship is between mentor and mentee. This is why a conflict among worship leaders, or a crisis of faith or breakdown in morality for the pastor, precipitates such a crisis in the church. It calls into question the truth or validity of the teaching. In other forms of worship, the personal lifestyles of priest or pastors are less significant.

FAQ

Lucinda: Does music have to rely on classical hymnology and instrumentations?

Tom: Not necessarily, but lyrics are more important than rhythms, and volume is a background for reflection. Music is a method of instruction and means to participate in beauty and truth. Anything else is mere entertainment.

The bedrock beliefs of the church are communicated through words and concepts, and through the examples of saints and martyrs. Eucharist is often important as a weekly or seasonal experience, but its meaning will be carefully explained. The eucharistic liturgy will therefore take longer, require more words, and involve very specific and repeatable rites. The movement of people, or sharing of elements, will often be well organized or ritualized. Seekers and visitors may experience educational worship as complicated and challenging, and many churches will provide study helps to understand terminology, rituals, or symbols. On the other hand, most members experience educational worship as simple, clear, and familiar. They feel right at home and readily fit in with any similar church in any location.

Worship Leadership

The primary worship designer and leader is the pastor or priest. Worship preparation often requires considerable time and energy through the week. A rule of thumb is that every minute of a sermon requires thirty to sixty minutes of individual prayer, research, and writing—and this is in addition to two to three hours preparing the liturgical process. That can mean that worship and sermon preparation for educational worship requires as much as twenty hours of individual work that may be spread out over the week. This time may be shortened by using prepackaged resources for sermon outlines and illustrations, or optional prayers and liturgies, provided by a denomination, publishing house, or website.

Preaching and worship design is a key area for seminary training and judicatory evaluation. Professional certification and ordination are important. Training helps the pastor or priest become an effective student of the Bible, systematic theology, and church history, as well as an effective communicator and teacher. Ordination places the leader in a system of accountability that regularly evaluates theological orthodoxy and obedience to ethical principles. Educational worship leaders often see themselves as peers for the wider community of public school teachers, professors, and critics of contemporary culture (media editorialists, politicians, and even consumer advocates). Continuing education is very important. Preachers often have an advanced degree beyond a basic master of divinity.

The Altered Call

Tom: *Great educational worship translates knowledge into accountability for mission attitude, high integrity, continuous education, and teamwork. This connection between understanding and accountability must be personified in the preacher, musicians, and liturgists.*

Lucinda: *In addition to my mentor, an absolutely confidential covenant community of eight ministry partners grew me back* *to integrity and revitalization. All of us were enriched by clarity about personal mission, learning experiences, intercessory prayer, and total honesty. No whining, complaining, or quick fixes . . . just high accountability to our individually set spiritual disciplines. Yes, this kind of community is really possible among clergy, and I am grateful for that five-year journey. Who would you invite to be in covenant alongside you? What would be the purpose, the values, and outcome expectations?*

The second most significant leader in educational worship is the music director (or choir director) and principal musician (or organist). The roles are often combined in smaller churches. This is a specialized field of sacred music, which is clearly separated from popular, secular, or profane music. The leader pays special attention to words and lyrics that reinforce the orthodoxy of the sermon and liturgy and to the instrumentations and genre of music that provides continuity with the history of the universal church and a particular Christian tradition. Just as the pastor requires special training and authority, so also does the music director. Moreover, just as the pastor must model the beliefs and values of the church, so also the music director must *model* the same integrity. Indeed, the spiritual and moral model of the music director can be more significant to the life of the church than the pastor, because the latter may change more frequently than the former.

Liturgists, sacramental assistants, and other assorted elders, ushers, and greeters (of any age) are all carefully selected and trained. Accountability is very important for volunteer leaders. Every leader is obliged to model a consistent behavior patter and communicate a consistent message that is tied to the doctrinal and ethical positions of the church. Teaching is therefore reinforced from start to finish in the worship service. This is why the biggest threat to educational worship is any accusation of hypocrisy. Seekers need to observe rigorous consistency among worship leaders.

Facilities and Technologies

The formula for educational worship is *continuity*, *predictability*, and *profundity*, and the facility for worship reinforces this. Externally, many church buildings are designed to clearly differentiate between sacred space and the surrounding buildings. Ecclesiastical architecture with steeples and towers, arches, and colored and stained glass is common. Alternatively, some church buildings are designed to clearly mark the building as an educational center. Architecture may be more utilitarian, but the building resembles a school or theater and has wide entrances, easy accessibility, and illumination. Exterior symbols tend to be classically Christian or denominationally distinctive.

The internal space for educational worship is designed for presentation rather than participation. Seating is in rows, so that attention is always directed forward toward a chancel, stage, or dais. Seating is often intentionally fixed, so that participants cannot move chairs or distort lines of sight. The first cluster of lifestyle groups and segments identified earlier (older, more affluent, and stable) often prefer ecclesiastical floor plans with pews, pulpits, lecterns, choir stalls, and organs, along with classic altars and fonts. The second cluster of lifestyle groups and segments (younger, single, upwardly mobile, and more transient) often prefer more utilitarian floor plans that are comparable to modern lecture halls or theaters (chairs with desks, stages with lectern and projection screens, contemporary altars and fonts). The third cluster (mixed ages, poorer, and struggling) can be comfortable in either setting, but still presentational. The facility eliminates distractions, and encourages participants to quiet down, pay attention, and take notes.

In the past, audio technologies have been the most important. Microphones tended to be more one directional, and considerable effort was made to improve acoustics and provide help for those with impaired hearing. Since the seating was intentionally restrictive, ushers were trained to guide traffic and offer assistance to those with physical handicaps. Lighting was also very important. The strategy for educational worship was often to spotlight speakers and dim the lights around listeners to facilitate essentially one-way communication.

Today, imaging technologies are becoming more important but primarily as a supplement to the spoken word. Printed books and liturgies are still the norm. Projection screens are used to facilitate the printed word, providing words to liturgies and songs or bulleting memorable points in the sermon. Images tend to be static or vague (rather than moving and sharp) so that worshipers are not distracted. Omnidirectional microphones are also more common, but primarily to blend and amplify music and lyrics or to capture dialogue that might be occurring at the front of the church for sacramental liturgies or children's lessons. Adjusted lighting is more sophisticated.

Heating and air conditioning is also becoming more sophisticated for educational worship. People who sit or stand in place for a long time tend to be more sensitive to cold and heat. Churches are improving air circulation so that participants can stay alert and listen longer. Many of the lifestyle segments that value educational worship are older or have special needs and limitations. Pews or rows will be shortened for wheelchairs, and aisles will be broadened for accessibility. Elevators and ramps are common upgrades for buildings designed for educational worship.

The printed order of service is often lengthy, but may parts of it may be standardized and reproduced from denominational sources. Many churches provide notepaper and writing utensils for participants, and more postmodern churches will provide abundant electrical outlets for laptop computers and wireless connections for participants to retrieve documents relevant to the sermon or liturgy from a digital archive. Eucharist may well be included weekly, or at least regularly through the year, and communion ware tends to be clearly and uniquely sacred.

The Internet is increasingly important for educational worship. Churches are designing websites that offer a library of sermons cross-referenced for topic and Christian season, along with many options for devotion, study in theology and ethics, and Sunday school lessons. Younger people interested in educational worship will look for online opportunities to participate in Sunday school classes, discussion forums, blogs updated regularly by the pastor, and so on. These tend to be text only. They also look for links to denominational resources, advocacy programs, and opportunities to lobby nonprofit or government agencies on ethical issues.

Timing and Timeliness

Educational worship usually follows an annual cycle with theological significance, so that sacred time and secular time are starkly contrasted. Timing itself is a method of teaching and helps participants order their lives in a clearly alternative Christian lifestyle. Indeed, some popular holidays may be intentionally ignored, and some more obscure Christian festivals may be intentionally emphasized. The cycle of religious significance may be enhanced by changing liturgies, vestments, colors, and so on. Worship design carries on despite behavior patterns in the wider community, and the church is more likely to accommodate school and work schedules, public holidays, and other local events through changes in hospitality or Sunday school than changes to worship.

Educational worship is often more sensitive to national and global events than to local events. World crises involving war, hunger, pandemics, and so on are often recognized in worship as general concerns for all people, and teaching can then focus on commensurate general, important principles or insights with which participants can interpret the significance of events. While coaching worship may help participants feed their family this week, educational worship helps participants understand how to feed the world for decades to come. While coaching worship may help participants change daily behavior, educational worship helps participants restore their overall relationship with God.

Worship is also sensitive to ecumenical or interfaith dialogue. Preaching and worship helps both define uniqueness and build partnerships. It contributes to a theological and ethical understanding about the differences and commonalities in wider Christendom or among world religions.

Sunday morning is the preferred day and time for educational worship, primarily because this preserves the habits of centuries of tradition. It also clearly and theologically sets the Sabbath as a day apart from the routine of the rest of the week. It is not just convenient. It is *significant*. Worship attendance itself is a countercultural action. For the pastor, music director, and other key leaders of the church, Sunday morning worship is the axis on which everything else rotates.

Educational worship may be at any time on Sunday morning. The decision about time of day is consciously made with reference to adult and children's Sunday school. Here again, each of the three clusters of lifestyle groups and segments may have different preferences.

- The first cluster (older, affluent, and more stable) often prefer educational worship late on Sunday morning (e.g., eleven o'clock), *after* Sunday school classes are over. In a sense, the Sunday school classes provide foundational education that prepares children and adults for worship. Children and youth are expected to participate in worship to further their education about Christian faith and practice.

- The second cluster (younger, single, upwardly mobile, and more transient) often prefer educational worship somewhat earlier on Sunday morning (e.g., ten or ten thirty). They are less likely to be up early for Sunday school; any children they have may be quite young and require a nursery or preschool during worship so that child care does not distract the adults from learning; and they are more likely to linger after worship to participate in a small group over lunch.

- The third cluster (mixed ages, poorer, and struggling) may not have a strong preference. Indeed, they might prefer worship even earlier but only because they intend to spend the entire morning worshiping, studying, and socializing. Depending on shift work, they may value Sunday as a true Sabbath and orient the day completely around worship, Bible study, or other opportunities for spiritual growth.

Whatever the preference, the timing of worship depends on assumptions about Sunday school and adult Bible study opportunities. This can also depend on the availability of the pastor as a teacher. It is common for the pastor (and other church elders) to teach a class before or after worship that is relevant to a seasonal theme (e.g., Lent, Advent, and so on), related to the lectionary scriptures used in preaching, or connected with membership training and assimilation.

Measurements of Success

Educational worship has been so much a part of modern and late Christendom culture that measurements for success are often taken for granted. Moreover, as public education standards have increasingly been under attack and as professional education has increasingly become more specialized, church leaders are often not surprised by lower participation in worship and may even see low attendance as a kind of affirmation of their faithfulness. They may perceive themselves as "holding the line" or "maintaining a higher standard" for thoughtful preaching or sacred music. It is very tempting for church leaders to interpret declining worship attendance as evidence of their success in being countercultural, and to use lack of popularity as an odd excuse for maintaining the status quo.

In part, the decline of interest in educational worship may be attributed to the aging and shrinking of particular lifestyle segments. Educational worship is no longer seen as a valuable extension of public or higher education in the post–liberal arts, postmodern world. However, there are younger and expanding lifestyle segments that are likely to be or become interested *if educational worship is designed well.*

Lucinda's Notes: You Can Do This!

Educational worship is often prone to factional fighting over music, preaching, liturgy, and anything innovative. It is very important to have common core values and bedrock beliefs alongside clear and memorable mission statements. Without it, factions emerge based on trendy theologies, pet peeves, aesthetic preferences, and personal privileges.

The existential anxiety over meaninglessness and the spiritual yearning for truth and authenticity in the postmodern world are as strong (or stronger) as in the modern world. A quest for quality in worship program, and a quest for credibility for worship leaders, can result in increased attendance for educational worship. Leaders will usually evaluate educational worship experiences every month (or perhaps every season) and integrate evaluation with leadership training.

There are seven key measures for success.

1. **The number of members/adherents in worship:** Success can still be measured by worship attendance. However, a simple measurement of average attendance is not very helpful because it does not take into consideration seasonal shifts in attendance. For example summer attendance in educational worship services is often very low, and late fall and early winter attendance is often much higher. There are two more useful numerical measurements.

   First, leaders can measure the proportion of members and visitors. If educational worship is really success-ful, there should be an increase in visitors because truly significant theological and ethical insights will create a buzz of discussion between members and nonmembers at home, work, and so on. A significant percentage of visi-tors should be tracked in every worship service. A bench-mark for successful educational might be that in any given worship service, 10–20 percent of participants are first- or second-time visitors, with an average visitor ratio of about 15 percent each year.

   Second, leaders can also measure *regularity* of atten-dance. If educational worship is really successful, members will be convinced that it is truly meaningful to follow the Christian Year, and participate in thoughtfully designed liturgies (including sacraments) each week of the year. They will not miss more than a few Sundays, and then only due to work schedules, illnesses, or brief holiday travel. They will not disappear for several months at a time to a summer cottage or winter home without remaining in long-distance, Internet contact with worship at the home church.

2. **Positive feedback about leadership credibility:** People who are driven by deep anxiety about meaninglessness make a connection between truth and the speaker of truth. Another way to measure the success of an educational worship service is to track positive feedback regarding the personal integrity and insightfulness of worship leaders, especially the pastor or priest and the music director. In educational worship, lifestyle credibility merges with theological and ethical insight. The preacher who "talks the walk" must also "walk the talk."

   Since the most significant relationships in educational worship are not *among* participants but *between* leader and listener, churches can track stories, comments, and reputation of the leaders in both the church and wider community. For example, a pastor or music director who is well known and respected among nonprofit, business, and government peers and visible in the media is a positive sign that educational worship is having an impact on the mission field. Also, for example, the moral breakdown or hypocrisy of a pastor or music director will be a negative sign of worship impact, and almost certainly lead to declining attendance *regardless* of the academic degrees, publishing history, and public honors that might be bestowed on him or her.

3. **The quality of eye contact:** A small but telling method of evaluation can be feedback from worshipers regarding eye contact from pulpit, Communion table, or chancel with participants in pews or chairs. This is why great communicators and entertainers avoid dark eyeglasses and shadowed spaces, and prefer clear lines of sight and excellent illumination. The eyes are windows to the soul. The mentees need to lock eyes with the mentor. They will often comment about how the leader "seemed to be looking right at me." It is a subtle, intuitive, but powerful litmus test for sincerity and authenticity.

4. **Feedback about memorable points:** Preachers already take notice of any postworship comments about key points from the sermon as people exit the church on Sunday morning. The success of worship really depends, however, on how memorable these key points are later in the week. Therefore, churches may deliberately test the success of educational worship through random surveys (using phone or Internet) later in the week. If people remember points from the sermon, or insights from the liturgy, that is a sign of success. If people don't remember much during the week, regardless of what they might have said exiting the church on Sunday morning, then worship was a failure.

5. **Spontaneous and unsolicited appreciation:** Sometimes an even more helpful measure of success is to count or describe spontaneous appreciation. Applause for a musical presentation or verbal affirmations ("Amens!") from listeners can be confirmation of the success of educational worship. This assumes, of course, that such responses have not become expected routines in worship.

   These can often be confirmed for authenticity by tracking unsolicited comments, e-mails, and other feedback during the week. Churches may keep a log of positive or negative e-mails, letters, and other feedback regarding sermons or music. Since it is human nature to criticize rather than praise, their benchmark for unsolicited responses may be about three to one. In other words, one positive comment for every three negative comments might be considered "normal," and lessening or reversal of this ratio is improvement.

6. **The number of Sunday school attendees:** By its very nature, educational worship is closely tied to Sunday school participation. However, success is not measured by Sunday school attendance by children or adolescents

but by older youth and adults. If educational worship is successful, it should motivate and empower participation of older ages in Sunday school classes. If it is unsuccessful, Sunday school may involve large numbers of children, but adult participation will be limited to seniors.

This is true regardless of scheduling Sunday school before or after worship. I indicated previously that older lifestyle segments (adults over sixty) might prefer Sunday school before worship, while younger lifestyle segments (adults under forty) may prefer Sunday school after worship. Ages forty to sixty might go either way. However, regardless of these choices, successful educational worship should prompt increased Sunday school attendance.

7. **Participation in midweek Bible studies and discussion groups:** In some demographic contexts, Sunday school (for any age and any strategic plan) may simply be obsolete. Low Sunday school attendance may not be a true indicator of the success of educational worship. In those cases, churches measure success by evaluating midweek participation, *specifically* participation in curriculum-based small groups (rather than affinity-based groups). In other words, they count participation in Bible studies, book clubs, discussion groups, and so on. They do not count participation in fellowship groups, craft groups, clubs, or service projects. If an educational worship service is really effective, a good benchmark is that 60 percent of the participants in that worship service can be tracked as participating in a curriculum-based small group each month.

In recent decades, many churches have made unwarranted assumptions about the success of educational worship. They *assume* that attendance alone, certification and advanced degrees for worship leaders, comments at the exit door, routine appreciation, children's Sunday school participation, and participation in large fellowship groups and clubs indicates the success of educational worship. It does not. Today churches need to be much more intentional to evaluate educational worship so that they can perfect programs and raise accountability for spiritual leadership.

Compatible Worship Options

A church can only blend two of the seven options
of worship successfully.
What are the easiest and hardest blends for educational worship?

Easiest Blend: Caregiving or Inspirational Worship
Difficult Blend: Coaching or Mission-Connectional Worship
Hardest Blends: Healing or Transformational Worship

Worship Option

Transformational Worship

Transformational experience brings people into direct and immediate experience of the Holy in such a powerful way that it dramatically changes or redirects an individual's life. It glorifies God by rescuing people from lives that are trapped by habits or circumstances that are beyond their control.

Entrapment can happen to anyone, at any time, and often unpredictably or accidentally. Therefore, at one time or another almost anyone in any lifestyle segment may feel compelled to seek out such a religious experience. However, there are some lifestyle segments that are particularly vulnerable to addictions, or enslaved by social, economic or political circumstances, that are likely to gravitate to transformational worship. Church leaders can discover whether or not lifestyle segments such as these are a significant proportion of their mission field by using the search engine at www.MissionInsite.com.[1]

Group D: Suburban Style

Middle-aged, ethnically mixed suburban families and couples
   earning upscale incomes

D15: Sports Utility Families

Upscale, middle-aged couples with school-aged children living active family lifestyles in outlying suburbs

Group K: Significant Singles

Middle-aged singles and some couples earning midscale incomes supporting active city styles of living

K39: Metro Fusion

Ethnically diverse, middle-aged singles living urban, active lifestyles

Group M: Families in Motion

Younger, working-class families earning moderate incomes in smaller residential communities

M44: Red, White, and Bluegrass

Lower-middle-income rural families with diverse adult and children household dynamics

M45: Diapers and Debit Cards

Young, working-class families and single-parent households living in small, established city residences

Group N: Pastoral Pride

Eclectic mix of lower-middle-class widowed and divorced individuals and couples who have settled in country and small town areas

N46: True Grit Americans

Older, middle-class households in town and country communities located in the nation's midsection

N48: Gospel and Grits

Lower-middle-income African American multigenerational families living in small towns

Group O: Singles and Starters

Young singles starting out, and some starter families, in diverse urban communities

O55: Family Troopers

Families and single-parent households living near military bases

Group P: Cultural Connections

Diverse, mid- and low-income families in urban apartments and residences

P56: Rolling the Dice

Middle-aged, midscale income singles and divorced individuals in secondary cities

P57: Meager Metro Means

Mid-scale African American singles established in inner-city communities

Group R: Aspirational Fusion

Young singles, couples, and single parents with lower incomes starting out in city apartments

R66: Dare to Dream

Young singles, couples, and single parents with lower incomes starting out in city apartments

R67: Hope for Tomorrow

Young, lower-income African American single parents in second-city apartments

Group S: Struggling Societies

Economically challenged mix of single, divorced, and widowed individuals in smaller cities and urban areas looking to make ends meet

S70: Enduring Hardships

Middle-aged, downscale singles and divorced individuals in transitional small town and exurban apartments[2]

Note the widespread appeal of transformational worship. It blesses people from many diverse economic, geographic, and cultural groups: suburban, urban, and rural; singles and families; wealthy and poor; dreamers and strugglers. Note also that these segments represent some of the largest proportionate populations. Combine this with the fact that literally anyone, at some time, feels *trapped* and yearns for *deliverance*, and we better understand why transformational worship is one of the fastest growing worship options in America and around the world today.

Life Situation and Compulsion to Worship

The lifestyle segments that most often gravitate to transformational worship commonly express feelings of *entrapment*. They are desperately looking for *deliverance*. A key word is often *desperation*. They may come to transformational worship as a kind of last resort. Not only have they experimented with other kinds of worship, but they may have also participated (or are currently participating) in various kinds of 12-step programs. Transformational worship is sometimes described as "recovery worship" because of its association with addiction intervention. However, the term *addiction* should be understood in the broadest possible sense. People are caught in a vicious cycle of self-destructive behavior patterns that they chronically deny until life becomes so unbearable or dysfunctional that they are forced to seek help. Many participants in transformational worship actually think that they are too late, and surprise and even shock may be associated with personal transformation. It feels like a miracle.

88

The story of Jesus walking on the water and rescuing Peter from drowning has been a popular subject for artists through the centuries precisely because it depicts rescue or deliverance from overwhelming peril.[3] The story is that after Jesus fed the five thousand, he sent the disciples ahead across the Sea of Galilee in order to make time for private prayer. He caught up to them in the midst of a storm, walking on water, crying out, "Do not be afraid! It is me!" Peter sought to prove himself and left the boat to join Jesus, but suddenly, overwhelmed by the wind and waves, began to drown. Jesus carried him to safety despite his lack of faith. My favorite depiction is *La Navicella*, a mosaic by Giotto (1266–1377) that was reproduced in oil by Antoniazzo di Benedetto Aquilo in the early fifteenth century. The terror of Peter, the strength of Christ, the surprise of the other disciples onboard, and the overall image of unexpected rescue capture the yearning for radical, personal transformation that this kind of worship is all about.

The existential anxiety of fate is this sense of personal doom or despair that drives people to transformational worship. The liberation they seek may be economic, medical, political, or even legal. They may be yearning for deliverance from poverty, drug abuse, oppression, or criminal histories. Whatever the trap is, they are looking for a new and fresh start on life. They readily use the language of being "born again."

Transformational worship powerfully connects with lifestyle segments that are vulnerable to any form of addiction. However, addiction (along with forms of economic or social enslavement) is really only a *symptom* of the deeper malady of original sin. The modern world assumes that humans can eventually escape all forms of entrapment through education, invention, willpower, and cooperation. Transformational worship appeals to a more primal instinct. This is the desperate realization that deliverance is completely and utterly beyond human control. No matter how educated, creative, intentional, or collaborative one might be, even the most intelligent PhD, business entrepreneur, professional, or team player simply cannot break free without the intervention of a higher power.

Therefore, transformational worship is perhaps the most egalitarian form of worship. It paradoxically connects with the social justice movement and may sometimes be blended with mission-connectional worship, because it gathers people together regardless of gender, race, income, occupation, or any other demographic factor that tends to stratify society. Everyone is equally helpless and completely powerless to change their lives and escape the trap of their existence. Everyone feels equally doomed, and everyone feels equally desperate, and everyone is quite honest about it. God's grace falls equally on the rich and the poor, the just and the unjust, and no one can make any claim to deserve what they receive.

The Altered Call

Tom: *Effective transformational worship changes lives. It is not based on the premise "I'm OK, you're OK." It is based on the confession that "I am really, really, really NOT OK! No therapy on earth can make me OK! And only the intervention of a higher power can accomplish the impossible."*

Lucinda: *Let's be honest. Traditionally trained clergy not only struggle to provide this kind of worship leadership but also are often terrified of it. First there is the fear that it will seem artificial or manipulative; then there is the fear they will mess with psychological realities that hurt rather than help; but finally they fear that they will look utterly foolish, naive, and unprofessional.*

My mentor helped me accept that mistakes will be made. I may look like an idiot. This altered call means that I have to be ready to shed tears, laugh at myself, absorb criticism, and utterly let go of my ego and my own addiction to "explain everything." Bottom line: There are unexplainable moments of grace. We all need the Savior—and then extra courage to live differently.

Transformational worship has a long and occasionally controversial history. Its spiritual roots lie in the Montanist movement of the second century, and although that was eventually declared heretical, the emphasis on the spontaneity and power of the Holy Spirit, prophetic or apocalyptic vision, and ascetic or conservative ethical behavior has influenced Catholics, Protestants, and Pentecostals. The apocalyptical quality of transformational worship is more personal than political. It's not just about speaking in tongues, odd behavior, or emotional outbursts. It's about turning the individual inside out and making dramatic changes in personal lifestyle.[4]

A variety of metaphors might be used to describe the incarnational experience of transformational worship. Early church authors described Christ as the "Lamb of God,"[5] or the rider of a white horse,[6] or the one who sits on a great white throne who ushers in the new heaven and the new earth.[7]

This more apocalyptic experience of Christ is beyond definition, and therefore beyond invocation and control. God is associated with suddenness, fire, whirlwind, and change. I have always favored the phrase *new being* to express the radical nature of divine intervention that has power to penetrate the very depths of our being.[8] The intervention of a higher power is a "Kairos moment" in which chronological time is penetrated by, or transparent to, the nonrational power of the infinite. All these metaphors emphasize an experience of God in worship that is uncontrollable and dramatic. Worship brings people into direct contact with God, and while the experience might be surprising and even painful, it is clearly positive and redemptive. Christ appears from out of nowhere, almost like a ghost or specter, walking out of the storm of our lives when least expected. He calms our fears with a promise, rescues us when we are drowning, and invites us into the boat with strange company to sail away to an unknown shore.

What It Looks Like

Transformation worship is all about surprise and surrender, dramatic change and spiritual renewal. What most forcibly strike the observer are the *lack* of structure and the *heightened sense of expectation*. Yes, there may be music, scripture, prayers, and message, but all these seem more incidental than necessary. Such activities are helpful but still seem to just fill in the time as people wait, often for considerable time, for something wonderful or awesome to happen.

Worship is intense. It is sometimes emotional, but it is always emotive. It speaks to the gut, and sometimes the heart, but is not primarily about engaging the mind. In any given worship service, participants may or may not actually be transformed (changed, liberated, converted, and so on), but the anticipation of such an intervention is constant. Yes, it is possible to "fake it," and lifestyle segments more committed to educational or coaching worship may be anxious or skeptical of transformational worship. Yet one can discern authenticity from fakery, primarily because authentic transformations are not tied to the charisma of any given leader or to the manipulation of any crafted liturgy. Worship is deliberately spontaneous and unpredictable, because fakery or authenticity is revealed in such a context.

FAQ

Lucinda: Is transformational worship always so emotional?

Tom: The personality of the one who receives a blessing makes every experience different. What makes the experience of Christ authentic is not emotion per se but dramatic impact that changes life completely. Is that emotional? You bet!

Transformational worship draws participants who are entirely transparent and honest about the trap that is driving their involvement. The worship service clearly names the trap (i.e., drug addiction, economic oppression, criminal behavior, and so on), and the participants are intentional about naming their fate. A sense of honesty pervades the experience, which is enhanced because worship leadership empathizes with it. Leaders speak from the same experience of life struggle but give personal witness to spiritual victory. The movement of the Spirit is always paralleled by the witness of the blessed. If people speak in tongues or prophesy about people or events, there is an interpretation or explanation. If people weep, faint, fall down, or are "slain in the spirit," there are counselors, prayer partners, comforters, and helpers to assist them.

Other forms of worship build community through structure, but transformational worship builds unity through chaos. Intense, personal dramas are played out everywhere and all the time. Participants may come and go; stand, sit, kneel, or lie prone; stand silent and still, dance or shout; and nobody really cares. A participant can feel completely anonymous and therefore become fully a part of what is going on. What is going on, the single thread of unity, is the common acknowledgment of desperation and the common longing for liberation. There is not the slightest hint of judgment or condescension, no distinction between member and visitor, no pretention of leaders.

FAQ

Lucinda: How do you prevent manipulation and deception?

Tom: Isn't it odd that clergy and churchy people in general only worry about such things regarding *this* kind of worship, when other forms of worship are just as susceptible? Accountability within the worship team for core values and beliefs still holds. And as in all worship, the litmus test is who claims the limelight. Is it the clergy, the supplicant, or Christ?

Transformational worship may resemble healing worship (as we shall see), yet it is quite distinct. In transformational worship, there is no intermediary, ritual, or therapeutic activity that channels the grace of God. God's grace is immediate, direct, and unpredictable, and frequently "blows you away." Moreover, the goal of transformational worship is not the healing itself nor is it any specific empowerment to overcome oppression or any specific strategy to escape poverty or any particular personal achievement. The underlying goal is the renewal of the inner spirit, the transformation of attitude, and the re-creation of life. People leave facing the same situations, but because their inner lives have been transformed they are no longer trapped and despairing. They have a fresh start. They are new creations.

This miracle may not happen *this* time, but it may happen *next* time. In this sense, transformational worship often functions in tandem with a support group or 12-step program. It can also help people who have been transformed to continue to endure, stay on target, and live "one day at a time." It has a motivational quality that keeps people alive through the week and makes them aware of the nearness of the Holy Spirit in ordinary living.

Hospitality

The most important priority for hospitality is to deploy a gifted and well-trained hospitality team. The *choice* of the team is crucial, and not any volunteer will do. Greeters and servers need to be utterly without bias (hidden or overt) regarding social class, economic status, sexual orientation, education level, occupational success, or residential stability. At the same time, they need to rigorously model and articulate the core values and beliefs of the faith community. On the one hand, they radically accept anyone and everyone to worship; but on the other hand, they guard boundaries of behavioral norms. For example, they welcome even the most eccentric and fringe elements of society addicted to self-destructive habits; but they also quickly block any behavior that might harm, denigrate, or prevent others from participation in worship. The hospitality team ensures that the worship center is both friendly *and* safe.

In addition to the usual greeters and servers, transformational worship requires a personal support team. This is necessary because worship is often emotional. The Holy Spirit impacts individuals in unexpected and sudden ways and their reactions may be equally unexpected or extreme. Their mission is to observe the people in worship and provide intentional, prayerful support as people interact with the Holy. Sit or stand with people who are tearful, laughing uncontrollably, or showing signs of negative or positive stress. Catch people that might be fainting. Pray with individuals during or after worship and in some cases refer them to counseling, coaching, or other spiritual leaders of the church. If individuals seem overcome by worship and leave the room, or even if they leave for coffee or the restroom, a member of the support team pays attention and is prepared to intervene for their health, safety, and spiritual support.

Even the serving team may be chosen and trained to do more than provide refreshments. They readily model and articulate core values and beliefs, engage in significant conversations, and smoothly refer individuals to talk with other spiritual leaders of the church. Given the extraordinary diversity of lifestyle segment participation in worship, the refreshment strategy should be to offer as many choices as possible. They need not be particularly expensive or elaborate. Provide plenty of space to move about and talk. Provide opportunities to smoke.

Hospitality team ministry is more challenging and stressful in transformational worship. The Holy Spirit breaks in and changes each worship service in unexpected ways. Participants react emotionally and behave unpredictably. Very little is routine for the hospitality team, and they need to intervene with creativity and integrity. After the service, or during the week, team members will gather to debrief, support one another, and pray for specific individuals and for the spiritual blessing of transformational worship.

Worship Format

There is no standard format for transformational worship because it is so radically open to expressions of the Holy Spirit. That does not mean that transformational worship *cannot* be structured, only that the structure is clearly subordinate to the whim or will or the Spirit. Worship is so powerful that structure fades to unimportance or disappears into a faint background. All that is really important is that the worshiper feels the fullness of God's immediate presence.

We often associate transformational worship with modern expressions of Pentecostal or charismatic worship. Yet transformational worship can also be designed with ancient traditions and Eucharist. Orthodox and old rite Roman Catholic worship may be intentionally shaped as transformational worship. Note that it is no longer important that worshipers *understand* the language, symbols, or rites that combine to create a sacred ethos. Chant, incense, icons, and rituals sweep the worshiper away to an alternative experience (perhaps even a sensation of alternative universe) that is permeated by God. It is not difficult to imagine worship in early medieval times as transformational, as people yearned to experience God as a liberator from barbarity, slavery, and epidemic and experienced the world more as entrapment by sin than as a life filled with opportunities.

Mainstream and evangelical Protestants in particular may struggle to understand Eucharist as a *transformational* event because for them the sacrament of Holy Communion is a *remembrance*. In the twentieth century, that remembrance is quite rational and intelligible. One remembers biblical stories, theological principles, or catechetical lessons. One remembers the mutual support and comfort of the body of Christ. One remembers with thanksgiving one's original baptism and the benefits of church membership. The original reformers remembered much more. They remembered the power of God that rescued them from prison or gave them courage to say "No!"

Eucharist is for many a nonrational, miraculous, and transformational experience. People can come to Eucharist with the same sense of expectation with which they come to more "Pentecostal" worship. They look for the real presence of Christ, the immediacy of grace, and personal transformation through the body and blood of Christ.

Regardless of structure, what makes worship transformational is that it is intensely personal, prayerful, and powerful. If these elements are emphasized, the tactical details can be adjusted for whatever lifestyle segment (or, in the case of Orthodox worship, whatever ethnic identity) is involved. Worship designers will be less concerned about the structure and more concerned about sincerity, authenticity, and the spiritual credibility of leaders. The prayerful preparation leading up to worship can be as significant, or even more significant, than the worship service itself. Whatever the vessel, and however imperfect the vessel, God will use it to fulfill God's purpose to change lives.

Keep it personal. A common criticism of transformational worship is that it seems more personal than communal. Participants may not be fully aware of others around them. However, transformational worship is in fact remarkably *selfless*. Participants are often as unaware of *self* as they are unaware of other *selves*. Their unity is not comprised of self-aware individuals self-consciously in harmony with one another.

Instead, their unity is comprised of self-surrendered souls who are all caught up in a heightened experience of the Holy Spirit. Participants often speak of "losing themselves" in worship, and therefore they lose any sense of time and place. There is a profound sense of mystery, and after worship is over participants may be at a loss for words to explain what exactly happened.

Keep it prayerful. Prayers may be structured or spontaneous, but what is most notable about prayer in transformational worship is that it is often *beyond words.* This is why people may speak in tongues or value liturgies in languages that they don't really understand. Prayer is a "sigh of the spirit." It is a communion with God. Participants feel that the prayers they utter are not even their own, but God speaking through and from their own being to God listening from beyond and in heavenly glory. The participant does not really *offer* prayers but *surrenders* to prayer.

The prayer that is most typical of *educational* worship is often the Lord's Prayer. But the prayer that is most typical of *transformational* worship is a form of the Serenity Prayer: "God give me the serenity to accept what I cannot change; the courage to change what I can; and the wisdom to know the difference." Indeed, the Serenity Prayer in its entirety is often memorized (and not just the abbreviated version). Worshipers often stress key phrases in the full Serenity Prayer, like "accepting hardship as a pathway to peace" and "trusting that you will make all things right if I surrender to your will."

Another prayer often used is the Jesus Prayer, repeated or chanted over and over: "Jesus, Son of God, have mercy upon me, a sinner." That's it. It might be reduced to two simple words like *sin* and *God* that become the focus of concentration. Individuals can literally lose themselves, and their awareness of their surroundings, in the experience of prayer.

Keep it powerful. This, of course, is the paradox of transformational worship. Leaders do not really *design* transformational worship. Transformational worship *grasps* worship designers. In some instances, a worship experience that is designed as coaching, educational, or some other form of "controllable" experience of the Holy is suddenly taken over by the Holy Spirit to become something else entirely. This can actually be quite terrifying to traditionally trained clergy. Once they "lose control" of the worship service, they fear the potential of harm or heresy. It will become all the more important to evaluate outcomes, so that worship leaders can discern the value of worship by the fruits of worship.

Transformational worship is intense and often dramatic. It may involve sensory overload as images (symbols, icons, and pictures), sounds (chants, singing, and constant music in multiple genres), touch (hands laid on foreheads and embraces), tongues (exclamations, sighs, or ecstatic utterances), and taste (bread and grape juice or wine) surround the individual consciousness. Yet it may also involve sensory deprivation as worship occurs in barren or ugly surroundings, in awesome silence, with little human contact, and as the culmination of fasting. Either way, it is the *impact* rather than the *insight* that is important.

All this makes worship awesome and to some extent appeals to postmodern interest in *interactive spectacle*. Transformational worship is not for observers. There is no critical distance in the experience, and if one does try to simply be an observer they will often feel let down, out of place, and disappointed. The spectacle of worship is not that of a modern concert that inspires and uplifts but in the end only sends the audience to dinner and drinks. This spectacle is more like a premodern revival or a postmodern rave that overwhelms and exhausts but in the end sends the audience to live in an entirely new way.

Worship Leadership

The *format* of worship must be open to the uncontrollable and unpredictable movements of the Holy Spirit, and therefore the *leadership* must be sensitive and flexible to discern and follow the Spirit. In this sense, the word *leader* is not quite appropriate to describe the key people who may be at the center of a whirlwind or at the nexus of an awesome mystery. It might be better to call them *first followers*. They are the first to be keenly aware of the movement of Spirit. They have a spiritual gift to "discern between spirits." In other words, these first followers must be able to tell the difference between mere emotion and genuine spiritual presence. They must walk a fine line avoiding manipulation and yet preparing for revelation.

This is not easy, particularly for church leaders whose identity and training is *professional*. Indeed, many of the best first followers that shape transformational worship are amateurs who are not especially trained or certified. They are strong models of spiritual life and usually speak from their own experience of addiction and intervention, entrapment and liberation, or sin and grace. In their personal lives, they are extremely prayerful. In their public lives, they are extremely humble. The often describe their leadership as "being used" as tools of the Spirit. They are often very independent and introverted. They may personally describe worship leadership as a burden, and often shun the limelight outside of worship.

In a sense, transformational worship leadership for such people is both blessing and curse. They may be called to lead transformational worship from a very humble and private faith but are often lionized by enthusiastic participants or vilified by the modern rationalistic media. They are tempted by praise and defensive about criticism and can adopt egos that contradict their very natures. The demise of a transformational worship service often follows a collapse in leadership credibility. This is the biggest reason transformational worship is hard to sustain for long periods of time.

Lucinda's Notes from the Mission Field

The spiritual authenticity of the worship team is so important! Picture this: *The tear-filled eyes, the clasped hands, all worshipers leaning forward, captured in heart and life by the power of God. They are all touched by the witness of a young worship leader's emotional story, and a trembling but powerful prayer by a former self-declared atheist team member. The praise band leader may not be the best musician in the world, but he has mentored both these individuals and is utterly sincere, brimming with hope, and expecting to see miracles all over again. The worship team's authenticity is what convinces every worshiper that maybe—just maybe—he or she can also change 180 degrees from a life of fear and turmoil to a life of hope and serenity.*

The pastor or priest often follows a neomonastic lifestyle. He or she tends to be reserved, watchful, compassionate, and sincere, rather than gregarious, confident, intellectual, or even especially articulate. This first follower is not an intermediary to experience the Holy but more of a visionary who discerns the movement of the Spirit and helps others immerse themselves in its flow. This person is central to prayer and Eucharist and may lead other rites (baptism, unction, foot washing, and so on). A sermon or meditation is usually fairly brief, informal, and personal.

In addition to the pastor/priest, there may be one or more witnesses who will share their story of liberation and hope. These people speak out of their experience of life struggle and spiritual victory and motivate participants. They intensify the sense of yearning and create an atmosphere of expectation. These witnesses may also be important to late counseling, coaching, and prayer with individual participants. They may be small group leaders for mid-week 12-step programs.

The Altered Call

Lucinda: *Clergy need to unlearn professional skills and shed ownership of worship design. On my best days, this kind of worship leadership is an opportunity to confess my need to control and desire to be the center of attention. On my worst days, I fall back to old clergy habits. Be prepared to stare into your soul and cry out for your own salvation. Deepen and strengthen your daily spiritual habits.*

There may be one or more people who have responsibility over the broader *ambience* of the worship experience. *Ambience* is more important than simply performing music or projecting visual images. For example, a music leader may prepare specific pieces of music in advance (solos, hymns, anthems, and so on), but it is more important that musicians spontaneously provide background music that is appropriate to the moment. They need to be versatile and intuitive to punctuate worship with praise, support worship with meditation, or sustain pregnant silences. Music may well include recorded sound effects (e.g., running water, bird and whale song, and so on). Other leaders may intentionally provide still and video images or other sensory stimuli.

It is perhaps more important for transformational worship than any other form of worship that leaders function as a team. There is an intuitive understanding among leaders and lots of nonverbal communication. They take cues from one another, especially the pastor/priest. The best metaphor for team leadership is the jazz ensemble. Good improvisational jazz band members intuitively listen and observe their partners. Each member steps forward and retreats into the background—takes initiative but supports the whole—sustaining an experience that is never the same twice. They rely on chords and phrases but together surrender to the music itself and improvise unexpected harmonies and poignant disharmonies. A good jazz ensemble does not make music. Their shared discipline and intuitive bond lets the music shape them.

FAQ

Lucinda: What is the function of music?

Tom: Music may contribute to ambience for worship and spontaneously follow the mood of worshipers. It may be meditative or joyous, lyrical or rhythmic. Quality is less important. Amateur musicians may be more authentic than professionals. Music tends to be more improvisational and spontaneous than practiced and rehearsed.

Facilities and Technologies

The classic strategic principle that *tactics are shaped by purpose* has been amply demonstrated in the descriptions of what transformational worship might look like. In this case, the *purpose* of worship is radical openness to God's unpredictable grace and urgent anticipation that

101

God will act to liberate people from traps that are beyond their control. There is endless variety in the format of worship so long as it is personal, prayerful, and powerful. The second classic strategic principle is that *form follows function*. This means that the facilities and technologies of worship can range from empty rooms and utter simplicity to highly symbolic spaces and poignant technologies that engage all the senses.

Transformational worship often takes place in a simple, multipurpose hall (convention center, arena, or converted retail or industrial space). Floor space is not cluttered with furniture, because people need room to move (stand, kneel, clap, dance, come forward, exit unobtrusively, or rush to the side of someone in need of support). There may be cushions for safety and comfort as people may fall or lie down. There is usually an elevated stage with microphone and spotlights to facilitate the message, witness, or prayers of a speaker. Sound may be amplified, but surroundings might be quite plain.

Transformational worship may also take place in highly symbolic surroundings. Again, furniture is often kept to a minimum to allow movement and protect the safety of participants. Walls, ceiling, and floor may be covered with icons, images, or mosaics. Candlelight and incense, surround-sound chant or sound effects, devotional objects, video projections, and the high drama of Eucharist can create an atmosphere of heavenly other-worldliness. A profusion of living plants, running water, and natural effects can also be used. The atmosphere can resemble a monastery, an arboretum, or other setting that seems most transparent to the Holy.

The environment, therefore, tends to be extreme. It may be extremely plain, simple, and ordinary, or it may be extremely ornate, complex, and extraordinary, but it is never institutional. The space rarely looks like a typical Western church building inside or out. When people today think of "church," they often associate the facility with Gothic windows, steeples, bells, pulpits, pews, hardwood, memorial plaques, and historical mementos. This is *not* the best space for transformational worship.

Music and musical instruments are usually electronic guitars, keyboards, and so on, or rely on vocals only. Music may be live or recorded, audio only or include video. Sound or sound effects are often pervasive as background to all worship. Music may be loud or quiet, lyrical or rhythmic, and often includes extremes of both.

It is important that the facility have excellent heating or air conditioning, good circulation of air, and easily available water and washrooms. Worship often lasts longer—sometimes much longer—than the standard hour in more traditional church institutions. There may well be adjacent rooms for individual or small group prayer, personal counseling, or quiet and rest. However, breakout space should always be monitored by volunteers to ensure the health and safety of participants.

Timing and Timeliness

The routine of transformational worship can be monthly or weekly, but it often follows the peaks and valleys of addiction. For example, transformational worship highlights periods of special indulgence or personal excess during the year: New Year, March break, St. Patrick's Day, local summer fairs, Thanksgiving, Christmas, and so on. It may also highlight periods of special crisis: February depression and suicide threats, April taxes and financial worry, or September stress and workaholism. Anxiety about entrapment can peak at any time, of course, and worship may be especially sensitive to the schedules of hospitals and clinics, prisons and correctional centers, retail and work cycles, and political events or elections.

Transformational worship is very sensitive to personal, relational, economic, occupational, and political stresses as they impact the daily lives and routines of individuals. It is not theoretical or speculative anxiety, but highly pragmatic and practical anxiety. Educational and coaching worship is sensitive to the occasions when people are wondering *how to live*, but transformational worship is sensitive to the occasions when people are panicking about *whether they will live at all*.

Therefore, transformational worship often connects with people who are not regular church attendees or who are disillusioned with church institutions or who feel alienated from "religions" in general. The best time for worship may not be a Sunday. A better day may be Friday evening (if worship is connected with 12-step meetings) or some other weekday. Saturday evening (among lifestyle segments with Roman Catholic backgrounds) or Sunday evening (among lifestyle segments with conservative Protestant backgrounds) may be effective. The time of day largely depends on the work schedules for the publics targeted.

The most important issue about timing is to allow *sufficient time*. Transformational worship is ultimately controlled by the Holy Spirit and not by the programs of a church or the timetable of a leader. One hour is rarely enough. Leaders should plan to arrive early and leave late. Participants may well forget the passage of time altogether because they become so absorbed in the worship experience.

Measuring Success

Transformational worship seems so inwardly focused toward personal change that it may seem to be difficult to measure success. It is important to remember that statistics are not the only things to measure. Leaders can also evaluate stories from the lives of participants and feedback from other mission partners and social agencies. Success is not measured by program quality (as might be true for coaching and educational worship) but by signs of authenticity, character, and credibility. In other words, the success of worship depends less on the quality of performance, preaching, or liturgical practice and more on the impact, emotion, and subsequent lifestyle changes among participants.

There are seven keys to success:

1. **The intensity of expectation:** Although it is difficult to quantify, the reputation of transformational worship creates a sense of anticipation that you can feel. The atmosphere seems to be electric: hopeful, energetic, and attentive. The sound level of conversation may be high or hushed, but it is not normal. People seem eager to press inside the worship space. In contrast, educational worship often has a "laid back" quality. Friends linger in quiet or jovial conversation; visitors maintain critical distance; par-

ticipants are in a reflective mood. Here people seem more "on edge." Conversation is brief and people don't linger. Visitors are ready to engage; participants immerse themselves in the experience. Hospitality teams can be trained to monitor intensity on a scale of 1–10 or simply provide intuitive feedback to leaders.

2. **Number of visitors accompanied by members:** A more quantifiable method to measure the intensity of expectation and the reputation of worship in the community is to track visitors and especially the number of newcomers that are accompanied by church members. If members are highly motivated to invite others, and if strangers are highly motivated to connect with worship, then expectation is more intense. Clearly, people actually believe that something extraordinary, positive, and even life changing can happen to them. This statistic may fluctuate from one service to the next, but a *trend* in newcomers over a period of six months to a year is revealing. It suggests the degree of confidence people have in the *effectiveness* or *significance* of worship in their lives.

3. **The number of lives transformed:** No matter how inspiring, engaging, weird, or wonderful worship is, the real point of transformational worship is to actually transform people. Therefore, church leaders intentionally observe behavior during worship. They track how participants interact with the Holy, the degree of their emotional engagement, and the number of participants who avail themselves of breakout rooms or relationships for prayer or counseling. There is certainly a risk of artificial behavior or self-delusion. Some participants may pretend to have transformational experiences in order to get attention, or they may simply misinterpret aesthetic enjoyment of music, images, and the environment *as if* it were the power of the Spirit. Counselors and observers can try to

discern what is authentic and what is not, although clearly this is blurred. After all, what begins as pretense can become authentic. It is neither possible nor desirable to judge others. Still, a transformational worship service in which nobody is significantly changed is not a success.

4. **The number of stories from the mission field:** Observations made at the time can be confirmed and enhanced by stories gleaned from the mission field. Church leaders evaluate success by keeping a kind of journal or history of lives changed. Transformations may not really become visible for weeks or months. Even the significance of an experience of the Holy in worship may not be understood, accepted, or applied until further counseling or small group support helps it bear fruit. These stories may be gathered through website and blog participation or through reports from small group leaders or simply passed on to the worship leaders.

5. **The recognition of cross-sector partners:** Transformational worship is connected to addiction intervention, economic and political change, neighborhood renewal projects, and other personal and community rehabilitation work. Therefore, the success of transformational worship can be measured by reputation and referral among other social service, health care, and law enforcement agencies. These agencies may or may not be faith based. They may not understand or endorse the beliefs of the church. Yet they will say positive things about the impact of the worship service on drug abuse, crime, poverty, violations of human rights, and so on.

6. **Percentage of worshipers in midweek recovery:** Transformational worship that is particularly tied to addiction recovery will be linked to midweek 12-step programs, therapies, or other peer support groups. These may be

sponsored by the church or beyond the church. Leaders should expect that transformation in worship will motivate higher, regular participation in such groups. The motivation may be to find peers who can interpret what happened in worship; or it may be to better prepare oneself to be ready for transformation at the next opportunity. Change is one thing; sustained change is another. Success is best measured by persistent changes in behavior, which rarely take place without a support group.

7. **The number of adult baptisms:** Worship that is particularly tied to conversion, new hope, and new life will be linked to sacraments of adult baptism, Eucharist, or both. Adult baptisms particularly and visibly mark the changed life of an individual, and given the growing unpopularity of Christianity in the secular Western world, it is more risky and daring than ever before. An adult who desires baptism is risking negative impact on his relationships, family, and even career. Similarly, success in transformation may also be measured by regular attendance and eager attention to the celebration of Eucharist. Transformational worship should lead to a rise in adult baptisms and weekly participation in Eucharist.

The modern world tends to assume that the world must be rational, events must be explainable, and people must be in control. Western people in particular are skeptical of transformational worship, and no measurements of success will be convincing. Yet our experiences with addiction, and deeper awareness of circumstances of entrapment, begin to undermine rationalistic and individualistic assumption. Rescue and liberation come in unexpected and unexplainable ways. In the end, our attempts to measure the success of transformational worship are themselves limited. What may seem like success may prove to be illusory; but what may equally seem like failure may become success. God works miracles.

Compatible Worship Options

A church can only blend two of the seven options
of worship successfully.
What are the easiest and hardest blends
for transformational worship?

Easiest Blends: Healing or Mission-Connectional Worship
Difficult Blends: Caregiving or Inspirational Worship
Hardest Blend: Educational or Coaching Worship

Worship Option

Inspirational Worship

Inspirational worship is an uplifting experience that gives participants new confidence, courage, and optimism for the future. It glorifies God by lifting people from cynicism and depression and renewing their energy for living and their hope for eternal life.

There is a sense in which *any* experience of worship (e.g., coaching, educational, transformational, healing, mission-connectional, or caregiving) can be "inspirational." Inspiration is often blended with other forms of worship. As a distinct worship option, however, it is uniquely and purely an experience of *celebration*. It is intended to motivate participants to new heights of optimism and joy. Whether it encourages people who are aging toward death or simply motivates people who feel "dead on their feet," it gives everyone life, makes them smile, and sends them on their way walking several inches above the ground. All people, in any lifestyle, periodically feel the need to boost their spirits. However, there are lifestyle segments that are more likely to experience chronic depression and yearn to be renewed.

A primary or secondary preference for inspirational worship makes this one of the most popular and significant options today. As many as fifty-six out of seventy-one lifestyle segments (and eighteen of nineteen lifestyle groups) have some preference for inspirational worship. It is the highest priority for some, but a blended priority for many others.

Whatever their worship preference (education, coaching, transformation, mission-connection, healing, or caregiving), they want this mission focus to be *inspirational*.

Many lifestyle segments prefer worship that blends inspiration and education. Such a blend is what denominations and established churches with over two hundred in worship often describe as "traditional." However, there is a clear trend among lifestyle segments to place *inspiration* ahead of *education*. What really matters is not what people *remember* following worship, but *how they feel* following worship. They may not recall the points of the sermon or be any clearer about doctrines and principles, but they definitely want to be uplifted, motivated, and more energetic for the coming week. A powerful and pure inspirational worship service is not dissimilar to great entertainment. Both provide lasting relief from despair and strengthen participants to engage the challenging week ahead.

FAQ

Lucinda: Is inspirational merely a "feel good" experience?

Tom: What's wrong with feeling good? There is so much worry and anxiety in daily living that people long for even a brief interval of happiness. Inspirational worship goes deeper that just feeling good. It provides the joy of the Lord that gives strength during the week.

There are some tangible patterns among the lifestyle segments that prefer a blend of inspiration and education. The following segments tend to be wealthier, and have much to lose in a volatile economy; or they tend to be better informed, and consequently have greater anxiety about threats of climate change. These tend to be people with a global consciousness and an assumption of entitlement. Their yearning for inspiration tends to be tied to reassurance for a stable and prosperous future.

Group A: Power Elite

The wealthiest households in the United States, living in exclusive neighborhoods, enjoying all that life has to offer

A01: American Royalty—inspiration, education[1]

Wealthy, influential, and successful couples and families living in prestigious suburbs

A02: Platinum Prosperity—education, inspiration

Wealthy and established empty-nesting couples residing in suburban and in-town homes

A04: Picture-Perfect Families—education, inspiration

Established families of child-rearing households living in wealthy suburbs

Group B: Flourishing Families

Affluent, middle-aged families and couples earning prosperous incomes and living very comfortable, active lifestyles

B09: Family Fun-tastic—education, inspiration

Middle-aged couples with large families and active lives in affluent suburbia

Group C: Booming with Confidence

Prosperous, established couples in their peak earning years living in suburban homes

C11: Aging of Aquarius—inspiration, education

Upscale boomer-aged couples living in cities and close-in suburbs

C13: Silver Sophisticates—inspiration, education

Mature, upscale couples and singles in suburban homes

Group D: Suburban Style

Middle-aged, ethnically mixed suburban families and couples earning upscale incomes

D16: Settled in Suburbia—education, inspiration

Upper-middle-class diverse family units and empty nesters living in established suburbs

D17: Cul-de-Sac Diversity—inspiration, education

Ethnically diverse, middle-aged families settled in new suburban neighborhoods

Group K: Significant Singles

Middle-aged singles and some couples earning midscale incomes supporting active city styles of living

K40: Bohemian Groove—inspiration, education

Older divorced and widowed individuals enjoying settled urban lives

Group L: Blue Sky Boomers

Lower- and middle-class baby boomer-aged households living in small towns

L41: Booming and Consuming—inspiration, education

Older empty-nesting couples and singles enjoying relaxed lives in small towns

L42: Rooted Flower Power—inspiration, education

Mid-scale baby-boomer singles and couples rooted in established suburban communities and approaching retirement

Twenty years ago the people in these segments might have emphasized *education* over *inspiration*. Today most of them have reversed that priority.

There is a second pattern among lifestyle segments that blends inspirational with educational worship. The following segments tend to be middle class, aging in place, and less mobile. Many of these are institutional church veterans and come from family traditions of regular worship attendance and sound stewardship. They once formed the backbone of denominations. However, they are particularly anxious about shifting public policies regarding ethical norms, increasingly alienated from denominational hierarchies, and disturbed by immigration. Their anxiety is more local than global. Their yearning for inspiration tends to be tied to reassurance about cultural homogeneity and standards of behavior.

Group H: Middle-Class Melting Pot

Midscale, middle-aged, and established couples living in suburban and fringe homes

H26: Progressive Potpourri

Mature, multiethnic couples with comfortable and active lives in middle-class suburbs

H27: Birkenstocks and Beemers

Upper-middle-class, established couples living leisure lifestyles in small towns and cities

Group J: Autumn Years

Established, ethnically diverse, and mature couples living gratified lifestyles in older homes

J35: Rural Escape

Older, middle-class couples and singles living comfortable
   lives in rural towns

J36: Settled and Sensible

Older, middle-class, and empty-nesting couples and singles in
   city neighborhoods

Group Q: Golden Year Guardians

Retirees living in settled residences and communities

Q62: Reaping Rewards

Relaxed, retired couples and widowed individuals in suburban
   homes living quiet lives

Q63: Footloose and Family Free

Elderly couples and widowed individuals living active and
   comfortable lifestyles

Q64: Town Elders

Stable, minimalist seniors living in older residences and leading sedentary lifestyles

Note that several of these lifestyle segments clearly prefer inspirational
worship but may opt to blend inspiration with caregiving rather than
education. This reflects their yearning for personal attention and the
fact that their churches tend to have fewer than two hundred members.

There is yet a third pattern among lifestyle segments that prefer
to blend inspiration and education. The following segments tend to
be poorer, less educated, and in some form of economic or cultural
transition. These people also have strong ties with denominations and

established churches but struggle to preserve those ties in the midst of changing or challenging circumstances. Their anxiety is neither global nor local but quite personal. They yearn for inspiration in order to maintain or renew ties with their past experiences of religion. They seek continuity with the past, and hope to build new patterns of meaning in their changing circumstances.

Group I: Family Union

Midscale, middle-aged, and somewhat ethnically diverse families living in homes supported by solid blue-collar occupations

I32: Latin Flair

Conventional Hispanic gen X families located in selected coastal city homes

I33: Hispanic Harmony

Middle-class Hispanic families living lively lifestyles in city-centric neighborhoods

Group S: Struggling Societies

Economically challenged mix of single, divorced, and widowed individuals in smaller cities and urban areas looking to make ends meet

S69: Soul Survivors

Older, downscale African American singles and single parents established in modest urban neighborhoods

These lifestyle segments tend to accept modern, North American assumptions that education is crucial to personal and family advancement.

Worship is often a supplement to other forms of education that aims to add skills and build language and communication skills. Education in this sense is not abstract but very practical. It is not an end in itself but a step toward personal and family independence and happiness.

Other lifestyle segments that prefer inspirational worship may seek to blend it with other options. In recent decades there is enthusiasm to blend inspirational worship with coaching worship. Such a blend is what new Christians and independent churches have often described as praise worship. This has contributed to arguments among and between lifestyle segments about worship style and to the battle between traditional and contemporary worship. *Both* are inspirational. The difference is that so-called traditional versions of inspirational worship are educational and therefore more about doctrine and continuity with the past, and so-called contemporary versions of inspirational worship are about coaching and therefore more about behavior and practical applications in the present. Obviously, the terminology of "traditional versus contemporary" is inadequate to either describe or resolve this tension.

FAQ

Lucinda: Why do churches fight over traditional versus contemporary worship?

Tom: Traditionalists prefer to blend their inspiration with education, because they value preservation of the past. Innovators prefer to blend inspiration with lifestyle coaching and value creativity for the future. They're both good, just different. Both can be forms of entertainment! The heat in this debate has more to do with aesthetics than theology.

The lifestyle segments that prefer to blend *inspiration* and practical lifestyle *coaching* tend to be younger, and many have households that contain multiple generations (children, parents, grandparents). Their careers, personal relationships, and educational training are often experiencing rapid transitions. Busy lives are punctuated by extreme recreational habits, and worship attendance is only one priority in competition with others. All of them, however, are looking for inspiration that provides motivation, energy, and direction. These segments include the following:

Group B: Flourishing Families

Affluent, middle-aged families and couples earning prosperous incomes and living very comfortable, active lifestyles

B07: Generational Soup

Affluent couples and multigenerational families living a wide range of lifestyles in suburbia

B08: Babies and Bliss

Middle-aged couples with large families and active lives in affluent suburbia

Group C: Booming with Confidence

Prosperous, established couples in their peak earning years living in suburban homes

C14: Boomers and Boomerangs

Baby-boomer adults and their teenage/young adult children sharing suburban homes

Group D: Suburban Style

Middle-aged, ethnically mixed suburban families and couples earning upscale incomes

D18: Soulful Spenders

Upper-middle-class African American couples and families living in the expanding suburbs

Group E: Thriving Boomers

Upper-middle-class baby-boomer couples living comfortable lifestyles settled in town and exurban homes

E20: No Place Like Home

Upper-middle class, multigenerational households in exurban areas

E21: Unspoiled Splendor

Comfortably established baby-boomer couples in town and country communities

Group F: Promising Families

Young couples with children in starter homes living child-centered lives

F22: Fast Track Couples

Active, young, upper-middle-class couples and families living upwardly mobile lifestyles

F23: Families Matter Most

Young, middle-class families in scenic suburbs leading active, family-focused lives

Group I: Family Union

Midscale, middle-aged and somewhat ethnically diverse families living in homes supported by solid blue-collar occupations

I31: Blue Collar Comfort

Middle-class families in smaller cities and towns with solid
blue-collar jobs

Group O: Singles and Starters

Young singles starting out, and some starter families, in diverse urban communities

O52: Urban Ambition

Mainly generation Y African American singles and single
families established in midmarket cities

O54: Striving Single Scene

Young, multiethnic singles living in Midwest and Southern
city centers

Group S: Struggling Societies

Economically challenged mix of single, divorced, and widowed individuals in smaller cities and urban areas looking
to make ends meet

S71: Hard Times

Older, downscale and ethnically diverse singles typically concentrated in inner-city apartments

Many boomers and busters, the economic middle class, are included
in these segments. Notice that many of these segments are in lifestyle
groups that gravitate to suburbs and exurban areas, satellite cities and
transitioning small towns, and are apt to travel around an urban belt-
way to a large church that has the resources to provide multiple program choices. The last two groups, however, reveal that more and more

lifestyle segments that are struggling economically, or that are exploring alternative lifestyles, are seeking the blend of inspiration and coaching.

Finally, there are more and more lifestyle segments that hope to blend inspirational worship and transformational worship. One might say that the once chaotic and ephemeral experiences of charismatic worship, and the once therapeutic experiences of 12-step programs and recovery groups, have combined to become better organized and mainstream. The blend of inspiration and transformation is no longer a fringe worship option, but an intentionally growing church movement. These segments include the following:

Group D: Suburban Style

Middle-aged, ethnically mixed suburban families and couples earning upscale incomes

D15: Sports Utility Families

Upscale, middle-aged couples with school-aged children living active family lifestyles in outlying suburbs

D17: Cul-de-Sac Diversity

Ethnically diverse, middle-aged families settled in new suburban neighborhoods

Group M: Families in Motion

Younger, working-class families earning moderate incomes in smaller residential communities

M44: Red, White, and Bluegrass

Lower-middle-income rural families with diverse adult and children household dynamics

M45: Diapers and Debit Cards

Young, working-class families and single parent households living in small, established city residences

Group N: Pastoral Pride

Eclectic mix of lower-middle-class widowed and divorced individuals and couples who have settled in country and small town areas

N46: True Grit Americans

Older, middle-class households in town and country communities located in the nation's midsection

N48: Gospel and Grits

Lower-middle-income African American multigenerational families living in small towns

N49: Work Hard, Pray Hard

Working-class, middle-aged couples and singles living in rural homes

Group O: Singles and Starters

Young singles starting out, and some starter families, in diverse urban communities

O55: Family Troopers

Families and single-parent households living near military bases

Group P: Cultural Connections

Diverse, mid- and low-income families in urban apartments and residences

P56: Rolling the Dice

Middle-aged, midscale income singles and divorced individuals in secondary cities

P57: Meager Metro Means

Midscale African American singles established in inner-city communities

Group Q: Golden Year Guardians

Retirees living in settled residences and communities

Q65: Senior Discounts

Downscale, settled retirees in metro apartment communities

Group R: Aspirational Fusion

Multicultural, low-income singles and single parents living in urban locations striving to make a better life

R66: Dare to Dream

Young singles, couples, and single parents with lower incomes starting out in city apartments

R67: Hope for Tomorrow

Young, lower-income African American single parents in second-city apartments

Group S: Struggling Societies

Economically challenged mix of single, divorced, and widowed individuals in smaller cities and urban areas looking to make ends meet

S68: Small Town, Shallow Pockets

Older, downscale singles and empty nesters living in modest exurban small towns[2]

Although these segments are an eclectic group, they are neither at the top nor the bottom rungs of society. They have just enough affluence to indulge in self-destructive habits, or just enough poverty to panic about the future. They also tend to be a multicultural and biracial cluster of people. Many of them are upwardly mobile but relatively immature and naive. They are easily caught up in circumstances beyond their control (debt, chronic health problems, substance abuse, racism, corporate glass ceilings, and so on). They want to be motivated, be uplifted, and experience ecstasies so that they can overcome terrible odds. However, they may not have the patience for education or confidence in coaching and need inspiration to come with transformational power that makes things right.

(There are also lifestyle segments that look for worship options that blend their passion for mission [social change, political reform, environmental correction, disaster relief, and so on] with inspirational worship. These are better discussed in the section for mission-connectional worship.)

Life Situation and Compulsion to Worship

Clearly, there are people in many lifestyle segments that might gravitate to inspirational worship. They might blend it with an educational focus on doctrines and moral principles; an emphasis on practical, lifestyle coaching; or high expectations for immediate experiences of the Holy and radical change. Today the blended elements may be less and less important, and people seek a pure and powerful experience of sheer inspiration. This may explain why the boundaries are blurring between worship, entertainment, spectacle, and sport. A concert (in any genre) or film (classic or avant-garde), a royal pageant, or a playoff game may combine the devoted fans, emotional highs, and uplifting experiences that are positively spiritual.

The yearning for inspiration is motivated by a growing sensitivity to death and dying. The aging population of North America (in particular) is increasingly aware of life as fragile, impermanent, and transitory. This is both a personal and a global health issue. There is a general sense that progressive science, universal education, social services, and international reconciliation efforts have failed to achieve the utopian vision originally promised. Of course the vision of a world

123

without poverty, hunger, war, crime, disease, and other evils was always idealistic. Yet the generations of fans who followed episode after episode of *Star Trek* still believed, deep in their hearts, that it might be achievable in the twenty-first or twenty-second centuries. Fantasy could masquerade as hope for a time, propped up by unending news reports of medical advances and scientific breakthroughs but has now been revealed as hopelessly naive.

The dominant attitude of affluent North Americans is cynicism, and their dominant worldview is skepticism. People fear global warming, pandemics, mortal diseases, terrorist attacks, economic collapse, marital betrayal, and sudden death. Gratuitous evil is the single biggest obstacle to authentic faith. People long for a good reason *not* to commit suicide or despair or a good reason to go ahead and get pregnant and raise a family in this emerging "disaster zone" called Earth. They want to be inspired. They want to have confidence about tomorrow, next week, and some form of positive eternity.

Just as the existential anxiety of fate compels some people to look for transformational worship, so also the existential anxiety of death compels other people to look for inspirational worship. The two anxieties are clearly related, and the two worship experiences are also related. The difference lies in the result. Inspirational worship is powerful but not necessarily apocalyptic. Transformational worship leads to rebirth and dramatic personal change. Inspirational worship leads to self-confidence and a better attitude.

The Altered Call

Tom: *Truly awesome worship focuses hope for tomorrow and gives you courage to continue. It's not about head trips, heart throbs, or body language. It's about guts . . . and glory.*

Lucinda: *The first forty-five days of a new pastorate is a kind of "boot camp" of seeker sensitivity. Walking side-by-side with people in their daily battle with life, and beyond the safety of church walls, is your real training ground. We see and feel the physical* *and mental wounds and scars of desperate people. They don't need instant gratification. They need long-term confidence*

Ask yourself: What mission targets am I missing? What new skills do I need to develop? Where is the greatest impact? How can I shape a worship environment that overcomes skepticism and cynicism? How can I empower seekers to keep going and stay hopeful?

Vincent van Gogh might be considered an archetype for misunderstood and ignored idealists today. One of his most inspirational paintings is *Starry Night*, which is said to have been inspired by the story of Joseph's dreams:

> [Joseph] had another dream and told it to his brothers, saying, "Look, I have had another dream: the sun, the moon, and eleven stars were bowing down to me." But when he told it to his father and to his brothers, his father rebuked him . . . [and] his brothers were jealous of him.[3]

Impressionist artists often try to soften sharp realities and capture hidden meaning and purpose. Van Gogh's *Starry Night* is one of the most inspirational paintings today. The night sky is filled with swirling clouds, a large and luminous yellow crescent moon, and eleven glowing stars. It conveys a sense of mystery and hidden purpose and seems to embrace the observer. A small town amid rolling hills sleeps peacefully beneath the sky. At the center is a traditional church with an elongated steeple that seems to connect the infinite and the finite. In the foreground on the left is a large, dark mass that clearly invites personal interpretation. It seems to stand apart from the harmonious surroundings, but its wavy lines match that of the clouds and sky above. For myself, I have always understood this ambiguous mass as the personality of Van Gogh himself (and therefore the person of the observer), who is connected, yet apart; flawed, yet hopeful. In his youth, Van Gogh had a strong social conscience for the poor; yet he eventually died from a self-inflicted wound.

I am not alone in thinking *Starry Night* a classic of inspiration for those who are burdened with the existential anxiety of death and looking for renewal, hope, and ultimate acceptance. Don McLean's popular song "Vincent" is based on this painting and compares the artist's vision with the contemporary experience of disappointed idealists. Whenever I hear the lyrics, I always think of the existential anxieties of emptiness and meaninglessness that shape the mind-set of many lifestyle segments today. McLean addresses the starry night, calling it to

> Look out on a summer's day,
> With eyes that know the darkness in my soul.[4]

Both painting and song capture the eternal cycle of life, death, and renewal. Inspirational worship is compelling for modern skeptics and cynics because it reconnects them with their original idealism and hope. It offers confidence in a higher state of being and a higher purpose.

The metaphor that best describes the incarnational experience of inspirational worship is Christ as promise keeper. God's real presence reassures us that death is not the end, either for ourselves or for our dreams. The many promises of God throughout the Old and New Testaments will be fulfilled, despite the corruption of time and the refusal of humanity to listen. God is eternally patient and persistent. God has created the universe in a pattern only partially understood by science and reason, and the ultimate victory of goodness, beauty, and truth is inevitable. Moreover, human beings can participate with God in the fulfillment of promise. Our idealistic struggles may fall short, but they are not in vain. We are a part (albeit a mysterious part) of God's plan. While we may feel isolated or alone, God draws us back into intimacy with the divine.

What It Looks Like

So many different kinds of people long for inspirational worship! Yet churches have such difficulty providing truly inspirational experiences. The most common complaint about worship is that it is boring and uninspiring and does little more than motivate people to go home to lunch. This may be because worship leaders think they are designing inspirational experiences, when in fact they are designing educational or caregiving experiences. They may misunderstand the real yearnings of the publics around them.

The biggest reason church leaders fail to design inspirational worship is that they are too busy using worship as a methodology to sustain the church as an institution. Worship is fragmented, sidetracked, or disrupted by institutional moments like announcements, offerings, introductions, and other additions that in modern life can best be compared to commercials interrupting the program. It is as if a musical drama like an opera were suddenly interrupted by invitations to meet the lead tenor or soprano over lunch, fund-raising appeals to renovate the opera house, introductions of celebrity guests in the audience, or opportunities to buy cookies from the youth group. Nothing should interrupt the power of inspirational worship, certainly not the relative trivialities of institutional maintenance. Worship must be dynamic and flowing. The moment anyone looks at his or her watch, the spell is broken.

FAQ

Lucinda: What is "flow"?

Tom: Inspirational worship is like flying in a glider. You swoop up and down, fast and slow. Flying in a glider is also silent—no engine noise. Worshipers should be completely unaware of the structure or mechanism of worship.

Again, worship is like a symphony. It will be alternately fast and slow, allegro and adagio. It will be joyous and introspective and joyous again. It shapes your mood and awakens all of your senses.

Inspirational worship can occur in many ways, using any musical genres and both very ancient and very contemporary symbols. Worship can be inspirational with large choirs, classical hymnology, and powerful pipe organs; and worship can be inspirational with rock bands, rap music, and electronic keyboards. The choice of genre, media, and actions depends on the worship designers' dual sensitivity to the life-style segments around him or her and the Holy Spirit's leading. Of all the different kinds of worship, inspirational worship requires the greatest surrender of ego and the greatest spiritual awareness.

There are at least four keys to inspirational worship:

1. **It is big:** Inspirational worship is often easier to create with a large group of people. The minimum number of people is probably around two hundred, and there is no maximum. The anxiety of death and dying (persons or ideals) is very widespread. More and more people are leaving small churches to attend big churches largely because they find the worship more inspirational. If the large church offers small group opportunities, they can fulfill their desire for intimacy that they may have sacrificed relocating from the small church. The primary need, however, is inspiration and not caregiving.

   Size does not really correlate to numbers of participants, however. It really correlates to *big sound* or to *big vision* or to *big emotion*. It is possible for a small church to generate a *big experience*. Yet it must be "big"! Participants must lose their individuality, self-awareness, and ego in a larger experience. They must feel immersed in something gigantic and mysterious. Those who are driven to worship because of the fear of death symbolically die in the experience of vastness that is provided by worship. When they emerge from worship part of the joy is that they died and yet live again.

2. **It flows:** Inspirational worship follows the logic of the heart, rather than the logic of the mind. In other words, it is not a carefully crafted liturgy that "makes sense." Nothing destroys inspirational worship more than quibbles over terminology and language or quarrels over politically or theologically correct formulations. Worship flows

like water in a stream, clouds in the air, and sunbeams through stained glass. There is a constant back and forth of anticipation and resolution. The heart expects something to happen without consciously realizing it, and fulfillment brings relief and satisfaction. Inspirational worship does not *use* music. It *is* music.

This is why inspirational worship relies on variations of volume and tempo. The worship service often starts with high volume and fast rhythm and later morphs into lower volumes and slower rhythms. Sometimes the pace of worship slows down, and sometimes it speeds up. There is never dead air as people wait for a speaker to adjust a microphone or a choir or band to prepare to sing. The moment anyone becomes conscious of the passage of time, inspiration is lost. Everything moves seamlessly, and there is never time to think. That comes later.

3. **It transcends words:** Therefore, inspirational worship is about images, not words. It is about poetry, not prose. It is about motivation, not instruction. It is not rational or a rationalizing event. It is an emotional or heartfelt experience. This is not at all to say that worship is without meaning. Instead, the meaning of worship cannot be summarized in words. Indeed, if you can say it all in words you have missed the point. The meaning of worship is always awesome. It fills people with such awe that it might even feel terrifying as well as exhilarating.

All communication is a combination of form, content, and import. Different kinds of worship emphasize one aspect or another. Inspirational worship generally sacrifices form and content to maximize import. Import is the power or impact of truth that motivates action. People may not be able to explain what happened or how the experience changes the way they live in the coming week. Yet it clearly impacts them in extraordinary ways. They

129

may not be any clearer about theology, but they are more courageous to confront evil.

FAQ

Lucinda: How many points are in the sermon?

Tom: One scripture, one point, emphasized and emphasized again. The sermon is not about teaching. It is about motivating. If people take notes during the sermon, worship is no longer inspirational but either educational or coaching. It no longer aims at the heart but at the head.

---

4. **It is always vertical:** Inspirational worship focuses and celebrates the vertical dimension. This is the connection between finite and infinite or between the worshipers' lives and the power of God. The horizontal dimension is much less important. It is less important for worshipers to introduce themselves to each other, know one another's names, share stories and current events, or even sit with their friends and families. Self-awareness, family friendliness, and friendship circles become unimportant. All that is important is the connection with God.

When you look back to the High Middle Ages in western Europe, you begin to understand why worship tended to be highly inspirational. Violent wars, sudden attacks, the Black Death, and innumerable threats made life fragile and death a constant threat. No wonder cathedrals and churches were built with soaring arches and spires, designed with vivid colors and tapestries, and celebrated the pageantry of the Eucharist. Today we are once again seeking inspirational experiences. Violent wars, pandemics, global warming, and innumerable economic risks surround us; people long for the same vertical dimension in worship.

The great challenge to inspirational worship is the institutionalization of the church. The overhead of church maintenance, the pedantry of church theology, and the politics of church life all intrude on the worship service and sabotage designers' best efforts to make it inspirational. The public often goes elsewhere, to other kinds of spectacles in other sectors, to experience the vertical dimension that overwhelms and overflows human understanding.

Hospitality

Since the horizontal dimension is less important than the vertical dimension, hospitality tends to be simpler and more easily organized. People are not coming to chat with each other. They are coming to be immersed in the presence of God. They do not need opportunities to dialogue with each other and interpret the worship service, for truly inspiring worship defies interpretation and seems diminished if overanalyzed.

Many people will arrive at the last minute, and they may leave immediately. Greeters set the stage by conveying a sense of anticipation and excitement. Greeters are never blasé about their welcomes. They convey enthusiasm. They communicate their own restlessness and eagerness to "get in there" and "get going" and "praise God." They avoid unnecessary or idle conversation. They are more likely to point out the entrance to the sanctuary than the way to the washroom or welcome center. They point to a guest book, but do not undermine the air of spiritual expectancy by asking visitors for their name and e-mail address.

Refreshments before worship are intentionally and thoughtfully relevant to the taste and experience of the lifestyle segments expected to worship. However, they may not be opulent. People are not expected to linger. Refreshments are always provided in containers that can easily and safely be taken into the worship center. The chairs inside may have cup holders so that participants can free their hands to clap and their bodies to move and dance.

Inspirational worship may have an intermission (comparable to a concert hall or breaks between musical sets). This is a time to calm down, cool off, and refresh oneself to enjoy another experience. Greeters are not necessary, and the church does not deploy leaders to intentionally mingle for provocative conversation. However, it is important to sustain the inspirational experience by providing background music, images, and streaming video related to the worship service. Even though participants are taking a break, their hearts and imaginations are still with the worship service.

Many participants do not want to simply return to their mundane routines following worship. They may not go home directly. However, people are more likely to find hospitality *away* from the church building following worship. The church will provide refreshments immediately proximate to the worship center (not downstairs or down corridors). The further away the refreshments, the more likely people will be to leave the building. Churches that really want to provide hospitality following worship will deliberately deploy leaders in various restaurants, coffee shops, or pubs following worship. It is especially helpful to deploy *musicians* and other *artists* that were visible in worship in these hospitality venues. Participants will approach them to talk about the experience. This is their opportunity to share their spiritual life and faith. The musicians and artists are the first line of evangelism because they can debrief with participants about their emotions and sense of awe.

FAQ

Lucinda: Should the pastor shake hands as people leave?

Tom: No. Nothing dampens enthusiasm like standing in a line. People want to get out, go out, let loose their emotion, and debrief. The worship leaders they really want to meet are the musicians, actors, and other artists. The best place to meet and mingle with them is offsite in a pub or restaurant. Preachers need to let go of ego, get out of the way, and stop blocking the exit.

Worship Format

Inspirational worship is about flow more than structure. This is why, for example, a high-quality sung Eucharist is more inspiring than a spoken Eucharist. Flow draws the worshiper into an experience in which he or she loses self-awareness and gains a heightened sensitivity to the mystery of God. Structure emphasizes the subject-object distance between the self-conscious worshiper and God as wholly other. This is not to say that liturgy is irrelevant. Liturgy needs to feel intuitive and follow the logic of the heart, and should not be so cumbersome as to actually get in the way of God. Inspirational worship is not a work that people do but a revelation that people experience.

Nevertheless, it is possible to *plan* inspirational worship up to a certain point. The structure follows the flow of anticipation, illumination, and celebration. Participants prepare themselves by raising awareness of the human predicament of death and dying, imperfection, and impermanence. Such confession can be expressed in silent or spoken words or through images and songs. This is followed by an experience of breakthrough insight or a flash of understanding. Call this an "aha!" moment. It may be tied to scripture or sermon or to a dramatic event or story and can only be partially explained. Yet it is a profound awareness of grace. Subsequent celebration is thanksgiving for fresh hope and renewed idealism. People always leave feeling better and stronger than when they came.

One reason critics complain that inspirational worship is entertaining is that the participants seem to be mere observers. This is not accurate. Inspirational worship (like great entertainment) is always participatory. Much of the participation, however, is inward. Worshipers pay rapt attention. They are absorbed by the spectacle. Subsequent applause, cheers, cries of "amen," powerful singing, and other outward expressions of participation are more like eruptions of pent-up emotions. You can see that inspirational worship (like great entertainment) can only be planned *up to a certain point*. What actually makes inspirational worship successful is beyond planning. It is the revelation of the Spirit that moves people to some catharsis of emotion. People may cry or laugh, sing or be silent, but it is never because of the worship

133

service itself. It is because God has used the worship service to appear in unexpected ways.

Keep it heartfelt. Designers plan worship to aim at the heart rather than the head. They set out to remove all barriers to honesty, and then elicit a totally sincere response. There can be no pretense, no hiding behind concepts and theologies; there must be complete transparency of the soul to God. Genuine emotion is both important and cathartic. It cleanses and restores. It allows the individual to shed cynicism and renew hope. This is why the atmosphere of inspirational worship is so intense.

Keep it gut level. Designers plan worship to motivate action. Participants are restless, urgent, and excited when they emerge. They are not passive, but energized. Their renewed positive attitude may lead in almost any direction, but whatever they do it will be with greater confidence and conviction. Therefore, the music, images, stories, and other dramatic events of worship appeal to deeper instincts about good and evil and avoid being ambiguous or ambivalent.

Keep it experiential. Designers plan worship to engage all five senses. Sound, image, taste, touch, and smell are all crucial ingredients to engage the heart. Inspirational worship is about nonstop engagement and assumes that participants will think about it, talk about it, and interpret it afterwards and in individual ways. Worship is alternately lyrical and rhythmic, and people respond with their bodies and movements in unthinking and spontaneous ways.

Eucharist is often celebrated in the context of inspirational worship because it is so dramatic and participatory. Powerful music, colorful images, and movement through processionals or liturgical dance all add to the spectacle of inspirational worship. Worship inspires awe. Participants forget themselves (and their troubles), and are carried away in exultation. Eucharist is a symbolic representation of the perfect joy and communion with God that can be expected after death or at the end of time.

Eastern Orthodox Eucharist, for example, is often experienced by visitors as extraordinarily *inspirational.* The structure of worship is complex, but invisible. It fills all the senses. One is caught up in a work of art, or a mystical communion, and is really not aware of liturgy as such. One does not *analyze* what is going on, but simply *immerses* in the experience of grace. It is timeless.

Inspirational worship is therefore similar to transformational worship in format. It is perhaps more controlled and more tempered in its expectation. Participants may not be born again, but they leave with new courage to live up to their ideals and risk their lives in faith. Today this is exactly what great entertainment can do. Great concerts, exhibitions, and public spectacles have become more intentionally *spiritual*, just as successful inspirational worship has become more intentionally *cultural*. The competition for inspirational worship today is not worship at another church down the street, but the cinema, concert, or theater going on across the city.

Worship Leadership

The participants' expectation of leadership is shaped by the nature of inspiration itself. Inspiration occurs when the finite becomes transparent to the infinite; the eternal promise of God overcomes doubt, failure, and death and people find renewed courage to believe and strength to continue. The leader stands at the intersection of this cathartic ("aha!") experience and inevitably has a priestly character. It is interesting to note that even in great entertainment venues today, performers often dress, behave, and even speak in caricatures of sacramental leadership. The preacher, pastor, or leader of inspirational worship has a priestly character.

This means that the credibility of the leader depends more on the force of his or her personality and on the function that they perform in worship. It actually depends less on their spiritual habits, personal morality, or professional training. Of course leadership credibility is lessened if he or she is a clear hypocrite, insincere, morally disreputable, or utterly incompetent. Nevertheless, it does not ultimately depend on these things. The leader is often quite open about his or her ordinary upbringing, modest education, struggles with spiritual disciplines, and even personal and relational mistakes. The fact that the leader is *not perfect* is part of his or her credibility for inspirational worship. His or her very leadership reveals how God uses ordinary, imperfect, and flawed things to reveal divine grace.

FAQ

Lucinda: Is it possible to transform a more traditional inspirational/educational worship experience into a more inspirational/coaching experience?

Tom: Yes, but leaders need to understand the different nuances of existential anxiety that compel people to worship. The former aims at the head (intellect and understanding), and the latter aims at the heart (passion and confidence). Preaching in particular changes to become very practical, not abstract, and more motivational, not didactic.

Preaching is motivational, not informational. It often refers to the speaker's own life struggles and spiritual victories. It makes *one point*. This is the "aha!" insight. It is the core message. The rest of the sermon is an embellishment of this one point. Stories and illustrations surround the one point; images and verses punctuate the one point; but in the end there is only one tremendously significant and uplifting point to be remembered. Participants do not take notes, because there is nothing to write down. The overall effect of the sermon is motivational and uplifting. It "fires people up." It is profoundly encouraging. People take the point home and bank on it. They risk the coming week on the truth of that point.

All other leaders in worship repeat and embellish that one point (much like jazz musicians take turns improvising on a single theme). Given the popularity of music today, the musicians who lead inspirational worship are perhaps next in importance. Their lyrics sharpen the point, and their rhythm enhances the urgency of the point. Musicians may speak or witness to the point, but it is usually brief and must be inserted seamlessly into the flow of worship. Therefore, any comment from a musician is always accompanied by background music. The musician often quite literally steps out from the choir or band, and steps back into their midst.

The enthusiasm, excitement, and keen attention of musicians, dramatists, dancers, eucharistic attendants, and so on are crucial to inspirational worship. They cannot look bored or tired, and they cannot be visibly distracted or inattentive to all that is happening around them. They are vessels for the expression of the Holy.

FAQ

Lucinda: What if my choir is not large or powerful?

Tom: The music requires more training and preparation because it is rehearsed and choreographed in advance. The self-awareness of many musicians must also change: they are not just performers but also spiritual leaders. If you have a small choir, it helps to have at least one strong vocalist to lead the singing.

The leaders up front, or on stage, always behave intentionally. In a sense, they are performing. In theological context, they are living symbols that by their very presence (active or passive) *signify* that something important is going on. Even if they are stationary and silent, they have a function in the worship service.

This means that inspirational worship requires a quest for quality. Liturgy, music, technology, images, dance, and drama must strive for excellence. Whatever they do must be so well done as to look effortless and spontaneous. If it is poorly done, the rapt attention of participants is broken and the worship service falls back into subject/object dualism. Churches usually invest more money to hire staff for music, drama, and imaging, and they invest more time for training choirs, bands, and ensembles.

Moreover, training for excellence must go beyond the particular skill any given leader is exercising. They must also be trained to model key values, convey sincerity, and reveal crucial convictions by the smallest action. They not only learn to do things well but also to do things with significance. Entertainers do things well; missionaries do things with significance. These two things merge in inspirational worship leadership. The performance is *persuasive*. It motivates people to go deeper into the experience of Christ and further in the mission of Christ.

Facilities and Technologies

Inspirational worship is usually presentational in appearance. It requires an auditorium or worship center with seating that faces forward to give excellent sight lines to a raised chancel or stage. Seating may be in rows or a half circle, and occasionally in the round. The chancel or stage should be quite versatile so that furniture and symbols (altars, lecterns, and other equipment) can be added or removed. There is often a backdrop to the stage to help frame or focus the spectacle of worship. This may be permanent (stained glass, life-size sculpture, icons, and other images). It may also be changeable like theater scenery (cityscapes, neighborhood streets, cafes, and other settings).

Acoustics are as important as sight lines. The worship center needs to accommodate different kinds of musical groups, and will need to offer a variety of options for microphones and speakers. Large projection screens or multiple, bright LCD screens merge still and moving images with the flow of worship. Remember, the goal of inspirational worship is to make a small space seem vast and full. Big image and big sound are important. Music is often both live and electronic, and rarely stops during the entire worship experience. Provide ample space for bands and amplifiers or grand pianos and string instruments.

Imaging technology should use basic, readable graphic text for songs and scripture, high-resolution still images, and quality video that enhances the theme. It may not need to be perfect, but it does need to be authentic and engaging, with no flaws or distractions that break the attention of participants. There should never be a blank projection screen, and images can both change and follow the flow of worship. Make use of spotlights to define speakers and soloists

Inspirational worship involves all the senses, and the interior design and symbolism of the worship center is important. Anything artificial should be avoided. Use natural, adjustable, or colored lighting rather than fluorescent. Use real flowers and foliage rather than plastic or fabric. Upgrade air conditioning and heating systems to avoid extremes. Eliminate strong smells from heating oil or cleaning fluids. (Technology to adjust aroma in large spaces is already being introduced in theaters in Japan.) Use higher quality wine or juice and fresh bread for Holy Communion.

FAQ

Lucinda: How do I create "big" with "small"?

Tom: Do it through technology. Use audio and video resources to introduce a bigger sound. Renovate and redecorate the sanctuary. Replace shabby furnishing. Reduce hardwood. Maximize space. Begin a quest for quality by creating lay-training budgets to coach volunteer musicians, tech teams, and worship leaders.[5]

This all means that inspirational worship requires a well-trained team of technicians. You can't leave adjustments to sound and lighting to untrained ushers or occasional volunteers. The team should be well briefed on the flow of worship, prepared to make timely changes and adjustments, and ready to respond quickly to fix glitches. Yet the team also needs to be trained to model core values and articulate bedrock beliefs. After the music personnel, the tech team is the next group of people that young seekers often want to meet. They need to have a mature and confident faith and see the Spirit beyond the technology.

139

Timing and Timeliness

The vertical dimension of inspirational worship means that designers pay attention to God's providence and God's miraculous interventions. Therefore, worship often follows a theme of faith formation. The liturgical Christian Year can be helpful, particularly if it is oriented around major holy days that are still meaningful to the general public (Christmas and Easter). Inspirational worship can also follow themes of salvation history, based on God's promises in the Old and New Testaments. Visible and powerful interventions in response to personal, public, national, and natural crises are also important, and worship designers should feel free to interrupt a theme in order to focus on some emerging situation that has shaken or disturbed the public.

Prime time for inspirational worship is usually ten thirty or eleven Sunday morning, and this is followed by coffee, tea, juice, and refreshments sensitive to lifestyle segment preferences. A common option is for the inspirational worship service to be Sunday evening at six or seven, followed by wine or coffee and excellent desserts and finger foods. Worship designers might take their cue from evening classical music concerts like Christmas and Easter worship with Handel's *Messiah*, or revivals of classic Christian rock, like recent performances of *Jesus Christ Superstar*. Observe both the scheduling of worship experience and refreshments.

The challenge for planning regular inspirational worship is to make every worship service special. Participants may well commit to weekly attendance, but it cannot feel routine. Worship leaders cannot lose their energy, and worship participants cannot feel bored. To paraphrase the old adage: "Every Sunday is a holiday, and every worship service is a feast."

Measuring Success

The most common way to measure the success of inspirational worship is to monitor the size of the congregation. The anxiety of death and dying (of both people and ideals) is common across a wide band of lifestyle segments, and therefore worship that is specifically targeted to be inspirational should prove to be popular. Large attendance is one way to make worship "big" in power and significance. In the post-Christendom world, however, the number of worship participants will never be as large as in the past. This is particularly true outside the United States (Canada, Australia, England, and western Europe). Can inspirational worship still be big, without large numbers of participants? Yes.

There are seven ways to measure success:

1. **The size and intensity of interaction:** If a small congregation is truly inspired, leaders will feel the intensity of concentration in the worship service. Think of worship as a "God quake," and measure the intensity on a spiritual "Richter scale." In an earthquake, people run away, fight each other, and curse their fate. In a God quake, people move closer together, embrace each other, and praise God. If leaders observe people sitting apart and at the margins of the room, watching stone-faced or spontaneously silent, then worship is not inspirational. If leaders observe people moving closer together, animated, and spontaneously clapping or shouting, then worship is a success.

2. **The visibility and diversity of emotion:** Emotion is occasionally observed as people weep or cry for joy, but many lifestyle segments are more reserved than this. Watch facial expressions and body language. Reactions to inspirational worship will be visible on faces. People will tend to lean forward. Heads, hands, and feet will move rhythmically to follow the music. Eyes will move back and forth from performers to video screens. All these subtle clues indicate that the congregation is emotionally engaged with worship.

3. **The power and commitment to singing:** Each lifestyle segment approaches the act of singing in different ways. Inspirational worship is often measured by the power of many voices singing hymns with boldness and confidence. Whether or not it is in harmony, it is loud. Other lifestyle segments only participate in singing through repeating

141

choruses or the refrains to songs, often from memory. And still other lifestyle segments spontaneously join a soloist or band in a single phrase or verse of song. Even those lifestyle segments that don't sing may demonstrate their approval of others' singing by clapping hands or stamping feet.

4. **The number of repeatable stories:** The distinctive motivational preaching of inspirational worship usually embeds particularly meaningful anecdotes or stories in the minds of worshipers. Leaders keep a log of feedback from subsequent small groups, mission projects, and mission partners. You can keep track of the number of times someone recalls a story or anecdote because it is relevant to his or her subsequent personal situation.

5. **The "buzz and bump" in the community:** The same log can keep track of the impact of inspirational worship in the larger life of the community and the various social services, health, and mission agencies. Inspirational worship should cause a stir. There should be reactions to it in the media, or among people in service clubs and agencies. The reaction may be positive or negative . . . but it should matter. Inspirational worship should motivate greater volunteerism in the community, larger donations to charities, or changed attitudes and priorities among community leaders.

6. **The number of second- and third-time visitors:** If there is a "buzz and bump" in the community, there will be a high proportion of second- and third-time visitors that can be tracked by church leaders. This can be done without disruption to the flow of worship as people enter or leave the building, or through later surveys and focus groups. Many first-time visitors arrive accompanied by church members who have invited them to worship. If worship has been successfully inspirational, these visitors will return. This is a sign of higher motivation and interest. There should

always be a significant proportion of participants who are nonmembers, and they may consider themselves to be adherents of the church. Inspirational worship should eventually cause an increase in adult baptisms and membership commitments.

7. **The number of people leaving with a smile:** Finally, inspirational worship can be measured simply by observing the joy of people who depart. Churches can simply deploy observers at the exits or in the parking lot to observe behavior. If people are frowning, arguing, or simply in a rush to get away, then worship does not seem to have been effectively inspirational. On the other hand, if people are smiling, laughing or playing, and lingering in the parking lot (or making plans to go to lunch and debrief), then worship has been effective. The weekly routine of counting smiles may seem like a rough estimate, but this estimate can be charted to demonstrate a stable or growing enthusiasm from people who participate in worship.

It is possible for a small church to be very successful at inspirational worship. The size of worship depends more on the power and presence of the Holy Spirit, mediated through the skill and enthusiasm of worship leaders, than on the actual number of attendees. Worship participation will grow to the size of its spiritual power. A church that thinks big, acts big, and worships big will often numerically grow to be big.

Compatible Worship Options
A church can only blend two of the seven options
of worship successfully.
What are the easiest and hardest blends for inspirational worship?

Easiest Blend: Educational, Coaching, or Transformational Worship
Difficult Blend: Mission-Connectional Worship
Hardest Blends: Caregiving or Healing Worship

Worship Option

Caregiving Worship

Caregiving worship leads people to experience the embrace of God as a constant companion, protecting power, and generous benefactor. It glorifies God by providing people with a sense of belonging and context of emotional stability. Worship is often compared to an "oasis" where otherwise hard-working and nomadic people can find rest and fellowship. It is also compared to a "rock" or "fortress" from which mutually supportive allies can confront challenges from a hostile world. These two rather distinct metaphors for caregiving worship help us understand the lifestyle segments that prefer it as a means to experience God.

Those segments that consider caregiving worship as an oasis tend to be more affluent, younger, or family focused. Their lives may be more secure, and their home environments may be more opulent, and they may even have more disposable income to enjoy life. However, they are often multitasking, struggling with time management, and having increasing difficulty sustaining their social status. They include the following:

Group C: Booming with Confidence

Prosperous, established couples in their peak earning years living in suburban homes

C12: Golf Carts and Gourmets

Upscale retirees and empty nesters in comfortable communities

C13: Silver Sophisticates

Mature, upscale couples and singles in suburban homes

Group D: Suburban Style

Middle-aged, ethnically mixed suburban families and couples earning upscale incomes

D16: Settled in Suburbia

Upper-middle-class diverse family units and empty nesters living in established suburbs

Group E: Thriving Boomers

Upper-middle-class baby-boomer couples living comfortable lifestyles settled in town and exurban homes

E21: Unspoiled Splendor

Comfortably established baby-boomer couples in town and country communities

Group F: Promising Families

Young couples with children in starter homes living child-centered lives

F23: Families Matter Most

Young, middle-class families in scenic suburbs leading active, family-focused lives

Group H: Middle-Class Melting Pot

Midscale, middle-aged, and established couples living in sub-urban and fringe homes

H26: Progressive Potpourri

Mature, multiethnic couples with comfortable and active lives in middle-class suburbs

H27: Birkenstocks and Beemers

Upper-middle-class, established couples living leisure lifestyles in small towns and cities

H28: Everyday Moderates

Midscale, multicultural couples and families living in midtier metro suburban settings

Group L: Blue Sky Boomers

Lower- and middle-class baby boomer-aged households living in small towns

L41: Booming and Consuming

Older empty-nesting couples and singles enjoying relaxed lives in small towns

L43: Homemade Happiness

Lower-middle-class baby-boomer households living in remote town and country homes

Group M: Families in Motion

Younger, working-class families earning moderate incomes in smaller residential communities

M44: Red, White, and Bluegrass

Lower-middle-income rural families with diverse adult and children household dynamics

M45: Diapers and Debit Cards

Young, working-class families and single-parent households living in small, established city residences

Group I: Family Union

Midscale, middle-aged, and somewhat ethnically diverse families living in homes supported by solid blue-collar occupations

I30: Stockcars and State Parks

Middle-class couples and families living in more remote rural communities

I31: Blue Collar Comfort

Middle-class families in smaller cities and towns with solid blue-collar jobs

A preference for caregiving worship is particularly noticeable among all the lifestyle segments that belong to lifestyle groups E (Thriving Boomers), H (Middle-Class Melting Pot), and L (Blue Sky Boomers). The negative reason for their preference is that caregiving worship can reinforce their sense of privilege and need for attention. The more positive reason for their preference is that they are often rootless because career ambitions have forced so many relocations, their children tend to be scattered across the country, and their middle-class lifestyle tends to be under severe economic pressure.

Those segments that consider caregiving worship as a rock or fortress tend to be less affluent, older, and family free. Their lives may provide more leisure or discretionary time, and they may maintain strong roots in their heritage or neighborhood. However, their lifestyles are often financially precarious, and their health may be at greater risk. They may feel that their heritage or neighborhood is threatened by diversity or that their values and beliefs are being compromised by culture. They include the following:

Group J: Autumn Years

Established, ethnically diverse, and mature couples living gratified lifestyles in older homes

J34: Aging in Place

Middle-class seniors living solid, suburban lifestyles

J35: Rural Escape

Older, middle-class couples and singles living comfortable lives in rural towns

J36: Settled and Sensible

Older, middle-class, and empty-nesting couples and singles in city neighborhoods

Group N: Pastoral Pride

Eclectic mix of lower-middle-class widowed and divorced individuals and couples who have settled in country and small town areas

N46: True Grit Americans

Older, middle-class households in town and country communities located in the nation's midsection

N48: Gospel and Grits

Lower-middle-income African American multigenerational families living in small towns

Group Q: Golden Year Guardians

Retirees living in settled residences and communities

Q63: Footloose and Family Free

Elderly couples and widowed individuals living active and comfortable lifestyles

Q64: Town Elders

Stable, minimalist seniors living in older residences and leading sedentary lifestyles

Q65: Senior Discounts

Downscale, settled retirees in metro apartment communities

Group S: Struggling Societies

Economically challenged mix of single, divorced, and widowed individuals in smaller cities and urban areas looking to make ends meet

S68: Small Town, Shallow Pockets

Older, downscale singles and empty nesters living in modest exurban small towns

S69: Soul Survivors

Older, downscale African American singles and single parents established in modest urban neighborhoods

Group O: Singles and Starters

Young singles starting out, and some starter families, in diverse urban communities

O55: Family Troopers

Families and single-parent households living near military bases

Group P: Cultural Connections

Diverse, mid- and low-income families in urban apartments and residences

P56: Rolling the Dice

Middle-aged, midscale income singles and divorced individuals in secondary cities

P58: Fragile Families

Multicultural singles and families with mid and low incomes living settled lives in urban apartments

P59: Nuevo Horizons

Middle-aged, midscale income Hispanic families living mainly within US border cities

P60: Ciudad Strivers

Midscale Hispanic families and single parents in gateway communities

P61: Humble Beginnings

Multiethnic singles and single-parent households with mid-scale incomes in city apartments[1]

A preference for caregiving worship is particularly noticeable among all the lifestyle segments that belong to groups J (Autumn Years), Q (Golden Year Guardians), and P (Cultural Connections). The negative reason for their preference is that caregiving worship perpetuates local traditions, family habits, and unique cultural mores that are deemed sacred. The more positive reason for their preference is that they feel heightened stress over cultural change, and higher anxiety about being alone and vulnerable.

Life Situation and Compulsion to Worship

The lifestyle segments that most often gravitate to caregiving worship commonly express feelings of guilt and loss. They have a strong sense of duty, and feel they have somehow failed to sustain and communicate social values, cultural heritage, and essential faith to the generations that come after them. The existential anxiety over being *discarded* (forgotten, left behind, set aside, and ignored) is particularly strong. This explains why certain elements of worship are so emotionally important:

- Children's time (sermon or story especially for preschool and elementary ages)

- Passing the peace (extended opportunities to greet one another before, during, and after worship)

- Announcements (opportunities to be visible as active, responsible church members)

People in these segments have a strong need to belong with an identifiable, mutually supportive, protective community. They prefer *smaller* communities of faith (usually with less than 150 participants) because few people can remember more than 150 first names. They often think of themselves as a faithful remnant of a movement that was once much larger. This self-identification means a rather paradoxical attitude toward church. They want new, and especially younger, people; but any growth with new people contradicts their identity as a remnant and exacerbates their anxieties about losing the past and fitting into the future.

People in these segments often refer to the church as a "family." They go out of their way to preserve harmony and avoid losing members. They prefer to gather in one multigenerational worship service that mixes tradition with some more contemporary styles of music or language. There is a strong atmosphere of mutual support as worship honors each member's journey through all of the life cycles. Births, wedding, graduations, and funerals are highlighted, and each individual receives prayer upon request. Families may sit in the same seat for generations.

The Altered Call

Tom: *Caregiving worship is at its best when it is more "liquid" than "solid." One droplet keeps absorbing more droplets to create an expanding puddle that has the potential of becoming an ocean. Caregiving is most profound when love for the stranger outperforms love among members.*

Lucinda: *"We do life together," says the bivocational pastor for a community of fifteen families. "Our rule of life is to dwell in his presence as abiding love; nurture that love through relationships with others; act out our faith in love. Church is not where we go—but who we are."*

A young mother of three (one of the children now sitting on the pastor's knee) shared how important "the table" is in helping her raise her children in faith, as her husband travels in his work. It was family night, and the children brought the word and assisted at the table. Jesus's incarnational expression was fully alive through the hands of the young ones.

The sense of belonging requires sustained harmony and sympathetic leadership. The image of the shepherd is a perfect metaphor for the experience of Christ of these segments, even among those lifestyle segments far removed from pastoral lifestyles or agricultural settings. There are three classic images of Christ the Good Shepherd that express the meaning of caregiving worship.

The first image represents Jesus with a shepherd's staff walking in the midst of the flock and usually holding a lamb in his arms. Such images emerged very early in Christianity (e.g., the catacombs of Domatilla). One popular depiction found in many churches in North America is by the German artist Bernard Plockhorst (1825–1907). This is a classic late-nineteenth century depiction of Jesus looking western European, with long hair, walking along a stony path in the wild, carrying a lamb and closely surrounded by docile sheep. The nostalgic atmosphere is deliberate. There is a strong sense of belonging to a community in inhospitable surroundings. The clear reference is to John 10:1-18: "I am the good shepherd. I know my own and my own know me" (v. 14).

The second image represents Jesus clinging to the side of a cliff, reaching down to rescue a stranded sheep. One popular depiction is *The Lost Sheep* by Alfred Soord (1865–1915). Jesus clings by one hand, leaning over a deep chasm, nearly overbalanced to reach the stranded sheep. The dizzying height of the precipice is emphasized by an eagle, normally viewed from the ground as high in the air, but in this image at eye level. Jesus is clearly risking his life to rescue a stray to return him to the fold. The reference is to Luke 15:4: "Which one of you, having a hundred sheep and losing one of them, does not leave the ninety-nine in the wilderness and go after the one that is lost?" The significance of the numbers *one hundred* and *one* is not lost on those who prefer caregiving worship. The small size of the congregation parallels the importance of a single participant.

The third image represents Jesus close up. A good example is *The Good Shepherd* by Philippe de Champaigne (1602–1674). Jesus is again carrying the staff of the shepherd and walking a remote or lonely path. In this instance, he is alone and carrying a single sheep across his shoulders. This is no lamb. Jesus has no difficulty carrying the size and weight of the sheep, and the sheep is perfectly content to rest on his shoulders. In this image, and others like it, Jesus looks directly at the viewer with both empathy and expectation. The reference is to 1 Peter 2:25: "For you were going astray like sheep, but now you have returned to the shepherd and guardian of your souls." The image reminds the believer that Jesus is both shepherd *and* sacrificial lamb.

Caregiving worship is a particular blessing for those lifestyle segments that experience physical, emotional, or relational stress. The stress is more *chronic* than *acute*. The grace experience is more *providential* than *immediately powerful*. God restores wholeness and harmony to the individual soul and to the gathered community.

What It Looks Like

Caregiving worship is often described as traditional worship. As such it is often blended with educational worship, especially in congregations with fewer than 150 participants. It is all about familiarity and family harmony. It celebrates multigenerational relationships and connects people with the culture, country, or heritage of their origins. In the past, caregiving worship was generationally diverse with the real presence of grandparents, parents, children, and grandchildren. Today caregiving worship is more nostalgic. Grandparents are often accompanied by grandchildren, but the parents may be missing. The congregation tends to be very old and very young.

People often chat and visit in the sanctuary before worship, connecting with friends and catching up with news. Caregiving worship is sometimes blended with healing worship, and there can be some occasional tension between those who want to visit and those who want quiet meditation before worship. The half hour preceding worship often feels like a rehearsal. Choirs and musicians may still be practicing; volunteers may be checking microphones and arranging flowers. This is why caregiving worship is often started with a processional, special music, or people stand when the pastor enters the room. There is an intentional call to worship that marks an end to informal visiting and the start of intentional conversation with God.

In the past, caregiving worship often gave great visibility to the choir and the elders of the board (who might sit at the front or apart) to emphasize their presence as role models for the core values and beliefs of the community. Today this may seem authoritarian, but in fact it was a means of declaring consensus around the behavior patterns and beliefs that gave harmony and strength to the community. It was a means of quiet accountability that communicated the boundaries beyond which behavior could not go and within which every person, young or old, healthy or infirm, married or single, was guaranteed safety and respect. Today those boundaries are often revealed through mission statements in the bulletin, images in the sanctuary, or assurances by the pastor as he or she welcomes people at the beginning of worship.

155

The offering is often a central rite of worship, and today this may be where church elders are most visible. It is a tangible sign of commitment to the church family. Churches that celebrate caregiving worship are often reluctant to publish any details of individual financial giving. They prefer to encourage young and old, rich and poor, to simply give as they are able. Most offerings, however, are given in sealed church envelopes, and cash often reveals who is a visitor or nonmember. The offering is more of a symbol of solidarity than a financial engine sustaining the church.

FAQ

Lucinda: How do you make a caregiving worship service financially sustainable?

Tom: Critical mass for a church today is about one hundred regular, generous worshipers out of 150 members who also pledge or leave bequests. Many family churches with caregiving worship services are unable to both maintain property *and* pay a full-time minister.

Clustering churches and bivocational clergy are common trends for this kind of church.

The psychographic profile of many lifestyle segments reveals that people tend to be followers rather than leaders. They are less likely to pledge, but more likely to give generously in response to a crisis and leave behind a generous bequest.

The closing moments of caregiving worship link worship with the pastoral care and visitation that can be anticipated in the coming week. The benediction uses traditional words, but the pastor often comes down from the pulpit to stand nearer to the people. The pastor always shakes hands at the door, and people will wait patiently in line for the opportunity to have a personal word or greeting (even if they then go downstairs for refreshments). Symbolically, they expect the pastor to be available through the week 24-7 for visits, conversations, interventions, and emergencies. The pastors or priests are often late to refreshments, because intimate conversations or special counseling delay them.

Hospitality

Greeters and ushers must be very friendly and natural. Churches that focus on caregiving worship are often afraid that hospitality teams might seem too "pushy" or "manipulative." They keep training to a minimum. The most important skills for greeters and ushers are to be generationally sensitive and attentive to strangers. Therefore, they must be smiling and friendly to children, tolerant of crying infants and preschool antics, and respectful to teenagers; and also avoid concentrating on their friends and intentionally greet singles, visitors, or loners who come to worship.

Caregiving worship lives or dies by the reputation greeters and ushers create for friendliness. Visitors will tend to evaluate a church based on their experience in the first five minutes before worship and also the last five minutes as they leave the building. Greeters are always on hand to say goodbye and often give newcomers generationally sensitive gifts to honor their visit (e.g., plush toys to children, computer gadgets for teens, music CDs for adults).

Given the family metaphor of caregiving worship, it is not surprising that refreshments are often homemade, potluck, or purchased from local markets, food stores, and pastry shops. In some churches, refreshments may be intentionally ethnic. Food is opulent and diverse but not necessarily healthy. Sugary treats make postworship hospitality a special occasion, and there is often a birthday cake or other tasty item that encourages people to linger and mingle. Liquid refreshments, however, are fairly basic: cold and hot coffee from large urns and pitchers, milk from cartons and powdered creamer, and so on. Today it is important for the servers to be both male and female, although a women's group often takes responsibility for refreshments to reinforce traditional gender roles. Always provide a separate, supervised serving station for children, allowing them space to run around, make a mess, and be themselves without risk of tripping or disturbing a senior.

As I suggested above, the pastor's presence is not really necessary for refreshments. This is clearly a time for the members to gather in friendship circles and for elders or greeters to introduce newcomers to the church family. It is often a time when opinions about church policy are shared and tested and the actual decisions are made outside of formal board meetings.

Special occasions are usually associated with food and entertainment. Special dinners and potluck lunches are common. Entertainment is usually unpaid and amateur and often provided by church members and their friends. Caregiving worship on regular Sundays and special occasions contributes to the socialization of newcomers, the assimilation of immigrants, and the indoctrination of young adults into the core values and beliefs of the community. Therefore, these events are profoundly, although not overtly, educational. Those who design hospitality will protect certain boundaries of accoun-tability. Behavior that is antisocial, or contradictory to community values and beliefs, will be corrected as quietly and generously as possible, primarily by lay leaders (perhaps matriarchs or patriarchs) rather than clergy.

FAQ

Lucinda: What is the biggest challenge to hospitality?

Tom: Churches are often too tolerant of insensitive behavior among greeters and ushers. Hospitality is often handed down over generations as a privilege. Wise churches make sure greeting and ushering teams reflect age, gender, and cultural diversity in the community.

Churches that emphasize caregiving worship often encourage an unusual paradox. They consider themselves extremely friendly, yet it is remarkably difficult for a newcomer to gain complete acceptance. This is especially true if the newcomer comes from a different socio-economic group or cultural tradition. This makes committee participation a form of assimilation. The best way to get accepted is to join a committee. Progress through the bureaucracy (starting with Christian education and outreach committees and progressing to trustee, finance, and personnel committees) reflects the degree of community acceptance and trust. These churches favor large boards and frequently appoint "members at large" to honor longtime members.

Hospitality via bureaucracy has broken down in recent decades. Today, church leaders are more likely to train and deploy "shepherds" who literally walk alongside newcomers on the assimilation journey. They explain the meaning of worship symbols and rituals, accompany newcomers to various fellowship and worship events, and generally smooth their path to acceptance and trust.

Worship Format

Caregiving worship follows a predictable and familiar format. There will be unison readings and responsive liturgies, traditional creeds, and hymns chosen from a denominationally approved book. Pastoral prayers, however, are often original and even spontaneous. Participants are often free to add personal introductions or footnotes to readings of scripture. Individuals usually make their own announcements from the pulpit or front of the church, so that announcement periods are often long and occasionally humorous.

In addition to the elements noted above (children's time, passing the peace, and announcements), caregiving worship is usually slow paced. It is marked by pregnant silences, and allows time for participants to collect their thoughts and focus their attention on symbols of faith inside the sanctuary. The liturgy is predictable but not as formal as is the case in educational and inspirational worship. Classic hymns punctuate the worship service and may be more important than the sermon. Caregiving worship is less concerned with unifying worship around a common lectionary and sermon and more concerned about unifying worship around traditional or doctrinal themes and an anthem. This is very evident in Advent and Christmas. Educational worship will focus on lesser-known Advent carols, and caregiving worship will focus on well-known Christmas carols. At important seasons of the year like Christmas and Easter, the worship service will exponentially increase music, rites, and images and decrease the time for the sermon.

FAQ

Lucinda: How do you make worship positive, healthy, and upbeat?

Tom: Whether in prayer or preaching, match every grief with a joy and every lamentation with a celebration. Music may be more lyrical, gentle, or slow, but keep up the tempo.

A support team is necessary to move from worship to visitation and pastoral care. Many churches create caregiving teams and recognize them often in worship. They bring Holy Communion to elder members in private and group homes.

Sacraments are particularly poignant in caregiving worship. Holy Communion (Eucharist) is often prolonged to allow personal attention from the pastor or priest to individual participants or time for personal meditation. It is a time when the real presence of the Good Shepherd is vividly, and perhaps emotionally, experienced. Baptisms become the centerpiece of worship, very accessible to children, and include many local traditions like candle lighting, choral responses, or walking the baptized infant or child around the sanctuary for all to see and smile. Confirmations and transfers of membership are special occasions. Weddings are always without financial cost to member families. Healing prayer may be offered after worship. Funerals are often celebrated in the sanctuary rather than the funeral home. The church anniversary worship service is an important homecoming.

Remember that the purpose of caregiving worship is to provide a sense of comfort, reassurance, and belonging to people who are anxious about being ignored, forgotten, or discarded or who feel isolated or vulnerable in strange or hostile environments.

Keep it personal. Encourage as much physical contact as possible. Move people forward and closer together. Make eye contact. Shake as many hands as possible. Remember people's names. Acknowledge birthdays. Celebrate wedding anniversaries and special occasions. Maintain the appearance (and hopefully celebrate the reality) of trust, overall friendliness, and mutual support.

Keep it in the family. Blend the elements of worship so that there is something for everyone. Even though music is generally classical, lyrical, and thematic, include some more contemporary rhythms and new songs. Give children and youth a visible role in worship. Honor the elderly. Respect traditions, and preserve and occasionally use historic artifacts for baptism and communion.

Keep it confident. Avoid sermons, prayers, or songs that cast doubt on important beliefs or poke fun at valued traditions. Communicate quiet courage and optimism. By all means include a sense of humor, but jokes and funny anecdotes should still uphold the essential truths of the faith. Connect Sunday worship with seven-day-a-week Christian attitudes and lifestyles. Never print budget deficits in the bulletin; always print celebrations and thanksgivings for the generosity of members.

The key words to describe caregiving worship are *family*, *friendly*, and *familiar*. People want to emerge from worship united, compassionate, and strong.

Worship Leadership

Pastoral presence is extremely important in caregiving worship. The pastor's sincerity and authenticity is often revealed in his or her empathy rather than his or her theology. People connect first with the pastor's *heart* and then later with the pastor's *mind*. Therefore, the pastor as prayer leader is somewhat more important than the pastor as preacher. Clergy do not have to be great orators, and long didactic sermons are counterproductive. Preaching is only occasionally prophetic and universally pastoral.

The difference between comfort and confidence can be a fine line for pastors. Caregiving worship does not help participants avoid or deny harsh realities. It helps participants face them squarely but with the encouragement that they are not alone. God is with them. The united congregation is with them.

It is helpful if pastor and lay worship leaders can speak out of their own experience of struggle and victory. Sermons and testimonies are often sprinkled with personal anecdotes, but the most reassuring illustrations of grace are usually taken from the history of the church in the particular cultural heritage of the participants (i.e., the times of their ancestors going back two or three generations).

The pastor is usually a seminary graduate and ordained. He or she has often taken clinical pastoral education and may have special training in marriage, family, and individual counseling. The preferred pastor is usually older rather than younger and has therefore had personal experience of parenting, child rearing, and life stages. If the pastor had an earlier career, it is often in health care, public education, or therapy.

Since Eucharist is often experienced as a time of communion with the Good Shepherd, the pastor is often seen as a priestly mediator or bridge to God. Robes and ritual are often very helpful, particularly if they rely on familiar Christendom symbols like the cross, praying hands, open Bibles, shepherd's crook, and so on. The same familiarity and symbolic power of vestments and rites make baptisms and all other sacraments more meaningful. People feel like the pastor is "welcoming them home" and connecting them with their spiritual roots.

FAQ

Lucinda: How does the pastor sustain emotional energy?

Tom: Burnout is a huge problem for these pastors. Caregiving worship is emotionally draining, and pastors often need to rest afterwards and postpone visits to Monday (which is supposed to be a day off).

It is vital for the pastor to develop a routine of self-care and to shape a lifestyle rather than work schedule. Develop a strong support group with other pastors or health care workers.

Some prayers are historic, familiar, and can often be recited by memory among older veteran members. However, many pastoral or intercessory prayers are quite original and are stamped by the personality of the leader. If these prayers are spontaneous, they must still be focused, concrete, and intelligible. Avoid rambling, stuttering, and trite phrases that might cause people to doubt the sincerity of the leader. Original prayers that have been written ahead of time are quite acceptable, so long as they are clearly honest and personal.

Music leadership is increasingly important in many options of worship, and this is certainly true here. People who seek caregiving worship would rather have unpaid, relatively amateur musicians who appreciate classic hymns and do their best at performance and prefer not to use paid, professional musicians who impose genres of music or instrumentations that are foreign to the heritage of the congregation. The credibility of music leadership is similar to that of clergy.

Caregiving worship encourages laity to contribute to leadership. Individual members often take welcoming people to worship, reading scripture, providing special music, and making announcements. Caregiving worship can seem tedious to visitors because there is often time "wasted" as people come and go from pew to lectern. For the veteran members, however, this is time well spent. It is a way to honor members of the church family and visible assurance that they do not bear responsibility for church life and mission alone. They are in it together.

Some training for readers, sacramental helpers, and others is helpful, especially if it teaches lay leaders how to show respect and communicate clearly. Beyond that, however, participants in a caregiving worship service are more than willing to accept whatever is the best that a volunteer has to offer—even if their best is relatively mediocre. This is particularly visible in music and reading.

The compassion and understanding they give is also the compassion and understanding they expect to receive. This can mean that the benchmark for quality is set rather low. It will only be raised by the role modeling of key volunteer leaders and not by denominational workshops or professional staff.

Evaluation and accountability practices are often difficult in caregiving worship. Participants tend to resist training. This is because a pastor can't evaluate a worship leader for something that has not been trained. Further down the road, the pastor cannot dismiss a volunteer for something for which they have not been evaluated. In caregiving worship, it is nearly impossible to fire a choir member or reader or greeter or usher. Ironically, lifestyle segments that prefer caregiving worship may contain professionals in social services and health care that routinely practice high accountability in their institutions, but they resist this in the church.

When caregiving worship is particularly successful and participation grows, the church may hire a second minister. This minister is usually an ordained generalist and called an "associate" or "assistant" minister. He or she may have some specialization of ministry (children and youth ministry was common in the past, and elder or visitation ministry more common today). However, the associate minister provides the same services, with similar skills and compatible perspectives as the senior pastor. He or she can seamlessly substitute for the senior pastor.

Facilities and Technologies

People who prefer caregiving worship usually gravitate to more traditional ecclesiastical structures that reflect their denominational or cultural heritage. They do not need to be particularly ornate or expensive, but the buildings need to "look like a church." The structures themselves often suggest the multigenerational sensitivities of the congregation so that styles and construction materials are inconsistent. For example, a fairly utilitarian education wing or gymnasium, in different color brick, might be attached to a more formal Gothic style sanctuary in dressed stone. The classic Christendom lines of a tall-steeple church might be broken by the later addition of an elevator or extended ramps for easier access.

The interior of older buildings may also reflect the changing needs of generations in the church family. Rooms may have been renovated several times, and hallways may seem to be a bit maze-like. Lack of signage reveals the assumption that members of the church family are already familiar with the space and don't need to be told how to get anywhere. The facility design suggests that while it is wonderful to be a member, it is hard for a visitor to find their way into the community.

The sanctuary is a sanctuary, and not a worship center. It may be highly decorated or quite austere, but it will look, feel, and smell like holy ground. Symbols will be familiar from both culture background and denominational tradition. Windows, tapestries, pictures, and sacramental ware are often memorials in loving memory of members of the church family.

Seating has traditionally been provided by rows of pews (with cushions added), arranged in straight lines or semicircles. The sanctuary often feels cramped or crowded because the chancel area is very close to the front pews. This is because caregiving worship is enhanced when people are close to one another and can readily see facial expressions and make eye contact. Even in declining churches, when worship participants are scattered or sitting to the rear, it is very controversial to remove pews. The nostalgia and hope of the church family is that the sanctuary will once again be filled.

The trend in renovation, however, is to replace pews with flexible seating. Caregiving worship is well served by comfortable, padded, individual "cathedral" chairs that can be rearranged in a semicircle. It is easier for worship participants to turn to one another for pre- and post-worship conversation, move about to pass the peace, and make room for wheelchairs and infant strollers.

On the whole, it is easier to augment audio technology than video technology in caregiving worship. Microphones and speakers, specialized hearing devices, and acoustical adjustments are common. Older generations in caregiving worship tend to think computer imaging and video screens are distracting. However, younger generations can also prefer caregiving worship and find it helpful. The normal compromise is to use video sparingly, and use projection to provide words and still images only.

The sanctuary used for caregiving worship is not designed to be multipurpose. It can be used for concerts and occasional lectures, but is generally reserved for Sunday worship and sacramental events in the life-cycles of Christian members (baptisms, confirmations, weddings, and funerals). The sanctuary also tends to feel somewhat messy. Artifacts from Christmas, for example, may be left out until Easter. Volunteers look after the building, clean and tidy the sanctuary on their own time-table and to the standards of their own households. Decorations tend to be an eclectic mix of old and new. The sense of belonging includes a feeling of ownership, and the privilege that any member can display or use whatever is particularly meaningful to their personal spiritual lives and individual family traditions. Old memorials are hard to take down, and new memorials are always publicly acknowledged and celebrated. The narthex often displays photos, communionware, images of past pastors, and of course, artistic depictions of the Good Shepherd.

The museum-like quality of the sanctuary often demands that re-freshments be served elsewhere. Hospitality space may have a family living room or parlor-like quality, and may be furnished with items donated from member homes. Alternatively, refreshments are often served directly from the kitchen in the basement or fellowship wing of the building. Members think nothing about walking down corridors, around corners, or to a different level of the building to mingle with their friends in the church family. Wise church leaders plan ahead to deploy volunteers to invite and escort newcomers to the fellowship area.

A second trend, however, is to encourage refreshments in the sanctuary. This may simply be permission to bring coffee and tea into worship or actually develop a serving station in the sanctuary. Flexible seating makes it easier to move chairs to create space for standing or provide seating for elders to chat comfortably. The merging of worship space and refreshment space may reflect the trend toward open space in family homes that directly connects kitchen, dining, and living rooms. It encourages even stronger fellowship and binds the different genera-tions in the church family more closely together.

Timing and Timeliness

I explained earlier that the Good Shepherd metaphor has the dual significance of abiding grace and timely rescue. This informs expecta-tions for worship attendance and the annual worship calendar. Care-giving worship assumes *constant contact*. Once you are a member of the flock, you are always a member of the flock, no matter how far you stray. The traditional assumption is that you will attend caregiving worship regularly. Even if you attend university, serve a tour in the military, or have a seasonal second home, you are still spiritually connected to caregiving worship. You will be remembered in prayer, receive a copy of the worship bulletin and newsletter, and participate in the stewardship campaign. Members will only be removed from the roll by death or specific request. They will often return to worship at church anniversaries, Christmas, or other special occasions.

The assumption of constant contact means that caregiving worship follows both the Christian Year and the life cycles of member families. Celebrations in worship and decorations in the sanctuary generally parallel household special occasions and decorating traditions. God's providence is emphasized. Holy Communion will be served weekly, monthly, quarterly, or following whatever established pattern is traditional. Baptisms, weddings, and funerals will be scheduled at the discretion of individual families, and accommodate the travel plans of distant relatives. The emerging needs of the members are almost always more important than the dogmatic or theological priorities of the institution.

Worship is always included in any gathering of the church community, just as fellowship is included in any Sunday worship service. This is usually more than a perfunctory grace or benediction, although it rarely involves a sermon. Worship usually includes a formal greeting and invocation, scripture reading, pastoral prayer, passing the peace, and benediction.

Among Protestants, caregiving worship occurs on Sunday morning (and Roman Catholics may add a service Saturday night). This is probably not because it is a sacred Sabbath, but because it is a traditional family day. The timing of worship is itself a compromise that recognizes the multigenerational nature of the faith community. It is not too early, in order to accommodate seniors and parents with young children; nor is it too late, in order to accommodate active young adults, singles, and parents with older children. Therefore, worship is usually at ten thirty or eleven. Sunday school occurs ahead of worship, so that all generations can worship together.

Given the decline of Sunday school, the current trend is to schedule caregiving worship at ten thirty. The church provides an excellent nursery and sends the younger elementary-aged children to classes or peer group experiences after the children's story and before the sermon. This maximizes time for fellowship and refreshments following worship.

Lucinda's Notes: You Can Do This!

Creating Your Own Lectionary

In this instance, I use the word "lectionary" loosely to refer to any worship service or preaching plan over one or more years.

A new "lectionary" for caregiving worship might include scripture studies about hope, such as the Psalms, Paul's epistle to Philippi, or Revelation. These might rotate through seasons of the year when comfort or inclusion is especially important, such as a "Blue Christmas" for those experiencing loss or February for people especially depressed or October's Cancer Awareness, and so on.

The entire congregation is expected to worship together in one place at one time. Churches that favor caregiving worship often resist multiple worship services. If they must add a worship service on Sunday morning, it will be the same service repeated. They will go out of their way to expand seating for special occasions and may even violate fire regulations to remain in one sanctuary or spend money to rent a larger space in order to gather the entire church family in the same place and time.

Measuring Success

Leaders of caregiving worship are often reluctant to even talk about measuring success. This is because worship is at its caregiving best when the congregation is 150 people or fewer, standards for performance are reasonably low, and budgets focus on maintenance rather than expansion. It is hard to measure the success of caregiving worship, because the feeling of belonging is so difficult to quantify.

However, churches that emphasize caregiving worship are facing severe challenges. They depend on facilities and symbols that provide continuity with the past and options for all generations, and they require pastors with specialized training in counseling and cross generational relationships. Overhead costs for maintenance and personnel are high. Meanwhile, the lifestyle segments most blessed by caregiving worship are shrinking. Neighborhoods are diversifying and generations are incredibly mobile. Marriage and parenting norms are changing. People are less likely to stick with one church and one kind of worship service and more likely to participate in multiple communities and migrate from one kind of worship service to another as their needs evolve.

Therefore, the critical mass required for a congregation to sustain facilities, personnel, and programs today is significantly higher than it was just twenty years ago. A congregation of 100 worshipers and 150 members is close to, or beyond, the breaking point for institutional viability in many regions of North America.

One of the most important conditions for survival (much less success) is the number, quality, and spiritual credibility of lay leaders. Churches that focus on caregiving worship require the board (a core of lay leaders) to step up. The tradition of low expectation, rotated classes, and micromanaging board members who are dependent on the pastor for all the caregiving and simply concentrate on property maintenance and fund-raising, won't sustain the church anymore. The core of lay leaders must rise to high expectations for pastoral care in their own right and delegate responsibility and authority to ministry teams.

Moreover, today it requires more intentional and hard work to maintain *trust* than to maintain *property*. Caregiving worship is especially vulnerable to any breakdown in accountability. The integrity of leadership is often a greater measure of success than even the competency of leadership. The trust that took generations to build up can be sabotaged in an instant by a clergy scandal, board mismanagement, or even the smallest perceived hypocrisy on the part of a secretary, choir member, custodian, or volunteer.

This is a challenge for the church in general.

When it comes to worship itself, there are ways to measure the relative success of caregiving worship.

1. **The number of people in worship:** Churches that focus on caregiving worship may well maintain "resident member" and "nonresident member" lists. That makes sense, because members will belong (and receive prayers, privileges, and communications) until death or request for removal. However, these churches should *never* keep "active" and "inactive" lists because inactivity contradicts the sense of belonging. Even disabled, senior, or institutionalized members still belong and are active in the sense that they interact with the church.

   As a rule of thumb, caregiving worship is successful when about 80 percent of the resident members participate regularly in Sunday worship. "Regularity" may be defined as worship attendance twice a month, or weekly for seasonal residents combined with weekly worship at their second home. It does not include sporadic worship attendance on selected holidays.

   If a caregiving worship service attracts fewer than 80 percent of the resident members, then no matter how friendly and supportive the remnant of worshipers may feel, they need to ask themselves why such a significant portion of the church finds it irrelevant or unimportant to worship together. Unfortunately, many small churches claim to be successful with caregiving worship, but only a small percentage of the membership actually participates. The problem is almost always a breach of trust. Factional frictions, misbehavior among leaders, aberrant beliefs, or controversial denominational policies have broken the spirit of belonging. Success is measured by participation, because that reveals the truth about real acceptance and belonging.

2. **The number and quality of participation of young children:** Successful caregiving worship will always include a significant number of preschool- and elementary-aged children. They may or may not have a thriving Sunday school, but young children will be quite visible in worship sitting with parents or grandparents.

    As a rule of thumb, about 50–75 percent of member families with preschool or elementary children will find a way to send their children to worship on Sunday morning. The parents themselves may be less disciplined, but they clearly believe that worship attendance is vital to a healthy upbringing, and they want their children to be raised in an environment of both cultural and Christian values that preserve roots and heritage. Parents will continue to take an interest in the fellowship, fund-raising, and policy development of the church, and are likely to remain connected with the church through coming life cycles.

    The *quality* of child participation is as important as the number of children. The fun and laughter of children lifts the morale of the congregation and gives adults more confidence for the future. The patience and forbearance of worship leaders with the noise, confusion, or interruptions of worship will test the sincerity of their compassion and tolerance for eccentricity.

3. **The commitment to accountability:** Harmony may be the hallmark of caregiving worship, but the best way to measure it is by observing habits of accountability. People truly feel like they belong when they are confident that they are in a safe, respectful environment. Worship leaders

clearly communicate boundaries for positive behavior and model that behavior primarily through spontaneous deeds and unrehearsed words. Leaders can quantify how many times positive values are reinforced or contradicted in the worship service by greeters and ushers, readers and preachers, musicians and artists. Vague ideals and idiosyncratic behavior diminish harmony; concrete values and role modeling increases harmony.

It is also possible to measure accountability by observing the deployment and speed of leaders that intervene to correct bad, judgmental, or exclusive behavior. Worship leaders are alert to any insensitivity based on age, race, gender, income, and even aesthetic taste. They respond as a team rather than as individuals and in private conversation rather than public discord and readily forgive mistakes when there is genuine repentance. The more fearful and hesitant leaders are to hold one another accountable to clear standards, the more harmony is shaken.

4. **The intensity of passing the peace:** Another way to qualitatively measure the sense of belonging in caregiving worship is by observing the passion and intentionality of rituals of passing the peace. Caregiving worship dedicates significant time and a great deal of enthusiasm to this ritual. People do not limit themselves to greeting immediate neighbors and do not stay within their friendship circles. They leave their seats, cross the aisle, and especially greet visitors and new members. Names are exchanged, along with personal words of encouragement.

The ritual of passing the peace is also an opportunity to share bedrock faith convictions. It is a spiritual exercise, not just a friendly gesture. Measure the intensity of the ritual by listening carefully to the expressions of faith people offer to one another. Conversations may be brief, but they are significant. They communicate concerns about life and death, health and happiness, peace and well-being, and do not just recite formulas or comment about the weather.

5. **The stories of mutual support:** Caregiving worship is successful if it motivates both reactive and proactive generosity. In other words, church members are responsive to each other not only in times of emergencies and in ongoing support for chronic illnesses and ongoing challenges but also in anticipation of stress brought on by life cycle transitions. This can be quantified in several ways:

   The number of visits by laity who visit church members at home or in hospitals or nursing homes or other institutions without being asked and from a sense of personal concern rather than duty to an office.

   Spontaneous generosity in times of crisis, not only to church members but also to neighbors and work associates, through gifts, prayers, fund-raising, and other acts of intentional kindness shared during the week rather than on Sundays.

   The ability to keep confidences and protect privacy by minimizing gossip, rumor, and petty backbiting or trivial competition.

   Stories can be gathered confidentially by the pastor or church office and selectively shared through newsletters and prayer chains.

6. **The reputation for friendliness and inclusiveness:** Many churches that emphasize caregiving worship believe themselves to be friendly, but do little to test the reality. Leaders can measure success by periodically using focus groups in the community or intentional interviews with social service and health care partners in the community. It is especially helpful to test feedback with demographics and

lifestyle segments that are underrepresented in worship. This can reveal whether nonparticipation indicates an intentional choice for another kind of worship or whether it indicates cynicism about the claims of inclusiveness and openness in the church.

7. **The loyalty to essential traditions:** The sense of belonging is enhanced by family traditions that are denominational or local. Usually, there is a rich blend of historic traditions with unique local applications. There are two ways to measure the depth and sustainability of such traditions.

    Keep track of the traditions that surround holy days in the Christian Year (e.g., Christmas and Easter), transitional moments in life cycles (e.g., births, weddings, and funerals), and annual cultural or community events (e.g., fairs and ethnic holidays). Caregiving worship encourages church members to find strength and hope through such events.

    Keep track of traditions that survive staffing changes. Although there is always openness to innovations with a new pastor, music director, or staff member, there is a solid thread of continuity from past, present, and into the future. Certain decision-making habits and assumptions remain constant, unify church members, and maintain alignment with congregational mission.

Churches that lose their sense of history tend to become divided, and caregiving worship becomes superficial. Churches that are too dependent on staff become less christocentric, unable to differentiate between shepherds and the Good Shepherd. Conversely, clarity about essential traditions enhances the sense of belonging and helps participants think of the church as home despite the changes going on around them.

Compatible Worship Options
A church can only blend two of the seven options
of worship successfully.
What are the easiest and hardest blends for caregiving worship?

Easiest Blend: Educational or Healing Worship
Difficult Blends: Coaching Worship
Hardest Blends: Inspirational, Transformational, or Mission-
Connectional Worship

Worship Option

Healing Worship

Healing worship is an environment that helps people experience physical, emotional, mental, or relational wholeness. It is more radical than caregiving worship because there is a clear expectation for the miraculous. However, it is distinct from transformational worship because the hope is not to become a new person but to restore the health and purity of the original person. Healing worship glorifies God by restoring health to people with chronic or acute illnesses of body and mind and then to emotions and relationships.

Of course, acute and chronic illnesses occur in every lifestyle segment, and at different times or in different circumstances, anyone in any lifestyle segment may seek healing worship. Yet there may be some lifestyle segments that are more likely to consistently gravitate to healing worship than any other alternative. These lifestyle segments do not necessarily fit typical stereotypes. Modern secular observers tend to assume that people who prefer healing worship are less educated, less sophisticated, or less affluent. This is not necessarily the case.

Instead, I believe that the lifestyle segments that tend to seek healing worship have a keen sense of helplessness. They may feel that the relational fabric of their lives across time and space is coming apart; or they may feel that social conditions are inexorably destroying their

177

well-being. These experiences of absolute brokenness or inescapable misery cross all boundaries of education, sophistication, and affluence.

Lifestyle segments that may be especially prone to anxiety over the relational fabric of their lives include the following. These are people whose interest in healing worship is not just driven by personal brokenness but by profound grief and empathy with loved ones for whom there is no hope. They turn to healing worship more out of desperate love than personal confidence.

Group E: Thriving Boomers

Upper-middle-class baby-boomer couples living comfortable lifestyles settled in town and exurban homes

E21: Unspoiled Splendor

Comfortably established baby-boomer couples in town and country communities

Group I: Family Union

Midscale, middle-aged, and somewhat ethnically diverse families living in homes supported by solid blue-collar occupations

I32: Latin Flair

Conventional Hispanic gen X families located in selected coastal city homes

Group M: Families in Motion

Younger, working-class families earning moderate incomes in smaller residential communities

M44: Red, White, and Bluegrass

Lower-middle-income rural families with diverse adult and children household dynamics

M45: Diapers and Debit Cards

Young, working-class families and single-parent households living in small, established city residences

Group N: Pastoral Pride

Eclectic mix of lower-middle-class widowed and divorced individuals and couples who have settled in country and small town areas

N47: Countrified Pragmatics

Lower-middle-income couples and singles living rural casual lives

N48: Gospel and Grits

Lower-middle-income African American multigenerational families living in small towns

N49: Work Hard, Pray Hard

Working-class, middle-aged couples and singles living in rural homes

Group O: Singles and Starters

Young singles starting out, and some starter families, in diverse urban communities

O52: Urban Ambition

Mainly generation Y African American singles and single families established in midmarket cities

O55: Family Troopers

Families and single-parent households living near military bases

Group P: Cultural Connections

Diverse, mid- and low-income families in urban apartments and residences

P60: Ciudad Strivers

Midscale Hispanic families and single parents in gateway communities

P61: Humble Beginnings

Multiethnic singles and single-parent households with mid-scale incomes in city apartments

Group Q: Golden Year Guardians

Retirees living in settled residences and communities

Q64: Town Elders

Stable, minimalist seniors living in older residences and leading sedentary lifestyles

Q65: Senior Discounts

Downscale, settled retirees in metro apartment communities

As diverse as these lifestyle segments might be, they all share strong priorities for personal, family, and neighborly relationships that span generations and can bond people emotionally across long distances. Their sense of helplessness in the face of acute health emergencies or chronic diseases threatens to disrupt a web of relationships that define them as human beings. The relationship is what matters: if they are sick, they feel alone and unsupported; and if they are well, they feel alone and powerless. Science and the promise of medical advance is not enough, no matter how well educated they may be. They look for a healing intervention that will not only restore health to a person, but also health to a relationship and their very sense of identity.

Lifestyle segments that may especially be prone to anxiety over social conditions that are inexorably destroying their well-being include the following. These are people who feel trapped by complex vicious cycles of poverty, underemployment, crime, prejudice, declining social services, decaying infrastructures, aging, and other socioeconomic conditions that seem inescapable. These circumstances are grinding them down, undermining their health, increasing their stress, and generally defeating the optimism that they have once had.

I single out in particular those lifestyle groups that tend to be at the bottom of the socioeconomic ladder and who may feel most desperate because of circumstances beyond their control.

Group R: Aspirational Fusion

Multicultural, low-income singles and single parents living in
   urban locations and striving to make a better life

R66: Dare to Dream

Young singles, couples, and single parents with lower incomes
   starting out in city apartments

R67: Hope for Tomorrow

Young, lower-income African American single parents in
   second-city apartments

Group S: Struggling Societies

Economically challenged mix of single, divorced, and widowed individuals in smaller cities and urban areas looking
   to make ends meet

S68: Small Town, Shallow Pockets

Older, downscale singles and empty nesters living in modest exurban small towns

S70: Enduring Hardships

Middle-aged, downscale singles and divorced individuals in transitional small town and exurban apartments[1]

People in these lifestyle segments may not *exclusively* participate in healing worship. Younger people in these segments may also connect with coaching worship, still hopeful to obtain life skills that might help them break out of the vicious cycles in which they are caught. Older people in these segments may also connect with caregiving worship to find mutual support and inner strength. Yet healing worship will always be important, and they may regularly participate in different worship services in different churches.

Life Situation and Compulsion to Worship

The lifestyle segments that consistently seek healing worship (and people in other segments that occasionally seek healing worship) all feel that their lives and identities are irreparably broken. This brokenness is associated with physical, mental, or emotional illness, but their anxiety is much deeper than this. Their soul itself is "broken." Their identity as a human being is at risk. The thread of meaning or life purpose that began at birth, and which should extend into the present, seems to have been cut. Physical, mental, and emotional healing is important in itself, but there is a deeper, spiritual dimension to it.

Healing worship, like many of the healing stories of Jesus, recognizes the subtle and complex connections between guilt and fate. Healing experiences always beg the question as to whether *healing* or *forgiveness* is the real significance of the encounter with God. This is because "wholeness" as a response to "brokenness" is so multidimensional.

The story of Jesus healing the paralytic in Capernaum conveys many of the key elements of healing worship.[2] The healing of the indi-

182

vidual has both a horizontal and vertical dimension. This is why healing worship is often so dramatic. The urgency of the situation and the expectancy of the participants sharpen the encounter with the Holy. Many depictions of the Capernaum healing capture the desperate urgency of suffers to get to Jesus and the wide-eyed anticipation of the audience. See, for example, the famous engraving by Bernard Rode (*Christ Healing the Paralytic at Capernaum*, 1780).

The horizontal dimension is about continuity, or lack of continuity, with human relationships. In this example, the healing occurs in the context of friends and relatives of the paralytic who care so much that they tear a hole in the roof of the building in order to let the man down by ropes to the feet of Jesus. In other examples (e.g., the healing of the paralytic at the pool of Bethsaida), the healing occurs in the context of isolation, and the sufferer complains that no one cares enough to lift him into the pool. Healing worship always happens with some reference to the horizontal network of human relationships and suggests that the healing of the individual is symbolic or talismanic of the healing of the world.

The famous Rembrandt etching entitled *Christ Healing the Sick* (the so-called *Hundred Guilder Print* of 1647) captures this horizontal dimension well. In a single tableau, Rembrandt captures the themes of Matthew 19: healing the multitudes, gathering the little children, mentoring the apostles, and rebuking the Pharisees. As always, Rembrandt captures facial expressions in such detail that one glimpses the inner life and complex relationships that are the background to healing. What you see is only a fraction of the real story. The same is true in healing worship. The mere description of "what happened" never comes close to explaining *what really happened.*

The vertical dimension of healing is about awesome grace. The encounter with God is overpowering and unpredictable. A depiction of healing that is more relevant to modern experiences of healing worship is *Christ Healing the Sick* by the modern African American artist Romare Bearden, painted in 1945. This abstract example of early cubism captures the intimate relationship between a single sufferer and Jesus. The sufferer is disproportionately small and his spiky arms reach out

183

toward Jesus, conveying feelings of jagged pain. Jesus towers over him, standing very close, invading his private space. The hand of Jesus resembles the petals of a flower, raised above the sufferer's body. The head of Jesus is tilted forward almost at a right angle—awkward, surreal, human and yet not human. The robe of Jesus swirls down to envelope the sufferer like a cord that binds. The overall impression is one of awesome and mysterious power that embraces and even cocoons the sufferer, promising some miraculous restoration to wholeness or full humanity.

The Altered Call

Tom: Great healing worship is wonder-full. Healing may be timely or timeless, dramatic or drawn out, but it is always beyond words. Perhaps this is why modern people raised in the public education system of America have such trouble with it. Healing worship only works in the expectation of miracles.

Lucinda: The expectation of miracles that are beyond our control slams into my assumptions of personal power. My ego is confronted by my altar ego. Healing occurs as God's movement and not mine. The Spirit moves where it will, and the movement cannot be designed. At best, the role of the worship leader is to get out of the way and let Jesus's presence be manifested at his will. The repetition of the Jesus Prayer or the Kyrie lowers my own barriers and empties the need to get results because of my own efforts. What will be your prayer or mode of self-emptying that allows the real presence of Jesus Christ to be known?

Healing worship, like transformational worship, is fundamentally and intentionally irrational and mysterious. It is not intended to be educational or practical, nor is it simply therapeutic like caregiving worship. It does not share assumptions about life processes, psychosomatic symptoms, and inevitable explanations that are typical of rational, scientific, secular cultures. People who seek healing worship may be well educated, but they have been pressed to the limits of rationality and find it wanting. They are convinced that there is something more.

Participants in healing worship are not troubled by theological conundrums over why some people are healed and others not, or why the same person may be healed today and yet suffer tomorrow. They may not have a strong sense of providential grace.

They experience the world as a crowded, crazy place through which the Son of Man is passing, and they will do whatever it takes to place themselves in the path of God and touch the hem of his garment.

What It Looks Like

One reason I think Bearden's depiction is so descriptive of healing worship today is that the artist was intimately connected with the American civil rights movement. Many of his paintings and collages captured the suffering and joy of African Americans in the Deep South and in Harlem. Bearden was a multidimensional artist who cowrote the classic jazz song "Sea Breeze" that was later recorded by Dizzie Gillespie. The jazz and blues genres connect with healing worship. I am not saying that such music should or should not be used in healing worship but that the improvisational nature of jazz and blues is like the improvisational nature of healing worship.

Authentic healing worship always seems improvised. The more it is planned, timed, and organized, the less expectant participants become. That is one reason why many church attempts to design and implement a regular, weekly, one hour "Healing Worship Service" fail to actually heal anybody. It becomes a caregiving worship service, not a healing worship experience. Healing worship feels like participants are primarily putting in time to occupy themselves as they wait for Jesus to show up. Yes, the singing, praying, meditation, and occasional preaching may be helpful in its way, but all this is really preliminary and probably nonessential to the main event. The main event is the mysterious encounter with the awesomely powerful God who actually does a miracle and heals someone.

Not everyone is healed, but no one doubts the wisdom of God. That is one of the wonders of healing worship. People rejoice for the one who is healed and plan on returning again and again to the "pool" waiting their turn for the "waters to be stirred." They come with their family and friends who will help them or all alone and without support. It is usually one or the other. Few people come to worship accompanied by fair-weather friends in their spare time. Few people come to meet the pastor or become familiar with an institution. They come to meet Jesus and to touch or be touched.

Therefore, healing worship can include any liturgy, activity, performance, or rite. It may be formal or informal. It usually emphasizes experience and drama rather than words and dialogue. Healing worship is an *environment* and not a *service*. It fills the senses. It may be "other worldly," with incense, chanting, candlelight, healing touch, and sacramental drama; or it may be "this worldly," with sweat, choruses, neon lights, upraised hands, and dance. Nevertheless, all this is *very* secondary. Once Jesus arrives and healing happens, all else ceases to be important.

FAQ

Lucinda: Is there a minimum or maximum number for meaningful worship?

Tom: Healing worship is often small: two or three people gathered in the name of Christ. The larger the size, the larger the pastoral support team must be. A good ratio is one pastoral support person for every ten participants.

Healing worship is often a smaller gathering, perhaps less than fifty people. The larger the gathering, the more organization seems to be required, and the seeming choreography of worship detracts from its mystery. The danger is that healing worship will become a spectacle, a carnival, and perhaps even a kind of "freak show" that invites cynicism and mockery. Once healing occurs in authentic healing worship, the healed person also seems to retreat into the background. They become anonymous again, not a celebrity. The focus returns to Jesus, or to the awesome power of God, in praise and thanksgiving. The healed person is a humbled person and not a focus of media attention. This is why Jesus so many times tells the healed person to remain silent, show himself to the priests, give thanks in the temple, and simply go about his or her life in wholeness and purity. Sin no more.

Hospitality

Healing worship has a horizontal or relational matrix, but it is not really about fellowship. Sufferers who are accompanied by family or friends tend to stay in their intimate circles. Individuals who are unaccompanied tend to value their privacy. Therefore, greeters are warm and friendly but do not generally try to engage participants in conversation, ask a lot of questions, or gather contact information. Respect privacy. Honor the single-minded, hopeful urgency that has brought them to worship. It is very important to avoid morbid curiosity. Do not be shocked, repulsed, or melodramatic at the appearance or demeanor of those who worship. Accept them completely as they are. Show compassion by gentleness, kindness, and respect.

Ushers should be especially attentive to little details. There may be many small ways to make a worship participant comfortable. If the room is crowded or relies on pews, ushers may respectfully store walkers, crutches, and canes during worship so that they do not block aisles or trip others and then return them to their owners during a final hymn or prayer at the end of worship.

Ushers often provide pastoral support during worship. They observe participants and are ready with a glass of water, tissue, helping hand, or private prayer. They should be prepared to accompany a worshiper who steps out of the sanctuary to offer encouragement or simply protect their safety and security. It is not just that participants may be vulnerable but that they are often immersed in the moment and distracted.

Refreshments may be basic but tend to be healthy. Be especially sensitive to allergies and offer alerts and alternatives. Serve small portions; provide plenty of utensils, including straws; use nonbreakable dishes; provide plenty of room to move about, ample space to store coats and hats, and a variety of seating (soft and firm, high and low, and so on). People may arrive early and linger longer simply because they need more time to come and go. Everything should be ready well in advance, and don't be in a hurry to clean up.

A cheerful goodbye and ready assistance to exit is as important as a welcome. Sometimes it is helpful to give some devotional object, spiritual symbol, or talisman to people as they leave. In a Protestant church, a cross-in-the-pocket or scriptural bookmark is encouraging. In a Roman Catholic or Orthodox church, an icon, holy water or oil, or some other significant gift sustains hope until the next worship experience. Prominently provide baptismal water before and after worship, accessible to anyone with physical disabilities.

Worship Format

Healing worship (like transformational worship) does not rely on any particular format. Indeed, attempts to plan, structure, and control healing worship often inhibit experiences of actual healing. This is because healing worship aims at a direct intervention of God that by definition is beyond human understanding and control. The healing stories of the Gospels constantly confound and even offend both institutional authorities and academic theologians.

Nevertheless, in practice I see three distinct formats for healing worship. Each one can connect with a form of healing in the Gospels.

The first format of healing worship is sacramental. Consider, for example, the healing of the man blind from birth in the Gospel of John.[3] Jesus encounters the man in passing, and his disciples make him an object lesson to discuss the connection between sin and health. Jesus focuses instead on suffering as an opportunity for grace, and will eventually use the healing of a blind man from birth as a metaphor to connect sin and spiritual ill health. The act of healing, however, is performed by mixing his own saliva with dirt and smearing the mud over the man's eyes. Scripture alludes to such odd rites more than once.

This is the essence of the sacramental act in healing. God takes the ordinary and profane, infuses it with his spiritual essence, and uses the sacramental act as a vehicle for healing. One format for healing worship is to use the sacrament of Holy Communion, or other rites of healing touch or anointing with oil or water, as a means to bring healing to one who suffers. The drama of the sacrament is important, and it involves all the senses. This is why incense, chant, touch, candlelight, icons, and other symbols define the atmosphere of healing worship. It is not even important to understand what is being said. It may seem odd to compare the sights, sounds, aromas, and drama as "mud mixed with God's spittle," but these ordinary things become a medium for divine power.

Healing worship is like one, great hyperlink inserted into an ordinary text. The significance of a hyperlink does not lie in the word itself, but in the connection to a vast library of knowledge that lies just a click away. Touch the forehead with holy oil, or taste the bread and wine, and instantly a conduit to God's power opens between sufferer and healing Christ.

The second format of healing worship is to focus everything on the person and presence of a healer. Consider, for example, the story of Jesus healing the centurion's servant.[4] In this story, and others like it, the act of healing depends entirely upon Jesus's command. There is no particular ceremony. Even the sufferer himself is invisible. The entire focus is on the healer and his action. In the same way, another format of healing worship is to spotlight a credible, spiritual person with a reputation for the gift of healing. Worship may be filled with song and prayer, and there is a clear sense of expectation that is encouraged by scripture readings, images, or testimonies. The real focus, however, is on the healer.

Clearly there is great danger for ego and manipulation in this format of healing worship. No doubt there have been many abuses. On the other hand, many examples of this form of healing worship still confound and offend because ego and manipulation are *not* present. The real focus is on the *gift* of healing, rather than the person who is *gifted*. Therefore, the healer appears quite ordinary in dress and manner and may have only modest speaking skills. He or she has a well-earned reputation for humility and personal spiritual discipline and is usually extremely retiring in life. In a sense, they have a neomonastic presence.

The healer shuns praise, may feel drained by the experience, and may retire quickly for private devotion.

The third format of healing worship I can best describe as incidental. Healing worship happens unexpectedly and unintentionally. In a sense, any worship can suddenly (often upsettingly) be transformed into healing worship. Consider the story of Jesus walking down the road and unexpectedly touched by a woman in the crowd.[5] He stops, exclaims that power has emanated from him, and asks who touched him. The woman, who was ashamed to appear in public, comes forth to confess. Jesus praises her faith and continues down the road.

Healing worship often transforms what is otherwise a gathering of thanksgiving and praise. Worship is usually spontaneous, often loud, and very participatory. Individuals may vocalize prayers or speak in tongues or meditate and focus on intense private prayers. Worship is not particularly orderly, but it is fervent and expectant. Healing simply happens. It may occur through a leader or participant gifted in healing, but they have no control, and sometimes no consciousness, of it happening. Healing may occur without much recognition in the gathering. People will find it *wonderful*, but not particularly *unusual*, because God is always walking in the crowd of humanity, and unexpected things happen.

Whatever the formats of healing worship, healing is both the goal and the verification of the experience. Despite modern, rationalistic attempts to dismiss healing worship as fake or psychosomatic phenomena, there are too many experiences that cannot be explained so easily. Indeed, the greater question is why so many modern, rational versions of healing worship fail to realize any actual healings. The reason is that all attempts to rationalize, structure, and manage healing experiences are shattered by uncontrollable and mysterious experiences of the Holy.

Worship Leadership

Leadership can be very different in each of the three formats of healing worship. This determines the choice, training, and accountability of the leader.

The sacramental format of healing worship requires a priestly leader whose personality is clearly submerged beneath the symbolic power of his or her presence. The personality is not important. The spiritual integrity that supports the sacramental experience is vital. In other words, the *demographics* of age, gender, race, culture, family status, and income and the *lifestyle group* defining aesthetic tastes, personal preferences, political perspectives are irrelevant. What is relevant is the leader's practice of spiritual disciplines and his or her standard of moral behavior. The leader intentionally retreats into the background so that the sacramental experience can be emphasized, but that means nothing in the life of the leader can contradict or detract from the perfection and mystery of Christ.

The credibility of spiritual life, and visible spiritual discipline, extends to greeters, ushers, and other assistants in the worship service. Leaders are chosen for their integrity, and in addition to any particular skills in hospitality, they are trained to develop spiritual disciplines and participate in mentoring relationships. Assistants in worship may be seen as apprentices or novices who are accountable to the priest, pastor, or spiritual leader. Their behavior in worship should never block, distract, or undermine the experience of healing worship.

The second format of healing worship requires a leader with the spiritual gift of healing, and the self-awareness and authority to mediate God's power to others. This is a very difficult and stressful position, which is why this person is often profoundly humble and prayerful. The leader is, after all, only human, and must walk a fine line between ego and self-surrender. The leader is often assertive in confronting obstacles that might block faith and surrender to God's will; yet the leader may be very open about their personal struggles and self-doubts. It is difficult to imagine how such a leader can be trained in any traditional manner. They often have a varied professional experience, and their lives have been shaped by circumstances or events beyond their control. They may refer to individual mentors who have influenced their lives.

The greeters, ushers, and worship helpers often feel an intense loyalty to the worship leader. He or she may be a kind of mentor to them.

Their main purpose is to facilitate access to the worship leader or counsel and support individuals as they come to terms with the implications of healing for their emerging faith and changing lifestyles.

In a sense, the third format of healing worship doesn't require leadership because worship is not particularly organized. The principal worship leader helps shape an environment or creates an opportunity but is well aware that someone else may be the instrument of healing. His or her role is to "keep the lid on," or to provide sufficient boundaries to keep everyone safe, mutually supportive, and focused on hope. The leader is like a facilitator, and when healing occurs he or she recedes into the background.

This leader, however, has the spiritual credibility to hold others accountable to the integrity of faith and the point of worship. He or she can intervene if the core values or beliefs of the community of faith seem to be jeopardized. The leader can help interpret what is going on for visitors and observers and prepare helpers to assist others when needed.

Facilities and Technologies

Since the environment of healing worship is so important, it is usually important to shape a clearly Christian context. The facility is often quite ecclesiastical, although in more utilitarian settings visual symbols may be more portable than permanent. Visual images may be fixed or computer generated. Lighting can be dimmed or filtered, and candlelight may be an option.

If the facility is more ecclesiastical, it is likely to feel more ancient than contemporary. A traditional altar and communion rail encourage participants to kneel for the sacrament. Baptismal fonts and other sacramental equipment will be at the forefront. A pulpit is less important because preaching may or may not be included in worship. There may be other denominational and doctrinal symbols or colors of the Christian Year. Although the sanctuary may be traditional, healing worship requires both freedom of movement and extended periods of meditation. Therefore, flexible, padded seating and individual kneeling pads are preferable to pews. Provide wide aisles, and make sure the floor is free of cables, electrical cords, frayed carpets, and anything that might trip or obstruct people whose attention is entirely absorbed by the worship experience.

Sound is very important, and there is usually an excellent audio system for voice, music, and sound effects. Healing worship can make use of projection or computer-generated imaging, but only if it is unobtrusive. Many worshipers may find video distracting, although still images can focus meditation.

The room is often arranged to encourage intimacy and participation. Seating may be in the round or semicircular. There may be separate stations or areas for healing prayer, candles for individual prayer offerings, and personal support. If the room is more utilitarian (like a theater), the seats are comfortable and roomy. Special seating may be designated for those with specific physical disabilities, and it may be necessary to augment the hospitality team with ushers who can assist or escort worshipers to and from seats.

Healing worship services may be located in facilities that are close to medical centers. They may even be located in hospital chapels, medical office buildings, and more secular structures. Portable Christian symbols become even more important, and worship leaders may intentionally wear vestments and use clearly sacred sacramental items to focus worship. It is important that the facility be as soundproof, safe, and confidential as possible.

FAQ

Lucinda: Can a healing service be financially self-sustaining?

Tom: Church administrators often think dedicated space for healing worship is a waste of resources. This is because healing worship is usually small and does not necessarily sustain a consistent membership. There is rarely an offering, and it takes time and emotional energy from clergy and volunteers who invest in people they may never see again. The only reason to do it is because Jesus wants it!

Timing and Timeliness

Healing worship can of course be at any time during the year. However, it is often particularly poignant for people in winter, especially months that are traditionally more depressing. Worship is often especially relevant in the weeks *following* cultural celebrations (e.g., Christmas or Thanksgiving).

The schedule is especially sensitive to local contexts and specific lifestyle segments. Earlier I described two particular sets of lifestyle segments than often value healing worship. Some people are motivated to seek healing because suffering has strained their relationships or they feel helpless and want to support a loved one. Healing worship is more of a special occasion than a weekly routine. The opportunities are well advertised, and people may make special travel and accommodation arrangements or drive long distances to participate.

Other lifestyle segments value healing worship because they live in a context of chronic pain or in conditions that are grinding them down or constantly difficult. They may feel more isolated from friends or family. Healing worship for them may well be a weekly spiritual habit. They tend to avoid weekday evenings for reasons of health, mobility, or safety. If healing worship occurs near a medical center, it may be scheduled on a weekday morning or over lunch hour to allow medical personnel to participate. Otherwise, healing worship is usually a regular option on Sunday morning. An early time on Sunday morning usually implies a simpler, smaller worship service, and a later time usually implies more music, diverse leadership, and dramatic ritual.

Measuring Success

Healing worship is often seen as the most difficult option for which to measure success. However, it is also the best example of why measuring success is so important in worship design. If only one person experiences healing, then surely the worship service is a success. But what if more people could experience healing? And what if that one single healing says more about the limitations of our planning and the inadequacy of our leadership team than it does about the power of God? Is healing happening through us, or in spite of us?

There are seven keys for measuring success:

1. **The number of actual healings:** It is always curious to note the number of churches that advertise "healing worship services" from which there are no actual stories of healing. People come and go with no apparent significant change to their state of being. The reputation does not fulfill the promise, and worship attendance plateaus or even declines.

   A successful healing worship experience always results in one or more people experiencing a significant and dramatic improvement in their physical, emotional, relational, or mental health. Worship creates a buzz in the community and beyond. There are many *credible* testimonies to healing, and individuals invite their friends and neighbors, as well as strangers they meet in clinics, social service centers, and so on.

2. **The stories of improved quality of life:** Since not all experiences of healing are sudden and dramatic, the success of healing worship can also be measured by stories of improved quality of life. For example, the specific health condition may not have changed, but it has stabilized or entered remission. Moreover, attitudes have become more optimistic, and people are more committed to maintaining a healthier lifestyle of diet and disciplines of medication and exercise.

   Feedback from health care and social service partners is that participants in healing worship have been encouraged to confront illness, worked harder to sustain wellness, and experienced positive changes both for themselves and in their relationships. Families function more effectively. Interpersonal relationships are more sensitive, honest, and supportive.

3. **Participation of people under sixty-five:** Worship in which there is no actual healing is more likely a caregiving worship

195

service or simply a small therapeutic support group. The difference can be seen in the diversity of participation. Caregiving worship tends to be very homogeneous, and healing worship tends to be very heterogeneous.

Caregiving worship often tends to be elderly, and healing worship tends to include many people who are middle aged and younger. The former tends to include grandparents and grandchildren. The latter tends to include parents and children, singles young and old, extended families, and friends escorting friends. Moreover, the mix of participants in healing worship tends to change from one week to the next. In addition to a predictable number of regulars, there will always be a variety of newcomers.

4. **The number of people fully engaged in prayer:** The people who attend healing worship are primarily hoping to connect with God, not with each other. Fellowship, circles of friendship, and mingling with recognizable neighbors are not that important. Talking to God, the immediacy of divine presence, and the experience of being touched by the Holy are urgently important. The success of healing worship is revealed in the passion, focus, and intensity of people in prayer.

    This is why healing worship is like entering the holy of holies rather than a community meeting or seminar. There is an atmosphere of expectation. People are looking for God more than they are curious about their neighbors. There may be a variety of postures or attitudes of prayer. Very little is done in unison; most worship is expressive of the individual's own need, hope, and religious background, and no one pays much attention or cares how others look or what they are doing. The attention is focused on God.

5. **The intimacy of priestly attention:** Healing worship is usually a smaller gathering, but even if it is a large gathering in a theater-style format, individuals feels like the

priest, pastor, or worship leader is peering directly into their individual hearts. The leader gives individual attention to each person who comes forward for the sacrament or healing touch. Time is taken with each person. Often words are exchanged in low, intimate voices. There is intimate contact by sight or touch.

The worship leader is perceived as a mediator to God and has a reputation as someone who is transparent to the Holy. That is, God is visible or accessible through his or her presence and behavior. Obviously, this profound relationship can be manipulated, but despite abuses there are many authentic examples of priestly intimacy that result in the glorification of God's power rather than the human presence.

6. **The reputation for moral integrity and unexplainable grace:** Successful healing worship develops a reputation for profound meaning and miraculous occurrence. It is revealed in focus groups, interviews with health care and social service partners, and respect from a diversity of religious groups. The reputation of healing worship is enhanced when it is scrutinized by the secular media without scandal, and, therefore, when it is ignored by the secular media because there isn't any scandal to uncover.

   Although it may seem surprising, healing worship can thrive side by side with the scientific research and practice of medicine. Worship services can thrive in medical centers. God's healing power in worship is an extension of medical treatments and therapies, and medical treatments and therapies can be interpreted as a means of God's grace. Sometimes healing worship is the next step when medical science reaches its limits, and sometimes healing worship can motivate participants to take medical treatment more seriously. Even when miraculous healings are explained as psychosomatic phenomenon, there is a deeper mystery and spiritual significance that lies beyond the explanation.

7. **The follow-up of spiritual life:** Healing worship is successful if it leads to a deeper, more disciplined spiritual life. Jesus often connected healing with the commandment to "go and sin no more." This does not mean that sin *causes* ill health but that failed health is another sign of the inevitable fragility or imperfection of life that results from alienation from God. Healing should lead to thanksgiving, and thanksgiving should lead to realignment of lifestyle with God's way.

Healing is most successful when the former sufferer aligns his or her life with God's purpose and then intentionally seeks to bless others. The person healed from cancer, for example, goes on to volunteer with the cancer society in order to bless others suffering from the disease. We do not just measure *stories*. We measure *journeys*. Healing that simply returns people to self-centered living is less successful than healing that turns people around to self-sacrificial service.

Once leaders understand how to measure the success of healing worship, and why it is important to do so, resistance to measuring success usually disappears. If it remains, one suspects it is because there is a hidden motivation of self-interest that is hiding behind platitudes. The leaders of healing worship, like leaders in all worship, must be accountable to God for the *magnitude* and *multitude* of blessings that are actually shared.

Compatible Worship Options
A church can only blend two of the seven options
of worship successfully.
What are the easiest and hardest blends for healing worship?

Easiest Blend: Transformational Worship
Difficult Blends: Caregiving, Inspirational, or Mission-Connectional Worship
Hardest Blends: Educational or Coaching Worship

Worship Option

Mission-Connectional Worship

Mission-connectional worship helps people both experience and participate in the power of God that vindicates people who have been abused, neglected, or persecuted. The participants feel a strong empathy with anyone who has experienced unjust treatment. This is sometimes because they have experienced such injustice themselves or they have personal relationships with others who are victims of injustice. However, their empathy extends to strangers whose plight has become known through travel, news reports, and digital networking.

Mission-connectional worship glorifies God by motivating and training people to advocate for the abused and the helpless. Worship may be described using metaphors like "launching pad" and "action center," because the activities of worship are so closely tied to commissioning missionaries and supporting outreach efforts locally and globally. Worship is tied to community development and social activism.

Of course, many lifestyle segments are very concerned about justice (helping the helpless, ending oppression, liberating victims, and so on). Yet some lifestyle segments are likely to make this the primary, even dominant, outcome of worship. Worship is all about mission—and very little else. This often means that these lifestyle segments are quite alienated from any form of institutional church and any kind of formal worship. The church often has difficulty reaching them because there is

199

nothing about the institution and its formal worship service that either attracts them or blesses them. They are more likely to connect with faith-based nonprofits that do effective social service and advocacy work.

One common feature shared by these lifestyle segments is that they all tend to be highly *mobile*. This can mean several things.

- Some are second- and even third-generation immigrant couples who are enjoying dynamic lifestyles in metro areas. These may be Asian, South American, or African people living in gateway cities on the West or East Coast, who maintain strong connections with family and friends scattered around the world and who travel regularly back to their roots.[1]

- Others are empty nesters with significant discretionary incomes and sophisticated cross-cultural tastes. They enjoy travel but prefer to mix tourism with social service. They donate to charities but often volunteer with those charities to do hands-on labor. They have the lifestyle flexibility to travel away from home for extended periods of time and explore the world or leave home to respond to emergencies anywhere in the world.[2]

Most of these segments are in specific lifestyle groups. They tend to be younger, urbanized, and starting out in their careers, with active social lives. Many are single or in nontraditional relationships, and a few have young families. They all enjoy friendships that extend beyond traditional boundaries of class, income, race, or culture. Their relationships are both physical and digital, and they are in constant communication with friends, following news feeds, and texting about life moment to moment. When bad things happen, they know about it instantly and want to take action. They tend to be educated or committed to ongoing education and have a strong sense of ethical obligation.

Group G: Young City Solos

Young and middle-aged singles living active and energetic lifestyles in metropolitan areas

G24: Status Seeking Singles

Younger, upwardly mobile singles living in midscale metro areas leading leisure-intensive lifestyles

G25: Urban Edge

Younger, up-and-coming singles living big city lifestyles located within top capital markets

Group O: Singles and Starters

Young singles starting out, and some starter families, in diverse urban communities

O50: Full Steam Ahead

Younger and middle-aged singles gravitating to second-tier status

O51: Digital Dependents

Mix of generation Y and X singles who live digital-driven, urban lifestyles

O53: Colleges and Cafes

Young singles and recent college graduates living in college communities

O54: Striving Single Scene

Young, multiethnic singles living in Midwest and Southern city centers[3]

People in these segments represent the core of young adult volunteers who take time off from university educations or interrupt careers in order to serve. They may also use their travel and service as a means toward vocational discernment. If they connect with a church at all, it is often with a spiritual leader who is a mentor or "pilgrim" rather than a traditional institutional church pastor.[4] They rarely connect with a worship service first, but only through a small group, outreach mission, or mentoring relationship.

Life Situation and Compulsion to Worship

If people in these segments commit to worship, they do so in extreme. In other words, they commit wholeheartedly to worship with a crusading spirit. They are not violent (and indeed, they are strong proponents of nonviolent protest) but feel a moral obligation to confront the perpetrators of injustice and liberate people who are being misused. Their core values often include behaviors that are open, inclusive, and nonjudgmental; and yet these are sometimes at risk to other core values for accountability.

The lifestyles of people in this segment often seem a bit contradictory. On the one hand, they expect societies to take them as they are, accept their nontraditional relationships and eccentricities without judgment, and allow them to test boundaries of good taste and legality. On the other hand, they readily challenge authorities, expect societies to change policies, and impose new definitions of moral behavior. Again, this makes it difficult for the church to reach them, because they usually associate the church with the status quo. Churches that attract their attention are ones that gain credibility shaking the status quo.

The Altered Call

Tom: *Mission-connectional worship is what happens when a nonprofit behaves like a faith community. It's all about social service and faith sharing as two sides of the same coin. There is no "me" or "us." There are only outreach leaders, teams, projects, intercessory prayers, and total sacrifice.*

Lucinda: *The calling to mission-connectional worship requires the skills and abilities of forming strategic community partnerships, rallying and motivating those who would serve the other, and the* *gifts of perseverance and unflappable optimism. At the same time, one must surrender one's preconceived notions of the needs and desires of others in order to deeply listen and respect where God's presence IS and is working.*

―――――――――

It is helpful for worship designers to understand the deeper existential anxiety that drives people who gravitate to mission-connectional worship. The passion for vindication is deeper than policy change and holding authorities accountable. It is about *overcoming shame*. Shame is very different from guilt. Shame is what happens to people who are robbed of their self-esteem, through no fault of their own. It is a result of victimization. Chronic victimization is a means to enslave whole populations over a long period of time. People may even lose awareness of their own victimization, even though they live in a state of chronic shame. Repressed shame brings about depression—and eventually anger that can erupt in violence.

Is there a connection between shame that has been experienced by people in these lifestyle segments, and the shame they try to confront in the social patterns and institutional policies of society? While the question is universal among people in these lifestyle segments, I think the answer is very individual. The connection may be stronger for some than others. The obvious biblical image that captures the imagination of people in these segments is the good Samaritan (Luke 10:25-37). Of all the depictions of the good Samaritan, I think the painting by Vincent van Gogh expresses the anxiety and hope of mission-connectional worship best. Perhaps this is partly because Van Gogh painted this in 1890 when he himself was in an institution for the mentally ill.

In this painting, the Samaritan is helping the victim onto his horse. The victim seems barely conscious: a dead weight leaning across the Samaritan's body and bending him over. The Samaritan is heaving with all his strength not only to lift the victim but also to stabilize him on the horse and prevent his falling down again. His muscles strain with the effort.

There is no evidence of the robbers, although an empty strongbox or looted travel case lies on the road. In the background one glimpses the priest and the Levite who previously passed by, and they are so indifferent that they do not even look back. The background is lonely and forbidding. Mountains rise on each side, and the road is little more than a track above a rushing river. All by himself, and at considerable risk and sacrifice, the Samaritan settles the victim on his own horse and will take him to safety.

The parable is an illustration of the adage, "It takes one to know one." Only the Samaritan, who himself has suffered prejudice against his people, has empathy with someone else who is oppressed. Many (although not all) of the lifestyle segments that gravitate toward mission-connectional worship feel powerless against economies, policies, and practices that denigrate or limit their hidden potential. By helping the powerless, they help themselves.

FAQ

Lucinda: Is mission-connectional worship an effective way to renew an established church?

Tom: No, because resources that are poured into mission cannot be siphoned off to sustain property, programs, and personnel.

However, this is a good way to connect an established church with a related outreach or nonprofit ministry, provided that church leaders understand the outreach is not intended to increase church membership or church finances.

What It Looks Like

The church usually interprets the parable of the good Samaritan as a call to social responsibility. However, it is important to understand that many in these lifestyle segments interpret the parable quite literally. It is a clear indictment of established, institutional religion. Therefore, worship designers go to extreme measures to eliminate any vestiges of Christendom rituals, symbols, and technologies from the worship experience. This usually makes worship ultracontemporary and exactly mirrors the circumstances, surroundings, and media that shape the daily lives of participants.

Worship is all about mission. The participants acquire urgent information about mission needs, pray for mission and commission, and send mission teams. Worship does not follow a Christian Year, the popular holidays of the year, or even the routines of education, work, and vacation. It is driven by whatever urgent issues are emerging in local and global contexts. The scripture will be brief and pointed and often paraphrased. Traditional prayers and creeds are only relevant if they are deliberately part of the cultural tradition or in the language of people who are the targets of mission. Otherwise, they are unnecessary. The traditional sacraments may not be celebrated, but religious rites indigenous to the mission field may be observed (e.g., burning "sweet grass" to honor American Indians).

FAQ

Lucinda: Is there preaching?

Tom: No. There may be a lecturer who teaches about mission challenges and opportunities. There may also be a storyteller who provides insights into cultures or emerging needs. Neither is necessarily connected to scripture or doctrine.

If there is a sermon, it is usually an ethical point of view followed by a call to action. People are expected to go out of worship and into the mission field to do something symbolic or dramatic that will influence social change. Some may follow worship with some form of Christian education, but for most this is too passive, and, besides, they can catch up with education on the web. Instead, worshipers go directly to march in a protest, join a work party to clean the environment, volunteer in a homeless shelter, and so on.

Charitable giving is important to these lifestyle segments, but they are more likely to shape a generous lifestyle than commit to percentage giving. Therefore, the offering is often not very important in worship. People are expected to give generously to a nonprofit or charity of their choice but are not highly motivated to give to the overhead costs of institutional church maintenance and salaries.

Worship is either *very* high tech or *very* low tech. This can change from week to week, but generally remains consistent.

- If it is high tech, then the room is filled with computer screens that are always running and display various websites and news feeds. The room is wireless, and participants are encouraged to use digital devices to surf, text, and share comments with the speaker as he or she speaks, other people across the room, and still more people a hemisphere away. Music is often electronically reproduced, and sound effects from birds chirping to whale song may be constant.

- If it is low tech, then the room is sparse and natural, or worship may be outdoors. All electronics are temporarily turned off. Worship is simplified to storytelling and dialogue between participants and a guest with expertise or experience to offer. Music is live, usually unplugged or acoustic. Music is often indigenous to whatever culture or context is the focus of worship. Worship can include dance and drama.

Mission-connectional worship is often thematic, but not highly structured. It offers a combination of mutual respect and vigorous interaction. It starts whenever people are ready, and ends whenever people are finished, but there is no time clock.

Hospitality

Relationships are very important for these lifestyle segments, and they look for plenty of opportunities to make, renew, or deepen friendships. Whether worship is indoors or outdoors, there is usually plenty of time before and after worship to mingle. Nothing is very formal. Greeters and ushers are often unnecessary, and if any information needs to be distributed it will either be available online or to pick up. An order of service isn't usually necessary, unless there are culturally sensitive prayers or unfamiliar rituals indigenous to the mission field to be observed.

It is often helpful for a team to be in charge of refreshments. Aside from coordinating potluck or preparing beverages and specialty food, servers are the most visible leaders to model the core values of inclusive, open, and nonjudgmental behavior. Food is usually multiple choice and a mix of food groups and cultural favorites. Leftovers are always given away as take out, and more than a few will supplement their low-income lifestyles with the food they take home. This includes coffee, tea, and other liquid refreshments. Make sure that food is prepared and served in ways that are environmentally friendly (and avoid Styrofoam, plastic, and so on).

A unique feature of hospitality for mission-connectional worship is that participants are willing to pay for their food, even at a higher cost than similar food purchased in a coffee shop or restaurant. This is because all or most of the income is given to specific charitable causes.

Refreshments enhance dialogue. Food and ambience encourage people to come early and leave late. Since worship is a call to action, the fellowship time is often an occasion for debate and strategic planning. Food is served in the worship area itself. If it is high tech, then the video screens with websites and news feeds provoke conversation. Conversation is always significant and not idle chatter or catching up with friends. There is a sense of urgency to conversation as well as to worship.

Hospitality can be expanded to include breakfast, lunch, or supper. For some segments, this is added incentive to attend worship in the first place. Many others see this as a way to avoid meetings, participate in small groups or mission teams, or connect with the mentoring leader who circulates among the participants. There may be additional teaching or sharing by the guest speakers out of their expertise or experience.

Hospitality spills over to the website. Real fellowship blends into digital fellowship. The website should be easy to navigate, provide plenty of chat rooms and blogs, and post podcasts of the message as soon as possible. There should also be room for posting images and videos and plenty of links to social service and other nonprofit agencies locally and globally. All information should be free and unencumbered by copyrights.

Websites also provide a method to make financial donations to a cause, project, or mission team. This can be extended to selling merchandise in support of a cause or products made by indigenous cultures of the mission field. Income all goes to support the mission itself or the people that benefit by the mission.

Worship Format

The format of worship is simple and fluid. Worship is passionate in the sense that it is a call to action. It is purposeful and often quite serious but not necessarily emotional. The gathering may begin with music, but this is more a means to summon people from food to pay attention to what is about to be said. The music may use lyrics, languages, rhythms, and instrumentations that provide a specific cultural ambience relevant to the mission theme of the service. However, the people have not gathered to meditate, theologize, or even be inspired. They want to get down to the business of liberation.

A glib way to describe the format of mission-connectional worship is, "preach, pray, and plot." Everything else is secondary. Worship is not particularly liturgical. It is more this worldly than otherworldly.

The message is actually more teaching than preaching. It may even be a lecture. Someone with expertise and experience talks knowledgably about the urgency of mission and the details of context. The message is more pragmatic than theoretical. No one needs to be persuaded of the *need* for mission. People want expert advice on how to focus it and carry it out.

Any announcements are focused on mission updates. Various projects will be spotlighted, along with any special requests to help refine and empower the work. There are no institutional or personal announcements. These can be posted on a wall or observed on a website.

FAQ

Lucinda: Is there serious prayer?

Tom: Yes! Prayer can be in any form, connecting social service with divine presence or intervention. This is what separates mission-connectional worship from a nonprofit strategic planning retreat. There are no atheists and very few skeptics in mission-connectional worship, only ardent believers.

Prayer is almost entirely intercessor, and very specific about the people, the situation they are in, and the kind of help they require. Prayer is also focused on missionaries or mission teams, and people pray for their safety, renewed strength, and eventual success. Compassion overflows, but it is often tinged with righteous anger toward powers and principalities that cause oppression.

The traditional sacraments are relatively unimportant, except perhaps a form of ordination or commissioning. Mission teams and missionaries will be acclaimed and may be invited forward for special consecration and intercessory prayer.

The final component of worship often resembles a meeting of a revolutionary council. Participants discuss or even debate different goals and approaches for advocacy and social service. People do not want to leave until they are clear about a plan of action or how they can support an ongoing plan of action. There may not be any formal benediction or dismissal. Worship ends whenever discussion ends and the plan begins to be implemented. People may leave worship directly to march, picket, protest, rally, sign petitions, do good works, or even fly around the world to help in relief efforts.

In high-tech versions of mission-connectional worship, participants may join their mission teams live, via Internet, wherever they are in the world. The mission teams update the participants and often pray aloud together. The participants affirm their ongoing support and pledge further action. In low-tech versions of worship, the participants read stories or listen to eyewitnesses talk about critical situations or emerging challenges.

Mission-connectional worship may be celebrated regularly (rather than occasionally in the context of crisis). It will always focus on some form of social justice and the perpetuation of a social justice *movement*.

Keep it focused outward. Avoid prayer concerns that focus on the individual needs of participants and their families, because this will seem self-centered. Avoid appeals for institutional support. There are no offerings for a general operating fund, no invitations to hold institutional offices, and no extraneous denominational themes.

Keep it sensitive to strangers. The core values to be open, inclusive, and nonjudgmental must be rigorously enforced. Equality of race, gender, and age and acceptance of other income brackets and classes (especially poorer people) must be readily apparent. The only thing that *must not* be tolerated is any form of *intolerance*.

Keep it spiritually respectful. Although there are still forms of triumphalistic Christendom worship that tend to have a condescending, adversarial, or crusading spirit, postmodern mission-connectional worship always demonstrates extraordinary respect for other religions. This respect is not based on similarities of belief but on compatibilities of values like generosity, justice, compassion, and so on. There is no passion to convert—only a passion to cooperate.

Almost everything else commonly associated with worship is unimportant. This is why the church seems more like a nonprofit charitable organization at prayer and the worship service seems more like an emergency meeting of a society or agency. From the Christendom point of view, it may not seem like worship at all. And yet there is a strong experience of the immanence of God as vindicator, conviction of divine purpose, and awareness of the presence of the divine Spirit infusing all interaction and conversation.

Worship Leadership

Earlier I alluded to the fact that the spiritual leader of mission-connectional worship is usually a mentor or pilgrim. These are unconventional leaders who may or may not be ordained and who do not often resemble in dress or demeanor a typical clergy person. They are not particularly interested in traditional church programs for generational ministries, faith formation, fund-raising, denominational heritage, or ecclesiastical details. They are not interested in developing a megachurch or even in recruiting church members or honoring membership privileges. They probably do not emphasize the traditional sacraments and do not celebrate weddings or funerals.

FAQ

Lucinda: What are the qualifications of the pastor?

Tom: These leaders are usually not seminary trained. They are more likely to have an MA in social work or an MBA than an MDiv. They are more likely to be engineers than educators.

They often have cross-cultural backgrounds, and may have lived in other countries or traveled extensively. They have expertise in nonprofit organizations and policy governance.

What exactly do these mavericks do? These leaders are very committed to individual mentoring that helps people discern vocation and pursue personal mission. They are dedicated to unlocking the hidden potential of others and empowering them to be servants. They may not be great preachers, but they are persuasive and insightful communicators to small groups. They equip individuals for social service but recognize their limitations and readily forward volunteers to an appropriate and expert source for training. In this sense, these leaders are often excellent administrators. Mission-connectional worship is often a part of a faith-based nonprofit organization that the leader manages.

These leaders are often widely traveled and have both cross-cultural and cross-sector experience. They are pilgrims in the sense that they have personal experience with the people and contexts that are the targets of mission. They are often perceived as countercultural in their hometown, neighborhood, or country. Their personal networks often facilitate mission. They may also be pilgrims in the sense that they have a good working knowledge of other religions and respect a variety of spiritual perspectives.

The spiritual leader may or may not be the main speaker in worship. This speaker is often a guest from the mission field, a mission partner, or another expert about the context or mission program. The spiritual leader is present to lead prayers, consecrate mission teams, and facilitate action plans. He or she is rarely paid *for worship.* His or her income is derived from the nonprofit outreach organization and is usually minimal to cover basic living.

There are only a few other leaders necessary for mission-connectional worship, and these are usually volunteers. The hospitality leaders (primarily those serving refreshments) are well trained to model core values and to assert authority during worship that holds participants accountable for positive behaviors. In high-tech versions of worship, there will be a technology crew that is adept at video and audio and that can sustain excellent live Internet connections with mission teams around the world. In low-tech versions of worship, there is usually a volunteer musician who provides basic instrumental and vocal music before and occasionally during worship.

In a sense, the mission team leaders related to the church also function as worship leaders because dialogue, debate, and planning are parts of worship itself. The spiritual leader mentors each one to model a spiritual life, articulate faith and values, and discern spiritual gifts in others. Therefore, they are not only coordinators of an action plan, but also spiritual leaders of a small group. Their ability to coach spiritual life, and hold others accountable to faith development and spiritual habits, is one of the ways mission-connectional worship defines the organization as a faith community and not just a social service agency.

Facilities and Technologies

The lifestyle segments that gravitate to mission-connectional worship usually prefer more utilitarian facilities. There may be outdoor gardens for meditation and worship, but there may also be storage areas for equipment related to outreach programs. Space in the facility may be dedicated to depot kinds of outreach ministries (food bank, used clothing, recycled furniture, and so on). The primary use of the building may be to house a nonprofit agency. It is better to say that the property is social service and fellowship space that can also be used for worship rather than worship space that can also be used for fellowship.

Both landscaping and facility will be environmentally friendly. Green space, for example, may seem overgrown or rustic because pesticides will not be used to kill weeds. Outdoor signage and symbols are usually not elaborate or particularly ecclesiastical. Parking will be reserved for visitors, and the property will be easily accessible for young families and people with disabilities. Anything that can be done to reduce overhead costs for maintenance will be done.

Even if the facility is an older church, the interior will be significantly remodeled to minimize Christendom symbols and create space for presentation and dialogue. Pews will be replaced by moveable chairs and stackable tables. The meeting space may well seem messy and chaotic. Audio, video, and Internet technology, however, will often be high quality and relatively new. Multiple video screens can display multiple websites and news feeds. Webcams and tabletop microphones will facilitate conferencing software. The entire building will permit wireless Internet access and easy cell phone use.

The organization usually supports itself through grants and charitable donations. In order to be competitive in the nonprofit market place they must spend money for essentials and never waste money on sacred cows. Participants tend to be reverse tithers. In other words, they don't give God a tenth of their money, time, and energy. Instead they give God everything and accept a tenth back again in order to live. Everything else is dedicated to mission in one way or another.

Timing and Timeliness

Mission-connectional worship is sensitive to global trends and community crises. Worship planners do not pay much attention to the Christian Year, changing seasons, or even the routines of work and

213

recreation. Worship is most timely as a response to acute crisis or chronic oppression.

The challenge facing many churches is whether or not this kind of worship can be sustained as a weekly event. In the early transition to the post-Christendom and postmodern world, this has primarily challenged more liberal mainstream churches; but as more conservative churches mobilize for social action, it is a problem for them as well. On the one hand, acute injustice has become so frequent, and chronic oppression has become so public, that a weekly worship service that is all about mission seems realistic. Yet on the other hand, the lifestyle segments that gravitate to such worship are so alienated from the institutional church that weekly worship is distasteful and objectionable. These lifestyle segments are worried that churches will play the "bait and switch" game. Their reputation as "liberal" or "conservative" doesn't matter. These people worry that they will be enticed into weekly worship participation, only to be manipulated into supporting institutional overhead.

It is also important to understand that this kind of worship is only sustainable as a weekly experience in contexts *where these lifestyle segments live*. They cannot be imposed by a denomination, or initiated by a small group of church members, on the assumption that anybody and everybody will come. True, a great many people who are moved by injustice support advocacy and action through charitable agencies. This does not translate, however, into support for weekly worship. The contexts where mission-connectional worship might most likely be sustained on a weekly basis are in urban areas or near universities and colleges. If worship is weekly, the best time will likely be in the evening. It might be combined with a free dinner and followed by additional refreshments (guided by the core values of the church).

Mission-connectional worship is often scheduled at irregular intervals, usually avoiding major holidays when the single and childless couples are more likely on the move. The worship service may be tied a nationally, internationally, or United Nations–sponsored day of awareness (e.g., for refugees, political prisoners, famine relief, child mortality, gay/lesbian pride, and so on). Worship is often nondenominational, and frequently encourages interreligious dialogue. It may also be tied to other seminars, projects, and events scheduled by a university or among social service agencies.

Measuring Success

In all my travels, I have found that leaders of *unsuccessful* mission-connectional worship *avoid talking* about measuring success. And leaders of *successful* mission-connectional worship *always talk* about measuring success.

The reason is that unsuccessful worship in this option is not only embarrassing but also downright hypocritical. The sincerity of leaders and participants becomes an open question. The publics that are the object of mission, and the publics that are outside observers of mission, become convinced that church people "talk the talk" but won't "walk the walk." For example, churches may focus on mission in worship. They may talk and pray about poverty, homelessness, war, racism, sexism, and other oppressive realities. They may even make charitable donations to various causes and agencies. Then they drive away in expensive cars, go home to lunch, depart for vacations, and get on with their lives. Measuring success is just too uncomfortable.

On the other hand, the leaders of *successful* worship are very public about how they measure success and how frequently they do so. Their self-respect demands no less. These churches even take pride in the fact that mission-connectional worship is one of the worship options that intentionally *is not financially self-sustaining*. In other words, worship operates at a financial loss. No clergy, music, or technical support staff receives any remuneration. No rent is paid or property owned. Everything is donated. The church may do things other than mission, but mission-connectional worship does not financially support any costs of overhead. In other words, *everything* about mission-connectional worship *goes toward mission and nothing else*.

The alienation of many of the lifestyle segments from institutional religion forces leaders and participants of mission-connectional worship to go to extraordinary lengths to demonstrate the integrity of this worship option. "It's not *church* . . . it's a *mission!*"

They measure success in seven ways:

1. **The stories of "unbalanced living":** While many lifestyle segments expect worship to help them live *balanced* lives, the people who opt for mission-connectional worship expect it to *unbalance* their lives. They tend to be extremists. They want worship to be radically countercultural. Worship should help them live very passionate, sacrificial, and risk-taking lifestyles. Therefore, leaders will track, catalogue, and often publish stories of radical living. They celebrate martyrs. They wear their scars, and tell their stories, and even share their arrest records for nonviolent protests publicly.

2. **The reputation for high accountability:** All thriving churches hold leaders and members accountable to standards of high integrity, rigorous mission alignment, competency, and teamwork. Leaders and participants of mission-connectional worship do this even more diligently. Any participant can challenge the sincerity and commitment of any other participant anytime and anywhere. Leaders are constantly teaching and modeling standards of conduct, depth of conviction, excellence skills, and selfless cooperation. They may even use military metaphors to describe themselves as "comrades" in a "war" against oppressive forces.

3. **The number of missionaries supported and teams deployed:** One of the most impressive visible features of mission-connectional worship is the rite of commissioning volunteers to work in the mission field, whether it is the neighborhood they are in or a country around the world. Volunteers are frequently in front of the worshiping body for prayer. Leaders track the individuals and teams who are in service and frequently include their reports—or join with them via Internet—to encourage, celebrate, and support the good work.

4. **The size of the mission field reached:** Size matters because diversity matters. Mission-connectional worship does not connect people to a program; it connects them to a movement. This mission movement is a juggernaut that is constantly moving into new neighborhoods and countries or crossing public sectors or influencing more and more lifestyle groups. Leaders often map their progress in worship. The map may be geographical, but it may also be some form of graph or flow chart that reveals how the mission is advancing.

5. **The impact on the mission field reached:** Of course, size is not the only measurement of success. Leaders also measure the extent and significance of social change. This is why leaders are often preoccupied with statistics and trends. They connect worship, for example, with diminishing crime rates (less prostitution, fewer drug overdoses, fewer sexual assaults, reductions in homelessness, and so on). More positively, they connect worship (and the mission teams they motivate) with peace and reconciliation efforts, immigration rights, family stability and child safety, and so on.

6. **The credibility of mission partners:** Mission-connectional worship is often tied to a faith-based nonprofit rather than a traditional church. Nonprofits always work collaboratively with other agencies, and this collaboration is far more extensive and demanding than the rather hazy ecumenism of church traditions. Leaders choose their mission partners with great care to be compatible with their own values and belief systems. They suffer from any breakdown of integrity from a mission partner, but they also gain traction and public support by being allied with other reputable partners.

7. **The amount of money given away:** Success is not only measured by the money *that is not sidetracked* to institutional overhead, but by the money *that is raised to support*

external outreach. It is not just the total amount of money given away that is tracked. Leaders always compare the total amount raised to the comparative size of the worshiping community to demonstrate the true sacrifice of the people. In the same way, they will track the percentage giving of leaders, members, and adherents.

Established churches that prefer to maintain confidentiality for member contributions always struggle with this worship option. To the lifestyle segments that prefer mission above all things, this lack of openness about personal financial giving smacks of insincerity and hypocrisy. Worse yet, they quickly suspect that there is a hidden institutional conspiracy that diverts financial giving for mission to pay for institutional salaries and organizational overhead. In a sense, the degree of absolute transparency in decision making and financial management is a way of evaluating the overall success of mission-connectional worship.

Compatible Worship Options
A church can only blend two of the seven options
of worship successfully.
What are the easiest and hardest blends for
mission-connectional worship?

Easiest Blend: Inspirational or Educational Worship
Difficult Blends: Transformational, Healing, or Coaching
  Worship
Hardest Blends: Caregiving Worship

Possibilities for Blending Worship

Worship is all about mission. It is how church leaders participate in God's mission to bless particular publics in special ways. People are *compelled* to worship by profound existential anxieties. In the midst of worship they are blessed by the immanence of God, or incarnational experiences of Christ, in uniquely relevant ways.

These anxieties are associated with lifestyle segments in distinct life circumstances, but anxieties are more fluid than that. People can migrate from one lifestyle segment to another, and their anxieties will therefore change. The reverse can also be true. Shifting anxieties may be the primary reason why people migrate to a different lifestyle segment

For example, a lifestyle segment in the group Thriving Boomers is called Unspoiled Splendor. These are comfortable and economically stable boomer couples who may be living in new homes on large acreage lots in the country, just beyond the urban sprawl. They often wrestle with the anxiety of meaningless and loneliness, and long for clearer truths and deeper friendships. They usually prefer *educational* worship with a strong *caregiving* component.

Their children, however, may belong to a different lifestyle segment in the group Promising Families called Fast Track Couples. These are young, active, and upwardly mobile couples who either have young children or are preparing the nest. They're more likely to live in urban or exurban townhomes and entry-level housing developments. They often wrestle with anxieties of emptiness and death and long for clarity of purpose and coping skills. They usually prefer *coaching* worship with a strong *inspirational* component.[1]

As children, they may have shared the anxieties and yearnings of their parents, but as adults their anxieties and yearnings have shifted and they look for a different kind of worship service. This is probably not a conscious decision. They just feel increasingly alienated from the worship experience of their parents. It is not just that the style, format, or denominational identity of the church of their childhood is uncomfortable. It is the mission or purpose of worship that is somehow missing the target. They might say they are no longer "fed" or "blessed" by the worship of the past and are looking for different worship outcomes for the future.

Churches have discovered that it is very difficult to address these different anxieties in a single worship service, no matter how worship designers tweak the music and adapt the sermon. An upbeat anthem and preaching without notes using contemporary illustrations won't satisfy the Fast Track Couples, and the addition of a classic hymn and unison reading of a creed won't satisfy the Unspoiled Splendor parents. These segments may worship together at Christmas, but otherwise they attend different worship services (and perhaps different churches).

The anxieties that drive people to worship are also fluid in the sense that exceptional circumstances can drive people away from the norm for their segment and toward a worship service with a very different kind of blessing. For example, a terrible accident, debilitating disease, or alcohol addiction can change the lives of both Unspoiled Splendor and Fast Track Couples. Their driving anxiety may then focus on brokenness, fate, or entrapment, and they then yearn for a different blessing of healing or radically new life. Ironically, the parents and children who formerly could not worship together now unite in a *healing* or *transformational* worship experience. Eventually this might push them to identify with a whole new lifestyle segment.

Worship, then, is what happens when profound human anxieties intersect with peculiar divine blessings. Incarnation occurs at that intersection of finite limitations and infinite possibilities.

In the past, the term *blended worship* has always referred to mixing styles. Blending was concerned with aesthetics or the stylistic preferences of different generations and lifestyle groups. Churches attracted a more diverse congregation if they were able to provide a mix of music, drama, and image or to shape environment with a different style of interior decorating, seating, and lighting or to accommodate different tastes in fashion or food. The goal of blended worship was to make worship family friendly, cross generational, or cross-cultural so that a larger diversity of people would feel comfortable, pay attention, and lower their resistance to the gospel.

In the waning years of Christendom, blended worship relied on the fact that most people still felt duty-bound to attend worship. In a world of church shopping, worship designers assumed that the real challenge was to make their worship service more attractive. Churches cast aside the restraints of denominational tradition, and many growing congregations became independent so that they could mix and match styles more freely. They even "displayed their wares" by giving away DVDs and promoting podcasts.

To their credit, denominational and independent church leaders reacted critically to this trend toward consumerism. Yet appeals to traditional music, liturgies, symbols, and ceremonies never really addressed the consumerism of blended worship. The debate was still about one stylistic preference over another. A style is a style, even if it is 150 years old. Music, images, furnishings, fashions (and indeed, any tactic involving the five senses) is traditional only in the sense that these were the aesthetic preferences of our ancestors preserved over time. The worship many leaders call sacred today started out as a pragmatic stylistic preference centuries ago.

Why is plainsong any more sacred than rap? Why are Lutheran and Wesleyan hymns that started out as the adapted pop music of the masses any more sacred than the pop music genres today? Why is Gregorian chant any different from a 1970s praise chorus? They aren't. Traditionalists find themselves open to the same charge of consumerism as their opponents. Handel's *Messiah* is just as much entertainment as *Jesus Christ Superstar* or any contemporary Christian heavy metal rhythm. And the *Messiah* is usually performed at Christmas and Easter for the same purpose of attracting mass participation in a world otherwise alienated from the church.

221

Now that post-Christendom is entrenched and spreading, worship designers can no longer rely on a sense of religious duty among the public. Church shopping is waning and already dead in most areas of North America, Australia, and western Europe. The old stylistic habit of blended worship is increasingly unsatisfactory. Lifestyle segments are increasingly competitive, and even combative, to get the worship experience they really seek.

Once we understand the existential anxieties that drive or compel people to worship, we understand why one size no longer fits all. There is no magical mixture of aesthetic tastes that will draw the diversity of the public into the same room. Different publics are seeking distinct experiences of incarnation, and they are not satisfied with a little bit some of the time. They want to immerse themselves in a uniquely relevant experience of Christ all the way and all the time. Much of what we call traditional worship is actually a blend of *educational, inspirational,* and *caregiving* worship.

The traditional sixty-minute service contains about thirty-minutes of education (e.g., sermon, readings, creeds, and doctrinally correct liturgy aimed at the head). The remaining thirty minutes is divided between inspiration and caregiving. Churches over 100 or 150 participants usually give twenty minutes to inspiration (e.g., preludes, anthems, hymns, dramatic rites, and postludes) and ten minutes to caregiving (e.g., prayers, children stories, and announcements). Churches under 100 or 150 participants balance it the other way. Small churches tend to expand announcements and children stories, encourage spontaneous prayer, and limit hymns to old favorites.

Traditional worship was designed to bless the lonely (looking for truth, relationships, and escape from meaninglessness), the aging and dying (looking for hope, confidence, and eternal life), and the discarded (looking for compassion, comfort, and a place to belong). At one time, these anxieties could all be met in a single worship service because the public was generally uniform, stable, and religious. Today this is not the case, and this traditional blend satisfies fewer and fewer people.

Established churches are discovering that they have to make a decision. People anxious about being discarded or dying are not satisfied with only ten to twenty minutes of worship time dedicated to their issue. Even people who are anxious about meaninglessness are not satisfied with just thirty minutes of worship time dedicated to their issue. Each wants the *entire* worship service to focus on their specific anxiety. It doesn't help to reproportion worship every month or rotate the focus of worship through the year. People want the *entire* worship experience to help them wrestle with the anxiety that is uppermost in their lives, and they want that experience *every* week and *all the time*. Churches that try to satisfy everybody end up satisfying nobody.

Moreover, the decision churches must make to focus worship on a mission target is even more complicated. There are *seven* fundamental anxieties that compel people to worship, not just *three*. The lifestyle segments of discarded, lonely, and aging people that still attend the traditional blend of worship often assume that they represent the majority of people and that their anxieties about meaninglessness, death, and displacement are typical. They are not as representative as they think, and their anxieties are not as widely shared as they assume.

The diversity of lifestyle and spiritual yearning today adds people who are *lost* (looking for direction, coping skills, and escape from emptiness), people who are *trapped* (looking for deliverance from addiction, new life, and victory over inevitable fate), people who are *broken* (looking for wholeness, healing, and forgiveness), and people who are *abused* (looking for justice, vindication, and cleansing). Established churches have been hard pressed to address these blessings in a "one-size-fits-all" worship service.

In the so-called traditional worship of Christendom, there was little time routinely dedicated to these blessings. Only a few minutes out of the sixty allotted to good worship focused on these anxieties. Perhaps a seminar or small group would be advertised to coach the lost after coffee hour. Perhaps an invitation to AA or a devotional handout would be distributed as a bulletin insert. Perhaps an opportunity for healing prayer in the chapel would follow the benediction. Perhaps prayers for peace and harmony would be included among all the other intercessions, and a "minute for mission" would inform the congregation of a social service program. Yet these bits and pieces do very little to bless the many lifestyle segments who specifically, earnestly, and even desperately long to be immersed in a more relevant experience of worship.

Churches face a difficult decision. Their church has limited resources and mission networks. Their reputation in the community for
any particular blessing is often foggy. Their clergy have limited skills
and diminished credibility. They *want* to *bless everybody in general*.
They are *increasingly ineffective* to *bless anybody in particular*. Blending
isn't working. They have to pick their mission targets.

This is a hard decision for Christendom churches that assumed "universal church" meant "universal appeal." A choice to focus on one mission target is a choice *not* to focus on another mission target. A choice
to design worship that profoundly and effectively blesses *these* lifestyle
segments is inevitably a decision not to bless *those* lifestyle segments.

Churches must enter the postmodern world of multiple options.
This is similar to the premodern world of Paul. Paul and his team had
to customize a worship experience for every cultural context and existential anxiety. This means that worship in one town might not resemble worship in another town. Each worship experience brought
people into the real presence of Christ, but each experience of Christ
was different. The church expanded its reach one lifestyle segment at a
time, and the menu of worship included a variety of quite distinct services. Even if each worship service included Eucharist, the sacrament
of Holy Communion was designed differently to connect people with
a distinct facet of the mystery of Christ in each context.

The multi-worship-service church is God's response to expanding diversity of lifestyle segments. Yes, this changes almost everything for the church. It means worship leaders are trained differently
and worship teams include more volunteers as credible spiritual leaders. It means that money will be raised by lifestyle segments in one
meaningful worship service, in order to bless other lifestyle segments
that the donors may not understand, or even like, in a different worship service. It means that "standardization" (in liturgy, music, message, space, and symbolism) is obsolete, and the only good worship is
worship that works. It means that clergy are no longer necessary for all
forms of worship, that seminaries are no longer necessary for all kinds of
spiritual leaders, and that denominations are no longer in the business
of franchising worship opportunities that replicate a single archetype.

Is blending a dead end for the postmodern church in the postmodern world? Yes, if by blended worship we simply mean a magical mix of styles, tastes, and aesthetic preferences that will please all generations and cultures at the same time. That kind of blending, which has been so popular with the church of the twentieth century, is disappearing. The more doggedly denominations and established churches cling to this kind of stylistic blending, the more rapidly they will sink into irrelevance. On the other hand, it is still possible to blend worship to address two related existential anxieties or to blend worship to include two or more compatible lifestyle segments.

A New Look at Blended Worship

Although the profound anxieties that drive or compel people to worship are distinct, they are often paired. In other words, there are similarities between two anxieties. The lifestyle segments that are anxious about one thing are often anxious about another.

Courage to Participate	Courage to Separate	Courage to Accept/ Acceptance	Courage to Trust and Be Trusted
Coaching Worship blended with Educational Worship	Transformational Worship blended with Inspirational Worship	Healing Worship blended with Mission-Connectional Worship	Caregiving Worship blended with Educatioal Worship
Merging people who are *Lost* *Lonely* *Discarded* *Broken*	Merging people who are *Trapped* *Dying* *Abused*	Merging peole who are *Abused* *Dying* *Lonely* *Lost*	Merging people who are *Discarded* *Abused* *Lost* *Broken*

The anxieties of emptiness and meaninglessness often go together. People who are lost are often people who are lonely, and people who are lonely are often people who feel lost. Their sense of isolation from truth is often accompanied by a sense of alienation from relationships. They have lost their bearings, and they are on their own. They feel disconnected from trusted principles of truth and distanced from enduring friendships at the same time.

People who are anxious about emptiness and meaninglessness often share a lack of courage to participate in critical interaction with the world and risky emotional investments in other people. They long to experience Christ as both mentor (guiding people to truth) and model (perfect companion for virtuous living).

Therefore, it is possible to blend *educational* and *coaching* worship. The same worship service that explains eternal truths and reliable principles with which to understand life can also provide practical skills with which to cope with life. Please understand that I am not talking about *adjusting* expository preaching to include contemporary anecdotes or practical tips nor am I suggesting clergy simply update the liturgy with contemporary idioms and reference to current events. The blend of *educational* and *coaching* worship is much more radical than this. It focuses totally on enlightenment and personal potential.

The anxieties of fate and death also often go together. People who are trapped by tragic circumstances or relentless addictions fear death; and people who fear death by war or disease often feel trapped by circumstances beyond their control. They are powerless to initiate change, no matter how educated, wealthy, or popular they might be. Both kinds of people know that only the intervention of a higher power can rescue them, and both look for reliable promises of new life or resurrection to give them hope.

People who are anxious about fate and death often share a lack of courage to make radical, risky, and even painful changes in their lifestyles. They long to experience Christ as one who can guarantee future redemption or who can shatter present realities. Promise and fulfillment are two sides of the same coin and can become twin pillars of the same worship experience.

Therefore, it is possible blend *inspirational* and *transformational* worship. The same service can celebrate hope and experience miracles. The presence of the Holy Spirit uplifts and encourages the powerless, and the power of the Holy Spirit accomplishes what is otherwise impossible. This blended worship is not simply about more music and uplifting stories. Worship is totally focused on anticipation and revelation.

The anxieties of guilt and shame often go together. People with broken health and fractured relationships often lose self-esteem, and people who have been abused or shamed often experience breakdowns in health and dysfunctional relationships. There is a strong empathy among those who have experienced injustice and lost personal wholeness. All of these people risk losing self-respect and often feel excluded.

People who are anxious about guilt, shame, or displacement may not only be excluded, but often lack courage to *believe* in their acceptance even when others try to include them. They long to experience Christ as healer, vindicator, and shepherd so that they feel part of God's realm.

Therefore, it is possible to blend *healing* and *mission-connectional* worship. Worship can help people heal and find acceptance through experiences of healing and opportunities to heal. The best servants are often former slaves, and the most compassionate missionaries are often those who have themselves known the worst abuse. Worship is totally focused on self-discovery through self-surrender.

Finally, the anxieties of displacement and meaninglessness often go together. The increasing numbers of people who feel discarded or forgotten due to age, immigration, mobility, and cultural diversity are often depressed by the meaninglessness of life; and those who lose continuity with tradition and search for meaning often feel marginal to society. There is a strong empathy between those who feel displaced and those who become cynical about life.

People who are anxious about displacement and meaninglessness often lack the courage to trust others or the self-confidence to be trusted by others. They long to experience Christ as a shepherd who rescues the marginalized and reunites them into community.

Therefore, it is possible to blend *caregiving* and *educational* worship. Worship can help people reunite and belong to a community of high trust and at the same time teach them to see hidden continuities of meaning across time and space. The experience of belonging combines a sense of identification with universal ideals and truths, with relationships that model or embody those same truths.

An Even Deeper Look at Blended Worship

That said, worship is a still more mysterious phenomenon. The more I have traveled among the spectrum of cultures and lifestyles that participate in the global Christian movement today, the more I am astonished by the varieties of worship. In the previous chapters of this book, I have tried to capture the nuances that define each worship option, and I ended each chapter with a preliminary indication of the potential for blending.

Anxiety is a complex experience. Yearning is a complicated quest. Christ is a multidimensional experience. Therefore, worship may be blended. The blend is not about style. It is about mission target. The success of blended worship is revealed by the proportions of specific lifestyle segments represented in the body and the nature of the blessings received.

Is there some underlying expectation or hidden pattern that guides the potential blending of mission-targeted worship options? I think there is, but it is not a pattern about form or content but import. In other words, it is not compatibilities of structure, technologies, or organization of worship that open the possibility of blending. Nor is it the similarities of topic, theme, or message that open the possibility of blending. It is the power of worship itself that elicits a particular attitude, posture, or stance toward existence on the part of the worshiper and that is able to gather diverse lifestyle segments, driven by related anxieties, seeking multiple blessings, in a common worship experience. This is called *import*, a word that comes from the same root as *importance*. It is the *significance* of worship in repositioning the worshiper's standpoint in life that matters.

My mentor originally described six existential anxieties over against which God elicited three acts of courage. Altogether they represented the fundamental attitude of faith or the *courage to be*.[2] God elicits the *courage to participate* in order to overcome anxieties of emptiness and meaninglessness, the *courage to separate* in order to overcome the anxieties of fate and death, and the *courage to accept one's own acceptance* in order to overcome the anxieties of guilt and shame. My experiences amid the growing diversity of cultures and lifestyles have led me to add a seventh anxiety (displacement) and a fourth *act of courage*, namely,

228

the *courage to trust and be trusted,* which God elicits to overcome the anxiety of displacement. The table below builds on the one at the beginning of this book.

Worship Options	Seeker Yearnings	Acts of Courage	Christ Experience	Existential Anxiety Resolved
Coaching Worship	Lost Looking for direction	The Courage to Participate	Spiritual Guide	Emptiness
Educational Worship	Lonely Looking for Rapport		Perfect Human	Meaningless-ness
Transforma-tional Worship	Trapped Looking for Deliverance	The Courage to Separate	New Being	Fate
Inspirational Worship	Dying Looking for Renewal		Promise Keeper	Death
Healing Worship	Broken Looking for Healing	The Courage to Accept Acceptance	Healer	Guilt
Mission-Connectional Worship	Abused Looking for Vindication		Vindicator	Shame
Caregiving Worship	Discarded Looking for Compassion	The Courage to Trust and Be Trusted	Shepherd	Displacement

I have already described how each anxiety is related to a spiritual yearning for a particular experience of Christ. This reveals four fairly obvious ways that paired anxieties might lead to a blended worship experience. However, it is these four acts of courage that open even more possibilities of blending worship services.

The Courage to Participate	The Courage to Separate	The Courage to Accept Acceptance	The Courage to Trust and Be Trusted
Blending worship for the . . .	Blending worship for the . . .	Blending worship for the . . .	Blending worship for the . . .
Lost	*Trapped*	*Abused*	*Discarded*
Lonely	*Dying*	*Dying*	*Abused*
Discarded	*Abused*	*Lonely*	*Lost*
Broken		*Lost*	*Broken*

Once again, this chart is inevitably a fixed table trying to represent a very fluid human experience. However, it reveals the underlying expectations and hidden patterns that open possibilities for blending worship.

Worship does not emerge from theology. Worship emerges from the human condition. The human condition that my mentor called finitude for all practical purposes can be described as the inevitability of being lost, lonely, trapped, dying, broken, abused, or discarded in the course of living. It is our reaction to this inevitability that drives our seeking. It is our intuition that this condition can, and indeed ought, to be overcome that compels us to worship.

Here I mean worship in the broadest way possible. Worship means standing at the intersection between the infinite and the finite. It is the expression of our longing for incarnation. It is our desire for God, or rather, our desire to experience the power of God (the touch of the Holy, or the real presence of Christ) that will somehow empower us to overcome the threats of emptiness, meaninglessness, fate, death, guilt, shame, and displacement.

What drives people to worship is hope. The one universal outcome of worship, in any of its forms, is that participants find courage. The worship experience may not immediately solve their problem, address their issue, or answer their question. The anxiety that compelled them to worship may not be eliminated at the time. But if they emerge with the *courage to be*, it will be a success and they will return again and again.

- *For the lonely and lost*, it will be the courage to participate. They will throw themselves back into the fray, continue to struggle in their relationships, invest in life, and embrace the world, even though its promises are ambiguous, because there is hope.

- *For the dying and trapped*, it will be the courage to separate. They will take initiative, step away from self-destructive habits, step out from the madding crowd, take a risk, express themselves, strive to achieve their human potential, and live like there really is tomorrow.

- *For the guilty and abused*, it will be the courage to accept their own acceptance. They will forgive and be forgiven, feel higher self-esteem, hold themselves and others accountable to higher ideals, stand up for what is right in a world that is so wrong.

- *For the displaced*, it will be the courage to trust and be trusted. They will clarify their values and beliefs and live within those boundaries. They will focus their vision and mission and align their lifestyles. They will keep trying to build community in the midst of social disintegration.

Worship attendance universally declines, among all lifestyle segments, when the church ceases to understand that the only compelling reason for worship attendance is hope and the only satisfactory result of worship is courage. Church institutions and denominations today try to shape worship in any number of forms and styles, and with an endless variety of sermons and messages, and every attempt fails to sustain an audience.

Compare worship services with sustainable growth, and it is hard to find any single common form or style, sermon or message, to explain it. The reason worship attendance grows is that people find it *important*. It receives them in hope and sends them out with renewed courage.

Blended Worship in Practice

In practice, this means that each worship option may be blended (with greater or lesser degree of difficulty) with another option, but some options are nearly impossible to blend. The degree of difficulty—or the practical impossibility—depends on several factors. First and foremost, it depends on the nature of the lifestyle segment itself and the nuances that are peculiar to each particular location of that segment in America. It also depends on the calling, talent, and "coachability" of worship leadership and available resources.

The table on p. 234 summarizes the guidance provided at the end of the previous chapters. It probably does not need to be said that this chart is intended as a *guideline*, rather than a *prescription*. The unknown factor in designing and celebrating worship is the power, creativity, and unpredictability of the Holy Spirit. Nevertheless, pastors and priests and worship designers can use this chart as they review the lifestyle segments in their primary mission fields to focus or diversify worship options. Even strongly eucharistic churches (for whom liturgy is less flexible) can see how to nuance sermons and prayers; or how to train greeters, ushers, and personal support teams; or how to follow up worship with small group, mentoring, or counseling opportunities.

There are several assumptions made in preparing this chart. The overlaps of hope and the expectations for courage (or encouragement) open possibilities for blended worship.

- It is usually only possible to blend *two* options of mission-targeted worship at the same time. Therefore, the choices below tend to be either/or when the list of possibilities exceeds two options. For example, it is possible to blend educational worship with *either* inspirational worship *or* caregiving worship, but not both at the same time.

- There is a *primary* and *secondary* mission focus for any blended experience of worship. If planners start with one kind of worship, they can discern the degree of difficulty blending others. The focus one starts with both limits and opens up other options, which might not be the same if you start with a different option. For example, it is much easier to make mission-connectional worship inspirational than it is to start with an inspirational worship service and make it mission-connectional.

- Every blend is stressful. Most established churches are trying to morph an existing worship service into *something more*. It is inevitable that some current worshipers will back away or leave worship entirely. They will inevitably make this *personal*, complaining that their needs are no longer being met or accusing the church of no longer caring about them. However, this is not a personal issue. This is a *lifestyle segment* issue. Whenever you include lifestyle segments currently under- or not represented in worship, some people in segments that are overrepresented in worship will leave.

- It is less stressful to start a new worship option than morph an old one. This table helps planners focus their *primary* mission and then expand the reach of the worship service by identifying the easiest lifestyle segments to embrace and the hardest lifestyle segments to avoid. Worship designers are forced to admit that only Christ can be all things, to all people, all of the time. We humans, with our limited abilities to plan and organize anything effectively, must be as humble in our faith and realistic in our planning.

Some blended worship expressions seem possible, but for practical reasons is nearly impossible. Much depends on the lifestyle segments involved, and the unique circumstances of microcultures in any given context. There may still be many barriers to blending due to demographic incompatibilities like language, culture, gender, income, and so on.

Worship Option	Easiest Blend	Difficult Blend	Hardest Blend
If you start with . . .	It is *often* possible to blend . . .	It is *sometimes* possible to blend . . .	It is nearly *impossible* to blend . . .
Coaching	Inspirational	Educational or Mission-Connectional	Transformational or Healing or Caregiving
Educational	Inspirational or Caregiving	Coaching or Mission-Connectional	Transformational or Healing
Transformational	Healing or Mission-Connectional	Caregiving or Inspirational	Educational or Coaching
Inspirational	Educational or Transformational or Coaching	Mission-Connectional	Caregiving or Healing
Caregiving	Educational or Healing	Coaching	Inspirational or Transformational or Mission-Connectional
Healing	Transformational	Caregiving or Inspirational or Mission-Connectional	Educational
Mission-Connectional	Inspirational or Educational	Transformational or Healing or Coaching	Caregiving

The more churches focus on the fundamental anxieties that compel people to worship, and the common yearning to experience divine blessings, the more churches can overcome demographic obstacles or stylistic preferences to help worshipers experience shared meaning.

The Easiest Blends

Some blends make good theological sense because they follow the obvious connections between existential anxieties that compel people to worship and the kind of encouragement that they receive from worship. What makes good theological sense, however, may not be so easy to accomplish. This is because traditionally trained clergy and established churches must change habits of thinking and behavior that have been engrained through traditional education and centuries of Christendom experience.

- Educational and coaching worship might be blended because the anxieties of emptiness and meaninglessness are similar and courage to participate is a common goal. The challenge is that traditionally trained clergy and established churches must change didactic, presentational, and authoritarian habits to become more dialogical, conversational, and egalitarian in their leadership.

- Transformational and inspirational worship might be blended because entrapment and death are similar and courage to separate is a common goal. The challenge is that traditional leaders and churches must surrender aesthetic expectations of uninterrupted performance and accept the possibility (and probability) of spontaneity and uncontrolled experiences of the Holy.

- Mission-connectional and healing worship might be blended because guilt and shame are related and courage to accept acceptance is a common goal. The challenge is that traditional leaders must become more than therapists to become change agents and traditional churches must become more than prayer partners to become advocates.

235

- Caregiving and educational worship might be blended because displacement and meaninglessness are often experienced together and courage to trust and be trusted is a common goal. The challenge is that classically trained clergy must reveal more vulnerability and humanity and liturgically minded churches must accept more diversity and respond more compassionately to skepticism.

These blends are common in the Christian movement but are often achieved by clergy who have come to leadership through nontraditional paths of career development and by churches that have a reputation for risk and innovation. Every blend makes the church appear to be a "maverick" in the eyes of its denominational and professional colleagues.

In practice, there are other blends that seem to work well. They may be theologically unexpected, but easier to accomplish. This has more to do with compatibilities among lifestyle segments. We often see specific lifestyle segments living close to one another in neighborhoods, towns, and cities. The same principle of "birds of a feather flock together" seems to apply to worship attendance as well as residency.

Coaching and inspirational worship often go together. Whenever boomer parents and their buster children locate near one another, this blend of practical advice for daily living and motivational storytelling and singing works well. A good example is worship that attracts the lifestyle segment Boomers and Boomerangs.[3] This lifestyle segment is growing in an economically challenged time, but the different generations actually live together quite harmoniously and may attend the same church (usually a larger or megachurch). The aging boomers confront the anxiety of death and are encouraged to separate (i.e., step out of their comfort zones); and the younger busters confront the anxiety emptiness and are encouraged to participate (i.e., step into relationships).

Educational and caregiving worship often go together. This blend works in demographic situations where liberal arts–educated professionals live in aging neighborhoods or high immigration regions. For example, the segment called Aging of Aquarius,[4] living in older urban single-family dwellings, often lives proximate to segments like Humble

236

Beginnings[5] in urban high-rise apartments. The former makes sense of the world by comparing religious sensibilities and cultural nuances, while the latter bonds in a new community and assimilates into a new culture.

You can readily understand which mission-targeted worship can be blended for other examples in the table above. Start with a thorough understanding of the lifestyle segments in any given mission field. Explore the anxieties that compel them to worship, and connect these with their current demographic realities and life situation. You begin to see how different lifestyle segments actually *help each other* find hope and courage. Regardless of discontinuities in age, income, language, housing, and other things, the anxieties and hopes that drive them to seek God can productively be blended into worship. They can bless each other.

The More Difficult Blends

Some blends are much more difficult. Despite theoretical commonalities in their search for God, lifestyle segments can approach worship very differently because they have different life goals, notions about truth, relationships with their environments, and social values. Demographers refer to this as *psychographics*. These nuances are particularly relevant in politics, social service, health care, and religious practice.

- Some lifestyle segments are motivated by similar hopes and require similar encouragement but for very different applications. In other words, some lifestyle segments want to be very *practical* and others prefer to be very *theoretical*. This is why it is harder to blend educational and coaching worship than you think. For example, worship designers simply cannot satisfy the practical lifestyle needs of Babies and Bliss[6] and the theoretical religious questions of Silver Sophisticates[7] in the same worship service. This is true despite the fact that the former may be the grandchildren of the latter and share a similar family history.

237

- Some lifestyle segments agree about the importance of faith and the significance of the sacraments but seek truth in very different ways. In other words, some seek truth in *rational propositions* and others seek truth in *mystical experiences*. It takes careful planning to coordinate preaching, music, and choreography for the same worship service to reach both groups. For example, it is very difficult to answer the reasonable questions of Small Town, Shallow Pockets[8] and the spiritual speculations of Dare to Dream.[9] They are both economically challenged and may live side by side in urban apartments. The former lifestyle segment is older and Caucasian; the latter are younger and multiethnic. But more separates them than this. The former may be blue collar, but they have grown up in the public school system of printed books and rational truth; the latter are have grown up in the school of hard knocks with multimedia and mysticism.

- Some lifestyle segments share certain aspirations for healing, self-improvement, social justice, and other needs but look for very different kinds of interventions. In other words, some seek grace through *natural laws* and others seek grace through *divine interventions*. This is why transformational and healing worship may be more difficult to blend with caregiving worship than you think. For example, the following three lifestyle segments may live in the same rural and small-town mission field: Settled and Sensible,[10] Stockcars and State Parks,[11] and Work Hard, Pray Hard.[12] The first segment may prefer a caregiving worship service, but it will intentionally bring people into a nice, homely, intergenerational, controllable, predictable experience of the Holy. Nothing unexpected or unexplainable should happen. But that will not interest its nearby neighbors in the other segments. The other segments might appreciate the fellowship but won't consider it worship unless a higher power intervenes to heal people or liberate them from their addictions.

- Finally, some lifestyle segments consider religion to be a private matter while others think of worship as a social contract. In other words, worship may be *personal* or *social*. This is why special celebrations like Christmas and Easter, and even cultural celebrations like Mother's Day and Thanksgiving, are harder to design than people think. For example, it is difficult for a single worship service to satisfy those who yearn for introspection and awesome silence and those who yearn for mutual support and energetic singing. This is always the contradiction between inspirational worship and caregiving or healing worship. Everyday Moderates[13] and Birkenstocks and Beemers[14] may be part of the same Middle-Class Melting Pot of "midscale, middle-aged, and established couples living in suburban and fringe homes,"[15] but have very different expectations on Christmas Eve. The former want to chat, hug, laugh, and sing before and after worship; and the latter want to sit in quiet mediation and enjoy a medley of carols to resurrect childhood memories.

It isn't impossible to blend such worship services, but it often requires more resources in skilled personnel, state of the art technology, and flexible space than many small and medium churches can afford. In the end and despite the best efforts by worship planners, the feedback for such worship services is always mixed. Some appreciate it a great deal, most are ambivalent, and a few are simply angry. It is difficult to sustain a worship service with such mixed reviews.

The Hardest Blends

The mystery of incarnation is that God can be experienced in paradoxical and even contradictory ways. This means that some worship alternatives are nearly impossible to blend, and on the occasions when they work, it has more to do with divine miracle than human planning. They are just too different. Some of these difficult blends may be surprising, because Christendom churches have consistently tried to achieve them.

First, it is extremely difficult to blend *educational* and *transformational* worship. The former is intentionally reasonable; the latter involves religious experiences that are essentially unreasonable. I commented earlier that educational worship is often associated with established Protestant traditions that were intentionally "word" based. Words (abstractions, definitions, or explanations) might be written or verbal, but words are the central building blocks of worship. Transformational worship is not based on words, but on experiences that are specific, paradoxical, and intuitive. The wordiness that makes educational worship rich actually blocks the power of transformational worship.

Educational worship aims at the head. It explains faith, interprets history, and defines morality. Educational worship makes religion understandable, so that God's actions are predictable and consistent. It follows that the structure of worship is quite orderly and logical and follows routines and patterns. Transformational worship aims at the heart. It anticipates unexplainable experiences of the Holy. It is irrational or beyond reason. It follows that the structure of worship is disorderly and even illogical. It does not follow a predictable routine and is full of surprises.

People who look for education in transformational worship often feel confused, bemused, or even amused. They expect worship to provide food for thought that leads to careful strategic planning but experience dramatic happenings that literally turn lives upside down and inside out in moments. Their anxiety grows because they are afraid such experiences might be more harmful than helpful. On the other hand, people who look for transformation in educational worship often feel hypocritical, distant from God, or belittled. Their anxiety actually grows as they feel trapped in a maze of impersonal concepts.

Second, it is extremely difficult to blend *coaching* and *healing* worship. The former is very pragmatic and interactive; the latter is more mystical and reflective. I commented earlier that coaching worship attracts ordinary people, trying to live ordinary lives, in faithful ways.

Healing worship, however, attracts ordinary people who find themselves in extraordinarily difficult circumstances, trying to establish or recapture normality.

Coaching worship helps people take charge of their lives, adjust their lifestyles, and take control. The topics may vary, but worship focuses on practical dilemmas, difficult decisions, training life skills, and improving effectiveness day to day. It emphasizes responsibility and control. Healing worship, on the other hand, encourages people to wait on the Lord. It is more passive. There is only one all-important topic (wholeness or health) that is addressed in every worship service. Worship emphasizes patience and surrender of control to the power of God.

People who look for practical coaching in a healing worship service often feel even more helpless. They are looking for tips and tactics. Their anxiety actually goes up because they don't know what to do. On the other hand, people who look for healing in a coaching worship service often feel frustrated. They have already tried therapies and medicines and followed tips and tactics to no avail. Their anxiety actually goes up because they are looking for miracles.

Third, it is difficult to blend *caregiving* and *inspirational* worship. I commented in my descriptions that Christendom churches commonly blended educational worship with one of these alternatives based on the size of the congregation. Small churches emphasized caregiving, while larger churches emphasized inspiration. This is because caregiving worship concentrated on intimacy, which is easier to accomplish in a small group; and inspirational worship concentrated on ecstasy, which is easier to accomplish in a large group.

Caregiving worship provides people with a sense of belonging. Participants tend to be very self-conscious. They are aware of their defects and vulnerabilities and strive for higher self-esteem and trusting relationships. This takes time and deliberation, so that worship tends to move more slowly in order to be excessively personal. Inspirational worship encourages participants to forget themselves. They are aware only of God and the gifts of God and celebrate a spirit of self-abandonment. This is instantaneous and spontaneous, so that worship tends to move very quickly to be excessively celebrative.

People who look for caregiving in an inspirational setting often feel left behind and confused. The sensation of being an outsider actually increases the anxiety. People who look for inspiration in a caregiving setting often feel selfish and depressed. The sensation of being vulnerable actually increases their anxiety.

Fourth, it is extremely difficult to blend *mission-connectional* worship . . . with any of the other kinds of worship. This is one reason that this type of worship is less common in the United States (where worship is still understood in fairly traditional ways) and more common in other countries (where Christianity is a cultural or religious minority and is forced to develop indigenous expressions of faith). Mission-connectional worship in the United States is often not considered "real worship." It seems more like a faith-based nonprofit organization that is serious about prayer and oddly preoccupied with sharing faith as a natural corollary to doing good. Meanwhile, mission-connectional worship in Australia or Canada is often considered *the only* authentic worship! Unless there is a direct mission impact on the world, it seems like a self-centered waste of time.

Mission-connectional worship has components that are educational, motivational, transformational, practical, and compassionate. It seems like this kind of worship might be blended with almost any other kind of worship. Yet there are practical problems.

- Mission-connectional worship is extreme in its external focus. Every other form of worship is still too internally focused. People tend to participate *for themselves* and place their personal needs and yearnings ahead of everything else. Participants in mission-connectional worship are entirely focused on people *other* than themselves. They are not looking for anything other than a means to serve.

- Mission-connectional worship is also extremely indifferent to ecclesiastical heritage and theological tradition. Ethical obligations are clear and often radical. Doctrinal assumptions are often quite simple, simplistic, or downright foggy. The participants try very hard to empathize with those in the mission field but are not interested in protecting continuity with a church tradition.

The difficulty in blending mission-connectional worship with other forms of worship is highlighted by the lifestyle segments most likely to prefer it. These people often represent the emerging generations that have no institutional Christian memory at all. Their whole lives have been spent outside of, and indifferent toward, the institutional church. Now that they have wakened to Christian faith, they are essentially starting from scratch to design worship and do not want to repeat the sidetracks of the past.

Multiple Options

The difficulties in blending worship only underscore the fact that we now live in a multiple-option world. People are compelled to worship for specific reasons. Worship can be blended only in the sense that it addresses deep anxieties that blend together. This is not a matter of style. It is a matter of blending certain expectations for grace. Churches today are forced to surrender one of the last Christendom assumptions, namely, that one worship service can be a blessing to everybody all the time.

Blending is one option among many, but it has limited application. Church leaders and worship designers only blend worship as part of a larger strategy to target worship to mission. It is vital to point out that the degrees of difficulty in blending are not the result of greater or lesser authenticity, profundity, or faithfulness. All options of worship are genuine, relevant, and faithful. One is not better than another. Christendom church people that once dismissed this or that worship option for stylistic reasons are finally realizing that they have actually been denigrating people whose anxieties are just as urgent as their own—just different.

Once church leaders shed this last vestige of Christendom, even small churches with limited resources will finding a way to offer at

least one distinctly different option of worship in order to bless another lifestyle segment in their community that is not represented or
underrepresented in their congregation. It does not necessarily require
lots of money or volunteers. The only essential requirement to start
another worship option is a heart burst to bless someone other than
yourself.

The Sunday Morning Experience

The expanding lifestyle diversity that has severely limited (and often eliminated) the possibilities of blended worship has forced church leaders to approach the entire Sunday morning experience with completely different assumptions.

At the start of this book, we observed that there is a direct correlation between the changing circumstances of life and the kind of worship a particular public seeks. And there is a direct correlation between a lifestyle segment, the anxieties that motivate it, and the kind of worship in which it might participate. The assumption of post-Christendom worship designers is:

$$\text{Seeker Sensitivity} + \text{Incarnational Experience} =$$
$$\text{God's Blessing through Relevant Worship}$$

In retrospect, many church leaders now realize that centuries of Christendom engrained hidden assumptions about the Sunday morning experience that they never realized. Whatever they may have thought they were doing in designing worship, the actual formula looked like this:

$$\text{Membership Privilege} + \text{Ecclesiological Principles} =$$
$$\text{Institutional Harmony through Consistent Worship}$$

In times of lifestyle homogeneity, when the diversity of the public was limited to a handful of demographic, racial, or cultural factors, faithfulness on Sunday morning could be expressed in this formula. Almost everyone was a member of some church that defined its institutional existence by certain theological principles. Worship across the country had to be consistent, so that no matter where any member traveled they would always be honored and "feel right at home." It is radical lifestyle diversity today, resulting from revolutions in immigration, mobility, communication, and economies, that changes how church leaders express "faithfulness" on Sunday morning.

Radical lifestyle diversity forces new assumptions about the overall point of Sunday morning hospitality, worship, and fellowship.

- In the time of lifestyle homogeneity, the point was always membership. The goal was either to assimilate new members or honor current members. The greeters and ushers were longstanding members or institutional officers. Parking spaces and sanctuary seating were designated for visitors on the assumption that most of the space had already been claimed by members. Worship tactics (like music) favored membership tastes and preferences. Even the patterns of refreshments and fellowship were unchanged from week to week (or season to season) to emphasize the continuity and harmony unique to the institution. Members and general public all assumed that *it was up to the visitor to adapt to the church.*

- In the emerging time of radical lifestyle diversity, the point is always seeker sensitivity. The goal is to bless strangers to grace and to create a conversation between more mature Christians who are further down the road in companionship with Christ and less mature Christians (or seekers) who are following behind (or just getting started) in their spiritual journeys. Establishing rapport, targeting questions and needs, creating supportive relationships, and engaging significant conversations are the means to measure success. Members and general public all assume that *it is up to the members to adapt the church to the anxieties and circumstances of visitors.*

This means that the overall Sunday morning experience is no longer about assimilating newcomers and cementing members into a harmoniously functioning institution based on sound ecclesiological principles. It is about blessing the diversity of the public, who are driven by distinct existential anxieties, helping them experience incarnation, and then coaching them to continue their spiritual journey with Jesus Christ.

Although we have placed emphasis on the *worship service* in this book, it should be obvious by now that we are really talking about Sunday morning (or any other occasion for worship) as a total incarnational experience. People do not just experience the real presence of Christ in worship. They look for Christ as they get of their cars in the parking lot, walk with Christ on their way to the building entrance, and meet Christ in the greeters and ushers.

They come nearer to Christ in the worship service. They experience Christ in the unique way that is most relevant to their compelling anxieties. They receive blessings in ways that satisfy their unique yearnings. They may say that they enjoyed the worship service, but what they really mean is that they were blessed by the presence of Christ.

The experience of Christ does not end there. They leave worship to enter a conversation. One might say that this conversation about Jesus (who he is, what he does, and why that is supremely important to you and me) has been going on for two thousand years. The buzz of conversation in the hallway or over refreshments nuances that historic conversation in different ways for different people. It continues as they exit the church and say goodbye to the greeters and as they drive away and as they invest themselves in the coming week.

It is not just worship, but the entire Sunday morning experience that is incarnational. People are compelled to come to church (even though today most people have more than enough reasons to stay away) because they are lost, lonely, trapped, dying, broken, abused, and displaced. They experience Christ as spiritual guide, perfect human,

247

new being, promise keeper, healer, vindicator, and shepherd. They go out with life purpose, truthful relationships, a fresh start, renewed confidence, restored wholeness, higher self-esteem, and a universal sense of belonging.

If Sunday morning has done some or all of that, it is a success, no matter how shabby the building or how poor the music or how dated the technology or how inarticulate the sermon. On the other hand, if all Sunday morning has achieved is to facilitate some chitchat among friends and powerfully motivate people to go home to lunch, then it is a failure even if the building is an architectural marvel, the music is professional quality, the technology is state of the art, and the sermon is a rhetorical and theological masterpiece. The formula for great worship is really quite simple: meet Jesus.

The recipe for Sunday morning, however, is now more complicated. It used to be that hospitality, worship, and refreshments all functioned independently. A separate committee managed each piece as a separate and unrelated program. There were occasional breaks in this routine for Christmas, church anniversaries, and other special occasions when greeters might wear a corsage or boutonniere and refreshments might include a special cake in order to commemorate a special worship service. Normally however, each program functioned autonomously.

No longer! Now that worship designers are clearer about targeting worship to address distinct anxieties and yearnings, all the components of Sunday morning must be designed together. There is an intentional flow of experience from radical hospitality, through life-shaping worship, and into mentoring conversations over refreshments. The *right* greeters and ushers are trained to say and do the *appropriate* things in anticipation of the anxieties that compel people to worship. Hospitality *prepares* people for worship that is now *intentionally focused* to help them *connect with Christ* in the manner that is most urgent. The experience with Christ *continues after worship* as people are encouraged to have *significant conversations* with more mature Christians who can help them *continue the process* to become faithful disciples seven days a week.

We have seen that different lifestyle segments prefer different kinds of hospitality. This not only involves refreshment service but also the manner in which layers of hospitality are developed before, during, and after worship. Greeters, ushers, and servers will be trained to be uniquely sensitive to newcomers and members in order to prepare them for mission-targeted worship experiences. Again, this is not just a matter of learning customs, habits, and mores for the lifestyle segments the church hopes to bless.

This involves deeper sensitivity to the anxieties that compel people to worship in the first place and that shape their expectations to meet Christ. Hospitality teams are doing ministry, not institutional tasks. The goal is not just to make people feel welcome but to introduce them to an experience of Christ. Every hospitality leader is like Andrew or Philip. Neither disciple *waits* for inquiries about Christ. Andrew proactively finds his brother Simon and introduces him to Christ. Philip finds Nathanael (whom he knows to be seeking God) and introduces him to Christ. Hospitality is all about *introducing* seekers to an incarnational experience in which they will connect with God in ways that especially bless their anxieties.

From the point of view of the seeker (whether member or non-member of the church), the options of worship are best described as life-shaping experiences of Christ. These experiences specifically address their anxieties by introducing them to distinct incarnations of the mystery of Christ. The outcome of worship is that people are empowered to customize, rearrange, redirect, and generally shape a different lifestyle. Call it a Christian lifestyle. Call it a spiritual life. Call it, as they did in New Testament times, simply a *different way*.

This means a third component of the Sunday morning experience is emerging as crucially important. Life-shaping worship leads to significant conversations. The moment worship ends, worshipers are engaged in conversation inside the sanctuary, hallways, and refreshment centers and at the exit doors and in the parking lot. If worship has been successful, these significant conversations will often be spontaneous. However, the conversations will also be initiated by teams who have been equipped and deployed to do just that. We have seen how musicians, artists, technicians and servers may become primary evangelists that seekers seek out for conversation. Elders, board members, staff, and other mature Christians might also be deployed.

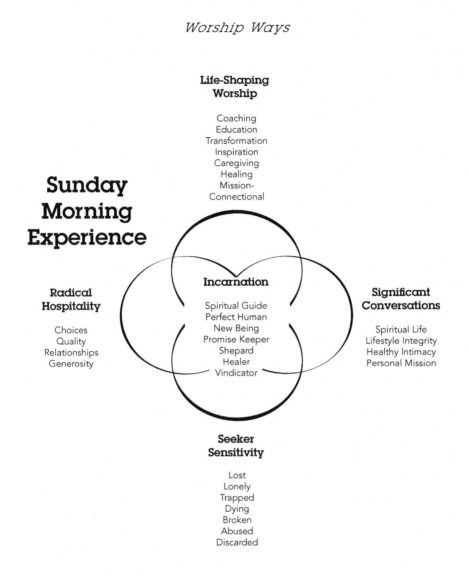

Life-Shaping Worship

Coaching
Education
Transformation
Inspiration
Caregiving
Healing
Mission-Connectional

Sunday Morning Experience

Radical Hospitality

Choices
Quality
Relationships
Generosity

Incarnation

Spiritual Guide
Perfect Human
New Being
Promise Keeper
Shepard
Healer
Vindicator

Significant Conversations

Spiritual Life
Lifestyle Integrity
Healthy Intimacy
Personal Mission

Seeker Sensitivity

Lost
Lonely
Trapped
Dying
Broken
Abused
Discarded

Pastors often invest vacation or sabbatical time to visit thriving churches of any tradition. One of the most common insights is that there is often no single tactic that makes churches thrive, but there is always one common outcome. There is always a buzz of significant conversation before, during, and after worship. These significant conversations are entirely different from the chitchat about weather, sports, and weekly events. People are talking about spiritual life; personal integrity at work, home, and recreation; trust and healthy intimacy; and their growing awareness of spiritual gifts and participation in God's mission.

Sunday morning—parking lot to parking lot—is a single incarnational experience. The gem at the center of it all is the real presence of Christ in worship. But worship is ineffective if hospitality does not create the environment of expectancy and the opportunity to meet Jesus. And worship is unsuccessful if it does not lead to significant conversations about God, life, and hope for the future. In the bygone days of Christendom, members and visitors could show up late and leave early, because all that mattered was the worship service. Today you want members and visitors to arrive early and leave later, because the incarnational experience is not complete unless both vertical and horizontal relationships are made. In the past we came to church to *wave* at Jesus and get on with our lives. Today (as in ancient times) we come to church to *meet* Jesus, *discern* where Jesus is going, and then *join him* on the journey of life.

What Is Sacred about Worship . . . and What Is Not?

Blended worship was the hallmark of the Christendom world that began with Constantine. One worship service blessed all people. Alterations to worship could only be small, and the growing diversity of the public had to struggle harder and harder to adapt to it. Mission-targeted worship (or multi-option worship) is the hallmark of the pre- and post-Christendom world. Different options of worship blessed specific groups of people. Alterations to worship could be large, and each public could connect with the experience of Christ that most urgently addresses their anxieties. In Christendom, church leaders maintained the status quo and expected the public to make all the sacrifices. In post-Christendom, church leaders have to work harder and make more sacrifices in order to remove barriers to seekers seeking God.

This transition is very stressful for many established churches, although many new church developments (church plants) seem to do it with relative ease. It forces church leaders to discern what is really sacred about worship and what is not.

The list of things *not sacred* about worship is disconcerting and occasionally shocking. Much of the property, technology, personnel, organization, programming, and procedure that we thought to be sacred are reduced to mere tactics. The truth is that God can use anything, anyone, in any way in order to bless people and redeem the world. It is only when we admit all that and set it all aside against (as Paul said) the surpassing worth *of knowing Christ, sharing Christ's sufferings, and participating in Christ's resurrection*, that we free ourselves to be instruments of God's mysterious presence. What Paul considered the "righteousness of the law" that blocked access to Christ, we might describe today as "sacred cows" of architecture, ritual, and style.[1]

In the pre- and post-Christendom world there are only three things sacred about worship: the experience of Christ, the blessing of Christ, and life with Christ. Church leaders need to ask and answer "sacred questions" before they take on the awesome responsibility of designing worship.

1. **What is the mission purpose of worship?** What are the compelling reasons that drive specific groups of people to worship? Which experience of Christ is most urgently sought, and what blessing of worship will measure success?

2. **How does worship emerge from the spiritual life of leaders and deepen the spiritual life of seekers?** Are leaders able to give out of the abundant grace they have already received? What spiritual habits will be reinforced, and what positive changes to lifestyle will result?

3. **How does worship drive people to serve in God's greater purpose to redeem the world? What significant conversations will emerge?** What social services will be encouraged? How will the community (or world) be any different because we worship?

Worship is sacred because Jesus Christ is really present. Wherever Christ is, people are blessed in special ways, go on to live life differently, and pass the joy on to others.

Everything else about worship is mere tactics. This includes the space, technology, music, language, leadership, food, and any other cultural form. It is all just tactics, regardless of history, familiarity, aesthetic appreciation, or institutional policy. When worship designers ignore or forget these fundamental questions, even the slightest change to worship tactics can be immensely controversial. When they focus on their answers to these questions, tactical changes can go far beyond the comfort zones of church members without fracturing the church.

Lucinda's Notes: You Can Do This!

Practical Tips for Forming the Initial Worship Design Team

- **Be intentional about selecting team members.** Team members are not just doing a task well. They are mindful of the overall mission goals of Sunday morning and focused on maturing participants deeper into discipleship.

- **Explore the mission field together** using demographic research. Take field trips to other congregations that are effectively reaching their mission targets; make prayer walks in the community; interview local business leaders, potential ministry partners, and nonprofits to test the validity of digital demographic and lifestyle segment research.

- **Focus, focus, focus!** Design worship to target the one or two lifestyle segments that are your primary heart bursts. Once you are successfully blessing one lifestyle segment, fall on your knees and let God reveal a heart burst for the next lifestyle segment.

- **Follow a discipline.** Design three to four weeks ahead for a theme or season of the Christian Year answering "sacred questions" and innovating relevant tactics. Use weekly communications with key leaders to evaluate previous worship and adjust for upcoming worship. Walk through the plan for the upcoming Sunday morning experience checking technologies, anticipating rituals, and confirming who will be where and when and doing what and how.

Coaching for the Tech Team

- Build relationship and trust by understanding the mission field, the gifts of each team member, and the mission of each worship service.

- Develop a style guide. For example, in healing worship it may mean using simple video images only, such as a candle, crosses, or images of Christ; limiting the number of lines of text to appear on the video screens; using prerecorded music to have a subtle surround-sound feel through careful placement of wireless speakers; or dimming the lights during healing prayer at the altar.

- Respect the tech's talent, be clear about the mission of each service and the feel and result you are going for but not every detail of how to do it!

- Make only one major change at a time, such as a flow to the worship service or a change in who will be providing pre-service recorded music, dimming the lights on cue, and so on. Rehearse these new elements.

- Celebrate the victories. Don't just lament the failures. Learn from mistakes. Worship leaders, show some grace! Everyone must have a backup plan when the technology goes down.

- And most importantly—respect the tech's time! Set the deadlines together for each team member to have materials ready and stick to them, clergy or worship leader.

The emerging post-Christendom and postmodern world has forced churches to clarify what is sacred and what is not. In the days when Sunday worship was culturally normative and people went shopping for the worship experience that they liked, churches could ignore the mission purposes of worship and concentrate on style. Now that Sunday worship is no longer culturally normative and church shopping is largely dead, churches cannot afford to base their reputations on style. They must base their reputations on mission purpose.

Each of the sacred questions above invites tactical creativity. Since the emerging postmodern publics have little church memory and may even be alienated by past institutional church practices, this creativity can be very diverse. The tactical issues for worship design are about *relevance, engagement,* and *motivation.*

Relevance is the tactical creativity that follows clarity about the mission purpose of worship. Relevance is all about using familiar, everyday things in a new and profound way. You might say it is about sacramentalizing life, or infusing life with new meaning. The challenge to worship design is that the diversity of lifestyle segments targeted is ever greater. More segments are involved and more detail must be mastered. This is why postmodern worship designers spend so much time prayer walking, listening, and keeping up with demographic trends.

Engagement is the tactical creativity that follows clarity about spiritual life. Engagement is all about addressing the questions, crises, and issues that specific lifestyle segments are dealing with right now. You might say this is about conversation. There is more to engagement than sending a one-way message. Worship must invent a method for two-way dialogue. The challenge is that lifestyle segments learn and interact in different ways. This is why postmodern worship designers spend so much time networking with partners in education, news and entertainment media, and technology development.

Motivation is the tactical creativity that follows clarity about human potential and social service goals. Motivation is all about compelling worship participants to learn more and serve sacrificially. You might say this is all about offering, but this is not just about financial giving. It is about developing a lifestyle of generosity. The challenge is that the philanthropic behavior of lifestyle segments is also very diverse. The boundaries between personal and family time, work and recreation, are increasingly blurred. Self-interest is more culturally normative for the postmodern world than community service. This is why worship designers learn from nonprofits that are successful in developing volunteers and spend so much time studying psychographic trends.

The simplicity of worship is that it is neither more nor less than meeting Jesus. It is an incarnational experience when God is fully divine and fully human and infinite grace intersects with human need. The simple point of worship is to meet Jesus. The complexity of worship is about what happens in that meeting. Each lifestyle segment, and each person, is touched by the Holy and changed by grace in different ways. How do we anticipate that moment? How can we prepare people for it? How can we shape lives and lifestyles because of it? How can we guide people to go deeper and further with Christ afterwards?

One final thing that is returning to the church in the post-Christendom world is the sacredness of *leadership*. We have gone through an extended period when worship leaders were reduced to mere professionals and task managers. They became interchangeable like cogs in a machine or recruited like corporate executives and retailers. That era, too, is ending. Today we are returning to a higher accountability. Worship leaders cannot answer the sacred questions above unless they themselves have experienced Christ in correlation to their own existential anxieties, have celebrated the blessings of Christ in their own life struggles, and at least strive to live life in Christ. They cannot just preach or perform on the stage of worship and then behave as they please.

What is sacred about worship leadership today is not that leaders are great theologians, great communicators, great therapists, great administrators, great fund-raisers, or even great friends. Leaders are sacred because they are, above and beyond the average church member and seeker, *courageous for Christ*. Whether they demonstrate (for any given lifestyle segment) courage to participate, courage to separate, courage to accept their own acceptance, or courage to trust and be trusted, their *courage* to design and lead worship stands over against the privileges, comfort zones, and selfish ambitions of institutions that would limit God's power to bless the full diversity of the mission field. Sacred leadership today has the courage to stake everything to be with Christ in doing whatever it takes to bless strangers to grace.

Notes

Introduction: Why Worship?

1. The most sophisticated research engine today is www.MissionInsite .com, which uses demographic, psychographic, and lifestyle data gathered by the multisector company Experian.

2. See the anonymous fourteenth-century work *The Cloud of Unknowing*, trans. Carmen Avecedo Butcher (Shambhala: Boston and London, 2009).

3. This dramatic shift is visible to Christian observers of religion and culture. For example, in 1965 Harvey Cox wrote *The Secular City*, anticipating the triumph of materialistic rationalism over religion. In 1995 the same author wrote *Fire from Heaven*, observing the resurgence of religion in a whole new way.

4. Demographers now can paint a portrait of peer groups that share similar attitudes, behavior patterns, spending habits, recreational priorities, media preferences, and habits of daily living. They tend to gather geographically, participate in similar activities, and follow predictable routines. They also share distinct outlooks, political perspectives, tastes, work ethics, and even religiosities.

5. See *See, Know & Serve the People Within Your Reach* by Thomas G. Bandy (Nashville: Abingdon Press, 2013) and "Mission Impact," a commentary by Tom Bandy on the ministry expectations of all the current lifestyle segments in the United States today (a resource found at www.MissionInsite.com).

6. Acts 19 and 18 respectively.

7. Paraphrase of Mic 6:6-8.

8. Tom first introduced these categories of urgency in his books *Talisman: Global Positioning for the Soul* (St. Louis: Chalice Press, 2006); and *GPS: Global Positioning for the Soul* (Amazon.com, 2010).

9. For example: Soren Kierkegaard, *The Concept of Dread*, trans. Walter Lowrie (Princeton: Princeton University Press, 1944); Viktor Frankl, *Man's Search for Meaning* (London: Hodder & Stoughton, 1946); and Paul Tillich, *The Courage to Be* (Yale University Press, 1952).

10. Tom provides a more detailed description of these experiences of incarnation in his books *Talisman* and *GPS*. They go beyond worship to orient experiences of Christ with the spiritual life in general.

Mission-Targeted Worship

1. See Tom Bandy's groundbreaking book *See, Know & Serve the People Within Your Reach* (Nashville: Abingdon Press, 2013) for a more detailed discussion of what a "lifestyle segment" is and how demographers define them.

Worship Option: Coaching Worship

1. These are all lifestyle segments identified by Experian in their resource "Mosaic 2010." Experian is one of a small number of international corporations that develops demographic and lifestyle segment information for business and public sectors, based on tracking credit card use and other surveys. Note that Experian updates and enlarges lifestyle segment profiles every few years, and that the descriptions above may change by 2020. A summary of the lifestyle for each segment, and a breakdown of their church preferences for leadership, hospitality, worship, Christian education, small groups, and outreach; and for church facilities and technologies, financial management and stewardship, and communications are found in Tom's resource "Mission Impact," available from www.MissionInsite.com.

2. Many national and regional denominations subscribe to www.Mission Insite.com, and their constituent congregations can obtain a password and training to access the search engine from their denominational office.

3. There is a large literature on Warhol's series of paintings on "The Last Supper." One of the most interesting is *Andy Warhol, Priest: The Last Supper Comes in Small, Medium, and Large* (Leiden: Brill Academic, 2001).

4. See Tom Bandy's strategic planning book, *Accelerate Your Church* (www.MissionInsite.com, 2012). He identifies the three ways for leaders to measure success: statistics, stories, and feedback.

Worship Option: Educational Worship

1. Experian, Mosaic 2010. Details may be found in Tom's resource "Mission Impact" at www.MissionInsite.com.

2. Experian, Mosaic 2010. Details may be found in Tom's resource "Mission Impact" at www.MissionInsite.com.

Worship Option: Transformational Worship

1. Many national and regional denominations subscribe to www.Mission Insite.com, and their constituent congregations can obtain a password and training to access the search engine from their denominational office.

2. Experian, Mosaic 2010. Details may be found in Tom's resource "Mission Impact" at www.MissionInsite.com.

3. Matt 14:22-36.

4. For further insight on the history and legacy of this perspective, see Harvey Cox, *Fire from Heaven* (Reading, MA: Addison-Wesley Publishing, 1995), especially 81–160.

5. John 1:29 or Heb 9:23-28.

6. Rev 19:11.

7. Rev 20:11; 21:1.

8. See Paul Tillich's use of the term in *Systematic Theology* (Chicago: University of Chicago, 1957), 2:118–36. I described it in metaphors like "earth shaker," "tsunami of grace," and (more biblically) "thief in the night" in my previous book *Talisman: Global Positioning for the Soul* (St. Louis: Chalice Press, 2006), 35–36.

Worship Option: Inspirational Worship

1. The ranking of "inspiration" or "education" after each segment indicates the probable priority that would be normative for the segment.

2. Experian, Mosaic 2010. Details may be found in Tom's resource "Mission Impact" at www.MissionInsite.com.

3. Gen 37:9-11.

4. Webmaster, "Vincent (Starry Starry Night)," Don McLean Online, last modified April 11, 2007, http://www.don-mclean.com/?p=107.

5. For an excellent resource about shaping worship space, see Kim Miller, *Redesigning Churches: Creating Spaces for Connection and Community* (Nashville: Abingdon Press, 2013).

Worship Option: Caregiving Worship

1. Experian, Mosaic 2010. Details may be found in Tom's resource "Mission Impact" at www.MissionInsite.com.

Worship Option: Healing Worship

1. Experian, Mosaic 2010. Details may be found in Tom's resource "Mission Impact" at www.MissionInsite.com.
2. Luke 5:17-26.
3. John 9:1-7.
4. Matt 8:1-12.
5. Mark 5:25-33.

Worship Option: Mission-Connectional Worship

1. In the 2010 Mosaic by Experian, B10: Asian Achievers is a good example.
2. E19: Full Pockets and Empty Nests; and H29: Destination Recreation are good examples.
3. Experian, Mosaic 2010. Details may be found in Tom's resource "Mission Impact" at www.MissionInsite.com.
4. See my descriptions of different kinds of pastors or spiritual leaders in *See, Know, and Serve the People Within Your Reach* (Nashville: Abingdon Press, 2013).

Possibilities for Blending Worship

1. I compare these two lifestyle segments more fully in my previous book *See, Know, and Serve the People Within Your Reach* (Nashville: Abingdon Press, 2013).
2. Paul Tillich, *The Courage to Be* (New Haven, CT: Yale University Press, 1952). My life, thought, and worship has been profoundly shaped by the anxieties and acts of courage described by Tillich and other colleagues like Rollo May, Victor Frankl, H. Richard Niebuhr, and Reinhold Niebuhr.
3. Experian C14: baby-boomer adults and their teenage/young adult children sharing suburban homes.

4. Experian C11: upscale boomer-aged couples living in cities and close-in suburbs.

5. Experian P61: multiethnic singles and single-parent households with midscale incomes in city apartments

6. Experian B08: middle-aged couples with large families and active lives in affluent suburbia.

7. Experian C13: mature, upscale couples and singles in suburban homes.

8. Experian S68: older, downscale singles and empty nesters living in modest exurban small towns.

9. Experian R66: young singles, couples, and single parents with lower incomes starting out in city apartments.

10. Experian J36: older, middle-class, and empty-nesting couples and singles in city neighborhoods.

11. Experian I30: middle-class couples and families living in more remote rural communities.

12. Experian N49: working-class, middle-aged couples and singles living in rural homes.

13. Experian H28: midscale, multicultural couples and families living in midtier metro suburban settings.

14. Experian H27: upper-middle-class, established couples living leisure lifestyles in small towns and cities.

15. Experian Lifestyle Group H.

The Sunday Morning Experience

1. See Phil 3:7-11.